André Gide

MODERN LITERATURES IN PERSPECTIVE

General Editor:

SEÁN HAND, Professor of French Cultural Studies, Department of Language Studies, London Guildhall University

Published Titles:

LILIAN R. FURST, *Realism*

JO LABANYI, *Galdós*

CELIA BRITTON, *Claude Simon*

ROGER PEARSON, *Stendhal: 'The Red and the Black' and 'The Charterhouse of Parma'*

ROBIN FIDDIAN, *García Márquez*

CHRISTINA HOWELLS, *Sartre*

MICHAEL TILBY, *Balzac*

MICHAEL WORTON, *Michel Tournier*

WILLIAM J. DODD, *Franz Kafka*

MICHAEL MINDEN, *Thomas Mann*

DAVID H. WALKER, *André Gide*

ANDRÉ GIDE

Edited by

DAVID H. WALKER

LONGMAN
LONDON AND NEW YORK

Addison Wesley Longman
Edinburgh Gate
Harlow, Essex CM20 2JE
United Kingdom
and Associated Companies throughout the world.

*Published in the United States of America
by Addison Wesley Longman, New York.*

First published 1996

**QM LIBRARY
(MILE END)**

ISBN 0 582 22774 7 CSD

British Library Cataloguing-in-Publication Data

A catalogue record of this book is
available from the British Library

Library of Congress Cataloging-in-Publication Data

André Gide / edited by David H. Walker.
    p. cm. -- (Modern literatures in perspective)
  Includes bibliographical references and index.
  ISBN 0-582-22774-7
  1. Gide, André, 1869–1951--Criticism and interpretation.
 I. Walker, David H.   II. Series.
PQ2613.I2Z578   1996
848'.91209--dc20   96-6230
                                                                  CIP

Set by 7 in 9/11½ Palatino
Printed & bound by Antony Rowe Ltd, Eastbourne

Contents

General Editor's Preface

Modern Literatures in Perspective is a series of collected critical essays on post-1800 European-language authors, works or concepts. It is designed to help the reader study these literatures in isolation and in context by selecting and presenting the most representative and inspiring reactions to the works in question from the time of their appearance to the present day.

A crucial feature of the series' approach is its open recognition of the critical revolution which has taken place this century and in particular in the last thirty years. Marxist, structuralist, psychoanalytical, deconstructionist and feminist theories have utterly transformed our assessment of literature. *Modern Literatures in Perspective* takes full account of the general issues raised by the revolution in theory, together with the practical effects which these theories have on the reading of the literary canon.

Recognizing the need for direction within this plural field of perspectives, each volume offers a high degree of critical guidance and advice in addition to presenting its subject in a methodical and accessible manner.

A substantial introduction outlines the historical and cultural contexts within which the literature in question was produced. It explores and explains the conflicting critical reactions to the literature in perspective and suggests ways in which these critical differences may be put to work. Each essay is prefaced by an introductory headnote setting forth the significance of the piece. A glossary of critical terms and cultural references provides further background information.

Modern Literatures in Perspective offers much more than textual analysis, therefore. It openly examines the relationship between literature and a range of wider issues. At the same time, its approach is more concrete than any history of literature. Rather than impose a synthesis or single methodology, the volumes in this series bring the reader into the heart of a crucial critical debate.

New critical insights, teaching practices and reading publics continue to transform our view of modern European-language writings. *Modern Literatures in Perspective* aims to contribute to this continuous transformation by disseminating and analysing the best modern criticism on the best modern literatures.

Acknowledgements

We are grateful to the following for permission to reproduce copyright material:
Anma Libri and the author, for 'Slips of the text' by Emily Apter from
Andre Gide and Codes of Homotextuality (Stanford French and Italian Studies,
1987) pp 110–124; the author, W.M.L. Bell for amended text from 'Religion
and its avatar in *La Porte Etroite*' in *Romance Studies* No 10, Summer 1987,
pp 7–10; Blackwell Publishers Ltd for 'Andre Gide's Shields' by Lucien
Dallenbach from *The Mirror in the Text* translated from the French by Jeremy
Whiteley with Emma Hughes (Cambridge, Polity Press in association with
Basil Blackwell, 1989); Doubleday, a division Bantam Doubleday Dell Publishing
Group Inc. for 'Gratuitous action and the aesthetic perspective in *'Les Caves
du Vatican'* by Jean Hytier in *Andre Gide* translated by Richard Howard.
Translation copyright (c) 1962 by Jean Hytier; the author, Professor Albert
J. Guerard for extracts from his *'L'Immoraliste'* in *Andre Gide* (Cambridge,
Mass., Havard UP, 1951); Alfred A. Knopf Inc for extracts from *Portrait of
Andre Gide* by Justin O'Brien. Copyright 1953 by Justin McCortney O'Brien;
The Lane Press Inc for extracts from 'Liberation from the existing social
order' by Mishca Harry Fayer in *Gide, Freedom and Dostoevsky* (Burlington,
Vermont, The Lane Press, 1946); Librairie Minard for extracts from 'La
Figuration due proces litteraire dans l'ecriture de *La Symphonie pastorale*' by
Alain Goulet, pp 27–55 in *Andre Gide 3: Gide et la fonction de la litterature*,
Claude Martin ed. (Paris, Lettres Modernes, 'La Revue des lettres modernes'
331–335, 1972) & 'Gide et l'autobiographie' by Philippe Lejeune, pp 31–69
in *Andre Gide 4: methodes de lecture*, Claude Martin ed. (Paris, Lettres Modernes,
'La Revue des lettres modernes' 374–379, 1973); the General Editor of
Romantic Review for the article 'On Readers and Reading in *La Porte etroite*'
by Albert Sonnefeld, originally published in *Romantic Review*, LXVII (1976)
pp 172–180. Copyright by the Trustees of Columbia University in the City
of New York; Societe de'Histoire Litteraire de la France for a slightly modified
version of the article 'Le Prodigue chez Gide: essai de critique economique
de l'acte gratuit' in the Andre Gide special number of *Revue d'Histoire
Litteraire de la France*, March–April, 1970, pp 209–229, translated by David
Steel as 'Gides Prodigal. Economics, Fiction and the *Acte Gratuit*; Rutgers
University Press for 'The Keyhole Metaphor and the Parable' by Vinio
Rossi in *Andre Gide, the Evolution of an Aesthetic* (New Brunswick, New
Jersey, Rutgers University Press, 1967, pp 128–142; the author David Walker/
Macmillans/St Martins Press Inc/Society for French Studies for 'Challenging
the novel in *Les Faux-Monnayeurs*' adapted from texts previously published
in *French Studies*, XL 1986 and *Andre Gide* by David Walker (Basingstoke,
Macmillan, 1990) pp 136–160; Yale French Studies for the article 'Time
sequences and consequences in the Gidian world' by Germaine Bree, first
published in *Yale French Studies*, 7, 1951, pp 51–59.

List of abbreviations

The French text of works by Gide is quoted from the following, to which page numbers refer:

André Gide, *Romans, Récits et Soties, Oeuvres Lyriques* (Paris, Bibliothèque de la Pléiade, 1958).

References to editorial material contained in this volume are indicated by the abbreviation RRS.

Other sources are indicated as follows. Full details are given in the bibliography.

JI	*Journal 1889–1939*
JII	*Journal 1939–1949. Souvenirs*
OC I, II, III ...	*Oeuvres complètes d'André Gide* (15 volumes)
J1, 2, 3, 4	*The Journals of André Gide* (4 volumes)

English versions of the texts are taken from the standard translations listed in the bibliography. Where these translations contain inaccuracies, omissions or turns of phrase which exclude a nuance present in the French and germane to the argument, modifications have been made which are printed in bold italics. Other editorial interventions are marked by square brackets around the material concerned.

Page references to both French and English versions are given wherever possible, in the form of a pair of numbers separated by a semi-colon. A colon following such numbers indicates an explanation of the source, date, etc. Thus (JI, 69; J2, 264: 1921) refers to an entry for 1921 appearing on page 69 of the French text, *Journal 1889–1939*, and on page 264 of the second volume of the English text, *The Journals of André Gide*.

Where no page reference is given for an English version, the translation is my own, or that of the named translator of the chapter.

Introduction

André Gide was born on 29 November 1869, of a father whose origins linked him to the traditionally protestant south of France, and a mother descended from a Norman family which though staunchly Protestant at the time of the author's birth, had been Catholic in earlier generations. Gide liked to present these circumstances as a vindication of his complex character: 'Is it my fault if your God took such great care to have me born between two stars, the fruit of two races, of two provinces, and of two faiths?' (*JI*, 959; *J3*, 84: 2 December 1929)

In fact this complex nature was in large measure the product of his efforts to free himself from certain predominant influences operating on him from an early age. His father died in 1880, a month before the boy's eleventh birthday, and André's mother, for all her inward insecurity and the great affection she bore her only child, adopted a rigorously puritanical and authoritarian approach to rearing him. The ethical teachings she derived from her religion emphasized duty, obedience and self-denial. The mark she and her attitudes left on her son was to prove indelible. During his adolescence, Gide experienced a phase of extraordinary religious fervour characterized by prayer and meditation, and quasi-monastic practices. Such tendencies were reinforced by his early love for his cousin Madeleine, a girl of similarly pious disposition with whom he was able to share his enthusiasms, both spiritual and literary: often, indeed, the two were indistinguishable, since the Bible was and would remain an important source of inspiration in both spheres. Quotations from the scriptures are scattered throughout his first book, *Les Cahiers d'André Walter* (1891), which Gide intended as a sort of marriage proposal to Madeleine. Like the autobiographical hero of this volume, Gide aspired to a communion of souls in a shared adoration of God.

However, this demonstrative piety was equivocal in its very intensity, for it was in large part a reaction to the stirrings of his sexuality. As an infant he had become an object of scandal and had been withdrawn from regular schooling following an incident involving so-called *mauvaises*

1

habitudes; throughout his youth he was haunted by guilt concerning masturbation and associated sexual phantasms. His particular religious formation complicated matters, for it is in the nature of protestantism to place the responsibility for salvation directly into the hands of the individual; and in moments of turmoil Gide had only his conscience to turn to. However, when he listened to this inner voice he heard murmurings which were entirely out of keeping with the conventional views of his mother and their milieu. He hoped that Madeleine would sustain him against his inner demons by agreeing to marry him; but she turned down his proposal on the advice of their respective families. In any case, like André Walter, the young author found that even his spiritual adoration for his cousin could not entirely supplant his other yearnings, just as the lip-service he paid to his mother's religion and morality could not stifle the voice of his instinctual revolt.

Madeleine's refusal did not extinguish his determination to marry her eventually; he resolved to wait, but in the meantime he was on the horns of a dilemma. His religious upbringing exhorted him to be sincere and to follow the promptings of his inner self; but at the same time the doctrines of that same religion imposed upon him a puritan orthodoxy which condemned him to outward dissimulation and hypocrisy. In an introspective manoeuvre also characteristic of Protestantism, he kept a diary which records his complaint, at the start of 1892: 'I am torn by a conflict between the rules of morality and the rules of sincerity. Morality consists in substituting for the natural creature (the old Adam) a fiction that you prefer. But then you are no longer sincere. The old Adam is the sincere man.' (*JI*, 29–30; *J1*, 19).

This debate with the principles of his family's creed would continue, in one form or another, throughout a large part of his life. In the early 1890s the dispute was temporarily displaced into the aesthetic sphere as he rallied to the symbolist movement and sought to rise above his private uncertainties in the service of art and the ideal. He impressed the élite circle of his literary peers with the languor, melancholy and sterile self-scrutiny evident in *Le Traité du Narcisse* (1891), *Le Voyage d'Urien* (1893) and *La Tentative Amoureuse* (1893) – and drew notable acknowledgement of his potential from Mallarmé – but he soon began to see that for literary as well as personal reasons he needed to seek out other horizons. By 1893 his mind was made up, and he determined on a journey to exotic north Africa, inwardly declaring: 'In the name of what God or what ideal do you forbid me to live according to my nature? And where would that nature lead me, if I simply followed it?' (*JII*, 550). In a different climate, amidst a different culture, perhaps he would find a way out of his inner conflict: 'I dimly saw at last that this discordant dualism might very well resolve itself into a harmony' (ibid.).

He was to devote most of the next three years to travel, spending three extended spells in Algeria. In the winter and spring of 1893–94 he fell ill and in the oasis town of Biskra underwent a *convalescence merveilleuse* which was like a rebirth into a renewed world. His senses, sharpened by illness and by the strangeness of a foreign land, brought home to him the sheer physical delight of abandoning thought and existing solely through the body. He chronicled this experience, and the life-changing impact of his subsequent journeys, in letters, notebooks and diaries which were to provide the stuff of *Les Nourritures Terrestres* (1897). On medical advice, he spent the winter 1894–5 in the Swiss mountains to complete his convalescence: the isolation in an environment he found profoundly uncongenial exasperated him, but the period was an intensely creative one in which he laid the foundations for much of his subsequent work.

Early in 1895 Gide returned to Algeria. If the first visit had led to his discovery of the life of the senses, the second visit took the form of a specifically sexual awakening. He met Oscar Wilde, then at the height of his fame prior to his disastrous downfall in the trials of May 1895. Gide had earlier met Wilde in Paris and Italy; but now the celebrated aesthete was recklessly indulging his homosexual inclinations among the Arab boys, and encouraged Gide to do the same. The ecstasy Gide experienced banished the last of his uncertainties as to his true nature. The Irish writer's influence on his life was to be commemorated in the character of Ménalque who features in both *Les Nourritures Terrestres* and *L'Immoraliste* (1902). Meanwhile, strengthened in his senses, confirmed in his sexuality, Gide adopted a more explicitly rebellious attitude towards the forces which had weighed on him up to then. Chief among these, of course, was his mother: Gide's letters to her now made it clear that the days when he submitted to her directives, observed taboos and respected authority were over.

However, soon after her son's return to France, Madame Gide died suddenly in May 1895. It was the moment of truth for Gide. He was compelled to recognize that a large part of his nature, and even his fledgling revolt itself, depended for their substance on what she represented. Stricken by grief and a profound sense of disorientation as an abyss opened up in his life, he proposed once more to Madeleine, who accepted him. The couple were married in October, after Gide had been assured by a doctor from whom he sought advice that his homosexual tendencies would disappear of their own accord once he became a husband. But by subconsciously casting Madeleine in the role vacated by his mother, he was merely perpetuating the framework of tension and conflict which would continue to structure his life and work.

In fact, Gide's intention on marrying Madeleine had been to open her eyes to the joys of travel and emancipation: with this in mind he embarked with her on a honeymoon journey retracing his own recent itineraries, from Switzerland, through Italy and on to north Africa. His hopes were not realized, however. He was unable to consummate his marriage: his relatively untested heterosexual drives proved incapable of coping with the great veneration in which he held Madeleine both for herself and also as the embodiment of a certain forbidding image of woman he had internalized from his mother. Moreover, he had to acknowledge that his yearning for the company of small boys had not abated, and the presence of Madeleine was obviously incompatible with this desire. In spite of this difficulty, which the couple seem not to have discussed, they did settle fairly happily into a pattern that their relationship would follow for the next twenty years. They appear to have come to a tacit agreement that Gide's life henceforth would have two centres. At one pole was Madeleine, the image of spirituality and selflessness, all that Gide had aspired to as a young man and would continue to adore, in his idiosyncratic way, throughout his life; at the other were Gide's sexual impulses and the anticonformist, antiauthoritarian reflexes they entailed.

His writing became the arena in which these urges played out their conflict. Prior to the turn of the century he experimented widely with forms and styles, testing out the literary, moral and psychological implications of the experiences and temptations his own life had afforded him. The explosive liberation of *Les Nourritures Terrestres*, with its incitement to disregard reason, morality and social convention in the pursuit of pleasure, was not without its inbuilt ironies; and even before its publication Gide had set about subjecting aspects of this book's message to searching critical scrutiny. He swung like a pendulum as the expression and exploration of one set of premises drove him towards the opposite extreme, in search of the harmony he had earlier fixed as his goal. This dynamic was to nourish almost the whole of Gide's ensuing creative work, emerging with particular clarity in the contrast between *L'Immoraliste* (1902), the account of a man's implacable quest for self-fulfilment – itself written between the lines of, and in reaction against, *Les Nourritures Terrestres* – and *La Porte Étroite* (1909), the story of a young woman's pious abnegation and unremitting self-sacrifice.

In these latter works Gide perfected the *récit* or first-person narrative, a form which he describes as '**ironic**' or 'critical' and which he uses as a means of showing how an individual can be excessively predisposed to a given idea or outlook. This mode of storytelling permits Gide to project his own experience and inclinations into a fictional context and have them worked through and recounted by a persona less lucid than himself, and more likely to go to irreversible extremes. The texts thus present **cathartic** cautionary tales, and for Gide himself, as he put it in *La Tentative Amoureuse*, 'every book is no more than a postponed temptation' (71; 19). In these narratives Gide reveals himself to be a peerless analyst of those tricks of the mind that make ethical obligations out of subconscious, unavowable inclinations, leading humans to conduct their lives in accordance with deluded, ill-founded conceptions of morality.

Gide's capacity to demystify these processes stems from his own radical reappraisal of the protestant ethic. The full implications of the protestant's freedom of conscience began to dawn on him in 1894, when he wrote to his mother that 'When Luther proclaimed free enquiry, the powers in the shadow must have laughed. The history of protestantism is a chapter in the history of free thinking';[1] and in 1896 he published a short essay on the subject called 'Christian Ethics', in which he quotes an article by Faguet:

> Since there is no limit to free enquiry, Protestantism created a limitless, hence indefinite, hence indefinable religion, which would not know, if free enquiry should introduce atheism, whether or not atheism is a part of Protestantism . . . . (*JI*, 95; *J1*, 77)

The logical product of freedom of conscience was the free-thinker: and Gide followed this logic through. He would repeatedly reiterate his belief that religious authorities obstructed access to the true liberating spirit of the Gospels: 'We shall soon come, I believe, to isolating the words of Christ in order to let them appear more emancipatory than they had hitherto seemed' (*JI*, 96; *J1*, 78). Saint Paul, Calvin, all the religious institutions deriving from them, falsify Christ's message: 'Catholicism is inadmissible. Protestantism is intolerable. And I feel profoundly Christian,' he later wrote (*JI*, 367; *J1*, 319). By the latter stages of his life, his emancipation from conventional religion – though not from religious sentiment – led him to formulate a virtually agnostic view of God as a product of man's aspirations, rather than vice versa.

This refusal to rely on preconceived formulations of belief and morality is a key to Gide's thought. His writing constantly seeks to question orthodoxy and doctrinaire or conformist attitudes. His refusal to align himself with any fixed scheme of values culminated, in 1914, in the epic farce of *Les Caves du Vatican*, which lambasts a whole host of what it terms *crustacés* – individuals who, out of laziness or the need for security, allow their lives to ossify into the conventional patterns of the bourgeois, the priest, the scientist, the novelist, or even the stereotype atheist or moral rebel. In *Les Faux-Monnayeurs* of 1925 a character sums up his own moral perspective thus:

> I said to myself that nothing is good for everyone, but only relatively to some people; that nothing is true for everyone, but only relatively to the person who believes it is; that there is no method and no theory which can be applied indifferently to all alike; that if, in order to act, we must make a choice, at any rate we are free to choose; and that if we aren't free to choose, the thing is simpler still; the belief that becomes truth for me (not absolutely, no doubt, but relatively to me) is that which allows me the best use of my strength, the best means of putting my virtues into action. (1089; 176)

As these final words indicate, Gide's concern is to develop to the full each human being's potential – precisely that which is restricted by prior notions of what a human being should be. 'Out of yourself create [. . .] the most irreplaceable of beings', he had exhorted the reader of *Les Nourritures Terrestres* (248; 136); and for himself he had formulated as his own credo, in the deceptively unassuming form of a note to his *Traité du Narcisse*, the injunction to make manifest, through his art, what it was in him that constituted his own individuality.

This aesthetic manifestation of the self is the stuff of all his writing. Using an image drawn from horticulture, Gide makes it clear that in his fiction he is cultivating what botanists call 'sleeping eyes': eliciting blooms from buds that would normally remain dormant, giving cathartic expression to elements of his self he is not prepared to live out in reality.[2] His novels are thus 'autobiographies of the possible'[3] rather than depictions of his actual life. Indeed, such is the complexity and multiplicity of the self that emerges in Gide's writing that he faces a dilemma in giving it expression. His autobiography, *Si le Grain ne Meurt*, on which he began work in 1916, indicates the nature of the problem that confronted him in a comment Gide added at the end of the first part. Complaining that the form he has had to adopt effectively defeats his intention to 'tell everything', he explains: 'I am a creature of dialogue; everything in me is at war and in contradiction', and points out that in the narrative of his memoirs 'the most awkward thing is having to present, as successive, states of confused simultaneity'. The notion of a unitary self comes under severe pressure as linear narrative and multifacetted self-expression struggle for preeminence. His tentative conclusion is that fiction may actually permit a closer approximation of the truth: 'It is possible indeed that one approaches the truth more closely in the novel' (*JII*, 547).

In fact, as Philippe Lejeune points out, Gide's work ultimately resolves this problem by effectively creating an 'autobiographical space' in which a composite self is constituted by complementary facets of his personality made manifest in his novels, his correspondence, his diary, his autobiography, critical essays and occasional writings as they enter into a complex and shifting system of reflections and echoes.

This system in turn gives life to the contradictions, inconsistencies, half-gestures, afterthoughts, errors and recantations which are the characteristic expressions of his personality. His novels are dominated by what one character sums up as 'Inconsistency of characters' (1201–2; 295): here too traditional conceptions of the stable identity of the subject give way to a shifting, fissile construction we nowadays recognize from the psychoanalytical theories of **Lacan**.

If Gide's concern with this manifestation of the self appears unduly egocentric, it should be stressed that from the outset he envisaged his life and his writing in a truly evangelical spirit: for him the artist's vocation – to which he attached extreme importance – was to dedicate his existence to the creation of an exemplary life, 'rather than recounting his life as he has lived it, he must live his life as he will recount it' (*JI*, 29; *J1*, 18: 3 January 1892).[4] For him 'Christ's saying is just as true in art: "Whosoever will save his life (his personality) shall lose it" ' (*JI*, 49; *J1*, 37: 1893). The title he gave to his autobiography equally aptly evokes the Gospel parable of the ear of corn which must die in order to yield fruit. In this sense the record of his life which Gide contrived to bequeath to posterity is our rich harvest of human creativity and moral insight deriving from his selfless courage and tenacity in the pursuit of a personal truth.

The seriousness with which he undertook the writer's mission is evident both in Gide's approach to his personal crises and in his later involvement with social and political issues. 'Woe unto him through whom the offence arises' but 'offences must arise' is the Biblical injunction he made his own in *Le Traité du Narcisse* and which can be appropriately applied to these aspects of his career (9; 12). Gide had given the title 'The value of ill health' to a text on the motivation of the great reforming thinkers and artists in history: Socrates, Christ, Rousseau, Dostoyevsky, Nietzsche and the rest, each had some characteristic abnormality which constituted their essential identity, authorizing them to speak up from the margins of orthodoxy and claim a place for hitherto unacknowledged aspects of humanity: 'Ill health offers a man a new restlessness that he is called on to legitimize' (*JI*, 98; *J1*, 80). Having established to his own satisfaction the legitimacy of his sexual inclination, he determined to present his own contribution to humanity's ongoing debate – in an attempt, as he would put it, to attain a harmony which would incorporate his dissonance.[5]

In pursuit of his vocation, he devoted himself to defining the distinctiveness of his position in reaction to the currents of thought prevailing during the last decade of the nineteenth century. Most notable was Maurice Barrès, a literary iconoclast of the early 1890s who subsequently turned to politics and evolved a reactionary doctrine based on 'the cult of the earth and the dead', an attachment to racial tradition and conservatism. In his 1897 novel *Les Déracinés* he denounced the centralized cultural system in France which he illustrated by showing a group of boys uprooted from their native province of Alsace and transported to the student life in Paris, where they become victims of the moral pitfalls and decadence of the capital. Gide saw in Barrès 'the enemy'[6] and hastened to signify his opposition with an article on *Les Déracinés* whose opening lines in particular were to become notorious: 'Born in Paris of a father from Uzès and a mother from Normandy, where, M. Barrès, do you expect me to take root? So I made up my mind to travel.'[7] Perhaps more striking to his opponents than the flippant tone aimed at an eminent figure was the challenge he was mounting in the name of emancipation, diversification, a refusal to conform or be tied down by norms: 'For want of being summoned up by something out of the ordinary, the most exceptional virtues may remain dormant', he asserts.[8] The writer for whom travel, change and variety were the key to personal growth was bound to jib at the exhortation to immobility. When Charles Maurras, the future founder of the reactionary *Action Française* and ultimately the ideologist for the pro-Nazi Vichy régime, weighed in in defence of Barrès, Gide made short work of him by demonstrating how horticulturalists agreed that the strongest botanical specimens are the product of repeated transplanting.[9]

During this era, Gide was actually struggling to extend his serious readership beyond the mere dozen or so he had despairingly supposed in 1898.[10] He set about creating a public for his brand of intellectual rigour and dedicated creativity, first by collaborating with the reviews *L'Ermitage* and *La Revue blanche,* and then, having gathered around himself a group of like-minded writers, by masterminding the launch of *La Nouvelle Revue Française* in 1909.[11] By the 1920s, this review was the dominant force in French intellectual life.

However, before attaining this cultural preeminence, Gide was to pass through a period of turmoil, coinciding with the First World War, which called into question the entire edifice of his life and thought. He worked in a centre for war refugees, and found himself succumbing to a contagion of despair and demoralization. All around him it seemed that friends and colleagues were turning to religion, and principally the Catholic Church, for moral sustenance and an escape from uncertainty. Gide himself had flirted with catholicism: he had been fascinated by the truculent fervour of the poet Paul Claudel who had tried to convert him. It had disturbed him only slightly when Claudel, horrified by the homoerotic implications of a passage which Gide refused to cut from *Les Caves du Vatican,* more or less consigned him to hell. But early in 1916 Gide received a letter from his friend Henri Ghéon announcing his conversion. Ghéon had been very close to Gide; he had the same homosexual inclinations and had accompanied Gide on many a furtive escapade in search of adolescent partners. Hence the news of his renunciation came as a severe blow. It triggered for Gide a period of intense guilt, self-doubt and even self-loathing.

He turned, as ever, to the Scriptures, recording his meditations in a notebook he entitled *Numquid et tu . . .?,* after the words addressed to Nicodemus in John 7: 52, challenging him to assert his allegiance to Christ. He pondered the Gospels in search of an answer to his anguish. At the same time, in early 1916 he began to write his autobiography *Si le Grain ne meurt*: and it was gradually borne in upon him, as he relived his childhood in the light of intervening events, that his ostensible liberation had not been as thoroughgoing as he had considered it to be. He had duped himself, in believing he could accommodate earlier influences within a more unconventional outlook. This sensation became so acute that he wondered frequently whether the inner voice he had heeded as a young man had not been, in fact, as his catholic acquaintances affirmed, merely the expression of a private demon. At all events, he had freed himself from orthodox morality only to discover that the so-called sincerity in whose name he had broken away brought its own dangers in the form of the manifold self-delusions the human mind is prey to. And after twenty years of marriage, Madeleine, who had virtually taken over from his mother as the embodiment of propriety and purity in his life, stood as a living reproach for his conduct. The struggle to reconcile once more the urgings of his instincts with fidelity to Madeleine, and the guilt generated by this inner strife, plunged Gide into a grave emotional crisis in mid-1916. Moreover, the love which, from his youth, had been a source of inspiration for the author, he now came to view as an inhibiting factor and a threat to the fulfilment of his creative vocation.

Confronted once more by moral and religious questions of the kind that had haunted his youth, Gide was in a sense reliving the traumatic experience which had preceded *Les Nourritures Terrestres*. Matters came to a head in May 1917, when he fell in love with the adolescent Marc Allégret. Up until this time Gide's homosexual partners had not really been rivals of Madeleine; he always maintained that his heart and soul were entirely hers, even though he had to go elsewhere for satisfaction of his senses. But his love for Marc represented a true infidelity to his wife; it was a love of his entire being, he felt – and it excluded her. Madeleine soon sensed that something was amiss, and the extent of her husband's betrayal was made brutally clear to her in December 1917 when she chanced upon a letter from Ghéon remonstrating with Gide for his past turpitudes and beseeching him to abandon the sinful *affaire* on which, he said, he could tell that Gide had embarked from the elated tone of his recent letters. The couple never discussed the situation candidly, but a gulf had opened between them. By now Gide seems to have decided that his personality had irredeemably outgrown his marriage in certain important respects, and that Madeleine could not furnish him with the renewal of artistic inspiration he needed. He later indicated that while all his previous work had been a form of plea inspired by and directed at her, from this point onwards he derived his creative powers from his homosexuality. In order to make this transition his life had first had to come full circle. Just as, some twenty years previously, he had fought off the influence of his mother in the first flush of homosexual experience, so now he was impelled to relive this trauma of separation so that he could finally put behind him the pious respectability that Madeleine stood for. Though in later years the couple did retrieve elements of the former harmony that united them, neither fully recovered from the moral mutilation which was the price of Gide's *disponibilité*. She destroyed all the letters he had written to her from their youth onwards, thereby wiping out a unique testimony of his love for her and expunging an essential figure from the pattern of his life; and he, after

Madeleine's death in 1938, published what survived of his own intimate diary of their difficulties, prefacing it with a self-incriminating obituary.

The other main outcome of this crisis was a new openness in Gide's stance on pederasty. He completed *Si le Grain ne Meurt* by writing a second part which dealt explicitly with his own discovery of his sexual orientation, and published the volume in 1920. He also returned to *Corydon,* a book he had kept secret by printing only a dozen copies of it in 1911. In 1924 he published a revized and expanded version, drawing on examples from natural history, science, sociology and literature to demonstrate the naturalness of pederasty and to argue for the beneficial effects on a young boy of the loving attention of an older man. The concerted culmination of Gide's self-assertion came in 1925–26, when, alongside a re-edition of his autobiography, he brought out his most ambitious novel, *Les Faux-Monnayeurs*, a wide-ranging tapestry deliberately intended to sum up and restate the complexities of his worldview. In it the homosexual theme has an unprecedented prominence: this was, as he put it, 'the first book I wrote while trying not to take her [Madeleine] into account'.[12]

Naturally, his public statements in respect of homosexuality provoked controversy: the appearance of polemical works such as François Nazier's *L'anti-Corydon. Essai sur l'inversion sexuelle* (1924) and François Porché's more subtle *L'amour qui n'ose pas dire son nom* (1927), show the extent to which Gide put homosexuality on the intellectual agenda during these years.

By the time Gide's writing became the object of such polemics these were themselves an indication of the intellectual authority his work had come to command. In 1921 he published a volume intended to constitute a considered reflection of his thought. Entitled *Morceaux Choisis*, it contained a representative anthology of his writings. It provoked resounding attacks from opponents, whose efforts, ironically, were to confer on Gide the notoriety that established him as the principal intellectual figurehead of his age. The onslaught was initiated by Henri Béraud, a not untalented journalist and minor novelist, winner of the Goncourt prize in 1922, who attacked Gide especially for his contribution to the preeminence of *La Nouvelle Revue Française*. His chief aim was to establish that the austere classicism and the cult of authenticity which were the hallmark of the NRF constituted a kind of Calvinist plot against the sense of fun and the robust *esprit gaulois* more congenial to French culture. Punning on the French version of the adage 'Nature abhors a vacuum' (*vide*), he hit on the slogan 'La nature a horreur du *Gide*' to sustain his denunciation of the writer's alleged snobbery and stylistic deficiencies. The tenor and content of his thesis are encapsulated in the title of his vituperative pamphlet, *La Croisade des longues figures* (The Crusade of the long-faced ones), published in 1924 as the culmination of a series of articles during the preceding two years. His were just some among numerous critical slatings Gide had to endure. In November 1921 he notes in his diary, 'For the last four months [. . .] I have received nothing but violent attacks. It is enough to make one think I am paying for them' (*JI*, 703; *J2*, 274–5), while he writes to a correspondent in February 1922: 'Yet more articles, ever more abusive [. . .] have been raining down on me in the past few days. My whole work is "merely a hollow shell in which all that is left of the nut is that black dust the worms have left behind" ', etc. It goes on like that for ten pages. And there are other articles every bit as bad. [. . .] 'They criticize me at one and the same time for wanting to recruit disciples (!) and for not having any [. . .] I can't open a review without finding some nasty remark about me.'[13] Elsewhere he transcribes the following comment by one René Johannet in an article of *La Revue Française*: 'His work is the most flagrantly unpunished intellectual and moral scandal of the century' (*JI*, 708; *J2*, 279: December 1921).

A specific feature of Gide's influence can be measured by the fact that the decade of the 1920s saw a broad, though often largely hostile, appreciation of his thought mounted by religious opponents. Pastor Eugène Ferrari published a pamphlet entitled *André Gide. Le sensualisme littéraire et les exigences de la religion* (1927), in which Gide acknowledged an argument mounted in good faith but lacking the subtlety of insight needed to see that Gide himself, through the ironic dimension of his creative writings, had actually anticipated and given expression to the reservations and objections his characters' behaviour calls for.[14] Father Victor Poucel, for his part, published a number of studies culminating in his book *L'Esprit d'André Gide* (1929). Here Gide was stung by the prejudiced and deliberate incomprehension which he attributed to the religious affiliation of the author who, on the basis of the controversial *Corydon*, *Si le Grain ne Meurt* and *Les Faux-Monnayeurs*, was prepared to deny any value to the whole of Gide's *oeuvre*, claiming to discern in it 'the fingerprints of a maleficent collaborator'.[15]

Underpinning the crude abuse of such texts is an antagonism of principle which was best and most tenaciously articulated by the Catholic critic Henri Massis, who pursued Gide with his hostility for almost half a century. The most subtle of Gide's opponents, he understood perfectly well why Gide had to be combatted: 'What is called into question here is the very notion of *man* on which we live.'[16] He attacks the novelist not merely on the grounds of immorality, but because Gide's zeal as a 'reformer' has even more radical implications, tending to 'break up the substantial unity of the human personality and in so doing destroy all logic and morality'.[17] When Gide finds in Dostoyevsky a confirmation of his theory of the 'inconsistency of human beings', Massis warns that this appeal to the sincerity of contradictory views simultaneously held threatens to undermine a fixed point of civilization: 'What then is sincerity for Gide? To be sincere is to have all kinds of thoughts, to grant them the right to exist merely because one finds them in oneself, for nothing which is within us must be deferred. And because he is unwilling to neglect any element of himself, Gide subordinates his aesthetic to the most unwholesome sources of his inspiration'.[18] Where Gide saw the potential for developing the hitherto unexplored riches of human nature, Massis saw an invitation to spiritual anarchy; the multiplicity of impulses that Gide perceived in human nature spelt the end for the Western notion of Man as a unitary being, as a monolithic Subject. Gide's exploration of the dynamics of the psyche, parallelling the discoveries of Freud, was a metaphysical rather than a purely psychological enterprise: it threatened to 'break the unity that intelligence and will introduce into the complex of sense impressions',[19] 'tear apart the unity of universal being [. . .] and the whole form of the human condition'.[20] At the same time, many of Gide's aesthetic pronouncements, and the terms in which his work was admired, were appropriating the tenets of classicism, the revered high point of French culture, and placing them at the service of this subversive conception of human reality.

> Gide clearly does not intend to dispense with our language, our genius, our classical canon of beauty, that art which contrives not to say everything, its modesty, its reserve, its moral qualities; but he only exalts them as a means of destroying that conception of life, of reason, of wisdom, of moral grandeur, of holiness, which they palpably derive from. The art of classicism, but not the humanity of classicism.[21]

As if this were not all, complained Massis, Gide sought actively to influence the young and win them over to this invidious worldview: in the critic's eyes this clinched the 'demoniacal character' of a work 'whose whole art is applied to corrupting'.[22] While responding with due severity to the ingenious distortions and misrepresentations with which Massis used Gide's texts to support his argument – 'If I weren't the one who had written them, I do declare I would believe you' – Gide paid Massis the compliment of requesting permission to quote from him in an epigraph for the forthcoming *Faux-Monnayeurs* and congratulated him on the intermittent perspicacity of his study: 'For the first time I have seen myself take shape from the scattered features brought together here. Thanks to you and since your study, I feel clearly that I have come into being'.[23]

The attacks by Massis and others provoked much more comment than Gide's work itself had done up till then; in spite of themselves they brought him to a wider public than he had known before, and he acquired a substantial serious readership. In fact, the urgency of his adversaries' polemic was already motivated in part by the fact that the younger generation was increasingly taking to his writings. Those who had survived World War One and conceived a profound hostility towards the society which had brought it about, began to turn to Gide's books for models of rebellion. *Les Nourritures Terrestres*, with its fervent incitements to emancipation, and the reckless disregard for convention depicted in *Les Caves du Vatican*, found an enthusiastic audience on a scale Gide had not previously known. André Breton, soon to be the leader of the Surrealists, eulogized the hero of the latter book in his early poem 'Pour Lafcadio', and organized the Dadaists' mock trial of Gide's *bête noire* Barrès in 1921. The young André Malraux, saluting in Gide 'a spiritual director' and 'the greatest living French writer' proclaimed that he was a prime source of 'intellectual awareness'.[24] Gide's major publications of the mid-1920s established him as the key figure in French culture, 'le contemporain capital' as André Rouveyre called him.[25] Marcel Arland was soon able to refer to him as 'the contested but veritable master of contemporary letters'.[26] A collective homage was published in 1928,[27] Gide was the subject of a special number of *Cahiers de la Quinzaine* in April 1930,[28] and a symposium on him conducted by the review *Latinité* in January 1931 further confirmed his status, eliciting testimonies to his impact from half a dozen countries. At a colloquium in 1935 entitled *André Gide et notre temps*, even Massis was prompted to acknowledge Gide's place at the leading edge of contemporary intellectual investigation, declaring that 'whenever criticism encounters Gide it inevitably touches something in the forefront of man's preoccupations today'.[29]

Gide had substantially realized his creative vocation by this time. Between his play *Oedipe* of 1931 and *Thésée*, his narrative 'testament' of 1946, he produced no major literary texts. However, his standing as a cultural luminary did not decline. His vocation took on a different colouring, establishing him as the prototype of what Jean-Paul Sartre would later call the 'écrivain engagé': he became an intellectual in the peculiarly French sense of an arbiter in intellectual debate, a commentator on current affairs and a spokesman for social reform.

Already in 1914 he had produced a book on the judicial system, based on his experience as a juror. *Souvenirs de la cour d'assises* was, however, but one manifestation of a lifelong interest in criminality and deviancy, reflected also in the *Faits divers* rubric he established in *La Nouvelle Revue Française* between 1928 and 1930, and the documentary volumes *La Séquestrée de Poitiers* and *L'Affaire Redureau* he published in 1930. After completing *Les Faux-Monnayeurs* he undertook a trip to French Equatorial Africa, initially in pursuit of *déracinement* and rejuvenation. However, the injustices he saw there, and the testimony he published on his return as *Voyage au Congo* (1927) and *Retour du Tchad* (1928), combined with his personal interventions, stirred up intense controversy and parliamentary debate, resulting in significant reforms that sought to put a stop to the abusive exploitation of the native populations by the companies holding colonial concessions. The early 1930s saw Gide campaign on behalf of the victims of emergent nazism in Germany and fascism in Spain; and his political notoriety reached its peak when he began to voice his support for the communism of the Soviet Union. Inspired, as he put it, by the Gospels rather than by Marx, his allegiance was of a piece with his discomfort at the privileges his own wealth conferred on him and with his hostility towards the bourgeois society whose institutions and hypocrisies had been the butt of so much of his writing. His many speeches and writings in defence of the revolutionary ideal culminated in a visit to the USSR in 1936. However, once there, and despite his sympathy for the régime's aspirations, he could not but notice its practical shortcomings. More importantly, he observed the installation of a new orthodoxy barely less rigid than those he had always resisted. Three months after his return to France he brought out *Retour de l'URSS*, in which he gave expression to his misgivings. His recantation proved no less sensational than his earlier conversion; in the face of violent controversy and savage polemics he reasserted his position one year later, this time extensively documented and confirmed by cross-reference to other dissidents, in *Retouches à mon retour de l'URSS* (1937). His point of view remained what it always had been, that of the individual seeking to remain faithful to himself, exercising the freedom to contradict himself, to admit to his mistakes and refuse to see the truth embodied definitively in any orthodox or institutional framework. He had already sounded a warning even as he announced his support for communism: 'Just like the conversion to Catholicism, conversion to Communism implies an abdication of free enquiry, submission to a dogma, recognition of an orthodoxy. It happens that all orthodoxies are suspect to me' (*JI*, 1175; *J3*, 276).

It is in this, more than in any particular commitment, that Gide continues to represent intellectual probity and to compel the respect of his peers and succeeding generations. The Nobel Prize of 1947 was followed, on his death in 1951, by tributes from younger luminaries such as Camus, Mauriac and Sartre, the latter, in particular, stressing the fact that Gide was an essential feature of the intellectual landscape: 'the whole of French thought for these last thirty years, whether willingly or not, and whatever other references it might have had, had to define itself also with reference to Gide [. . .] Gide is an irreplaceable example because he chose to *become* his truth'.[30] Of the next generation, Roland Barthes chose Gide as the subject of the first article he wrote[31] and was repeatedly to acknowledge Gide as a primary influence, as his 'original language'.[32] Michel Tournier in turn hailed him as 'the first *engagé* writer of his time' who 'deliberately identified himself with a range of causes he believed just', and praised his 'readiness to face up to discomfort and his willingness to make enemies on all fronts at once'.[33] In an era when it has become customary to question the status of the intellectual in France and to bemoan the absence of commanding figures of his kind, it is almost inevitably to the example of Gide that the contemporary philosopher Bernard-Henri Lévy turned for inspiration in his book and television series *Les Aventures de la Liberté*.[34] It is evident that Gide remains as much as ever a key reference point for French culture.

Notes

1. Letter reproduced in JEAN DELAY, *The Youth of André Gide*, abridged and translated by June Guicharnaud (Chicago and London, University of Chicago Press, 1963), p. 367.

2. Letter to SCHEFFER, *OC IV*, pp. 616–17.

3. The phrase is by ALBERT THIBAUDET, quoted in *Journal des Faux-Monnayeurs*, p. 87; 51.

4. This theme is pursued with exemplary thoroughness in DANIEL MOUTOTE, *Le Journal de Gide et les problèmes du moi* (Paris, Presses Universitaires de France, 1968).

5. *Dostoïevski, OCXI*, 294.

6. Letter to HENRI GHÉON, 7 January 1898, quoted in Claude Martin, *La Maturité d'André Gide* (Paris, Klincksieck, 1977) p. 244.

7. *Prétextes*, p. 29.

8. Ibid., p. 31.

9. See 'Autour de M. Barrès', *Prétextes*, pp. 29–38. For a recent overview of the question, see PETER SCHNYDER, 'Gide face à Barrès', *Orbis Litterarum*, 40, 1 (1985), pp. 33–43.

10. Cf. MARTIN, *op.cit.*, pp. 302–4.

11. MARTIN, *op.cit.*, pp. 433–4. See Auguste Anglès, *André Gide et le premier groupe de 'La Nouvelle Revue Française', I. La formation du groupe et les années d'apprentissage* (Paris, Gallimard, 1978).

12. *Ainsi soit-il*, in *JII*, 1157; 77.

13. Letter to Fr.-P. Alibert, 21 February 1922, in *Correspondance Gide-Alibert*, éd. Cl Martin (Lyon, Presses Universitaires de Lyon, 1982), p. 246.

14. Gide's response was published in the *NRF*, 1 July 1928, p. 46–8; and in *OCXV*, 531–4.

15. See *JI*, 863–4; *J2*, 424: November 1927; *OCXIV*, pp. 404–12; *L'Esprit d'André Gide* (Paris, A l'Art Catholique, 1929), p. 53.

16. HENRI MASSIS, *Jugements II* (Paris, Plon, 1924) p. 48; the remark was quoted with pleasure by Gide in a letter dated 25 January 1924, *OCXII*, 553–5.

17. Ibid., p. 46.

18. Ibid., p. 13.

19. Ibid., p. 46.

20. Ibid., p. 48.

21. Ibid., p. 52.

22. Ibid., pp. 29–30, 21.

23. Letter of 25 January 1924, *OCXII*, pp. 554–5.

24. ANDRÉ MALRAUX, 'Aspects d'André Gide', *Action*, 3e année, March–April 1922, p. 20.

25. This was the title Rouveyre adopted for a series of articles in *Les Nouvelles littéraires*, October–November 1924, later published in his book *Le Reclus et le retors* (Paris, Crès, 1927).

26. In the *NRF*, XXXVI, February 1931.

27. *André Gide*, Editions de la Capitole, coll. 'Les Contemporains'.

28. *Cahiers de la Quinzaine*, 6e cahier de la 20e série.

29. *André Gide et notre temps*, Entretien tenu au siège de l'Union pour la Vérité, Paris, U.V. *Bulletin*, 42e année, no. 7–8, April-May 1935, p. 19.

30. 'Gide vivant', *Les Temps modernes*, no. 65, March 1951; *Situations* IV, (Paris, Gallimard, 1964), pp. 85–9 (86, 89).

31. 'Notes sur André Gide et son Journal', *Existences*, no. 27, July 1942, pp. 7–18: reprinted in *Bulletin des Amis d'André Gide*, vol. 13, no. 67, July 1985, pp. 85–105; translated as 'On André Gide and his journal' in *A Barthes Reader*, ed. Susan Sontag (New York, Hill and Wang, 1982), pp. 3–17.

32. *Roland Barthes par Roland Barthes* (Paris, Seuil, 1975), p. 103.

33. 'Five Keys for André Gide', translated by Penny Hueston and Colin Nettelbeck, *Partisan Review*, vol. 54 no. 1, Winter 1987, pp. 35–56 (50–1); in French in *Le Vol du Vampire: notes de lecture* (Paris, Mercure de France, 1982), pp. 212–238.

34. *Les Aventures de la Liberté. Une histoire subjective des intellectuels* (Paris, Grasset, 1991). The publication of this book coincided with a four-part television series under the same title, broadcast on Antenne 2.

Part One

Aspects of the Work

1 Justin O'Brien on From Pagan Daemon to Christian Devil*

Gide's initial conditioning by Christian religion was to prove ineradicable. However, his treatment of religious themes is both creative and subversive. Creative, because he brings urgency and vigour to the theological issues he deals with: Gide is drawn to biblical texts and religious motifs because, for him, they correspond to deep-seated psychological and moral questions which remain crucial to human existence and retain an enduring relevance. Even some of his Christian detractors, such as Mauriac, conceded that his readings of the Scriptures brought the texts to life and demonstrated their contemporary pertinence despite his unorthodox, sometimes heretical, exegeses.

His approach to these matters is unconventional and individualistic partly because he exploits to the full the protestant principle of free examination of the scriptures. For him this makes it possible to liberate Holy Writ from the stifling dogma of institutionalized religion. The essential point for Gide is that Christian mythology, like ancient Greek mythology, gives up its riches when it is considered rationally, not as a repository of ineffable mystical truth or intimidating doctrinal authority, but as a rich store of psychological insight. Indeed, Gide brings to his reading of the Bible a lesson he has learned in examining Greek mythology: one has to believe in it, but not sacrifice one's intelligence to it. (See 'Considérations sur la mythologie grecque', *OCIX*, 147–154.)

Perhaps his most provocative application of this principle emerges from his preoccupation with the Devil, in the course of which, in effect, he combines both the pagan and the Christian traditions, the better to confirm their abiding richness. A parodic reflection of this method can be discerned in *Les Faux-Monnayeurs*, where Lilian Griffith accuses Vincent Molinier's musings of having bred 'a monster [. . .]. A cross between a bacchante and the Holy Ghost' (979; 60). Justin O'Brien examines this hybridization in a chapter of his

* Originally published in *Portrait of André Gide. A Critical Biography* (London, Secker and Warburg, 1953), pp 284–297.

critical biography, one of the first major contributions in English to Gide
studies, which is informed throughout by a close acquaintance with Gide
himself and with his writings – in particular the *Journal*, which O'Brien
translated into English in four volumes.

> . . . I had no sooner *assumed* the demon than my whole biography was
> at once made clear to me: [. . .] I suddenly understood what had been
> most obscure to me, to such a point that this assumption took on the
> exact shape of my interrogation and my preceding wonder.

> There is no work of art without collaboration of the demon.[1]

For some time André Gide's belief in an active force of evil served as a
stumbling-block for many readers, who noticed with what disconcerting
frequency the words Demon, Devil, and Evil One occur in parts of his
work. 'Satanism' implies worship of the Devil or at least trafficking with
him; it suggests witchcraft, black masses, and such infamous figures as
Gilles de Rais and the Marquis de Sade. Indulgent readers of Gide set it
down as just one more of his contradictions that, by resurrecting the figure
of Satan, he should seem to ally himself with such as these while spending
much of his life combatting superstition. But since the novels of such
Catholics as François Mauriac, Georges Bernanos, and Julien Green in
France, since *The Screwtape Letters* of C. S. Lewis and the novels of Charles
Williams and Graham Greene in England, there is a tendency to take more
seriously this aspect of Gide's work. Both Denis de Rougemont, an eminent
Swiss Protestant, and Claude-Edmonde Magny, writing in a French
Carmelite review, have described Gide as one of those rare spirits who
show great familiarity with the Devil and talk intelligently of him.[2]

Without ever worshipping Satan or, for that matter, dealing with him
any more than the average man does, Gide certainly gave him his due. In
fact, to write about the Devil in literature today without discussing Gide
would be tantamount to omitting Milton or Blake or Dostoevsky. It is in the
company of such writers that he belongs, in this regard, rather than in that
of the fifteenth-century Bluebeard and the man who gave a name to
sadism, with whom one otherwise intelligent critic associated him on the
grounds of a necessary link between Satanism and homosexuality.[3]
Nonetheless, Gide's sexual orientation does enter the discussion because it
was the constant current of pederasty in his life, his ambivalent attitude
toward his wife, and his consequent guilt-feelings that made him attribute
a decisive role in his biography to the Devil. In the Spring of 1919, when he
began to write the second and capital part of his memoirs, he had to make
an effort to exclude from the drama an important actor – the Devil – whom
he did not identify until long after the events.[4] He complained to his friend,
Roger Martin du Gard, that his task would be so much easier if he could

bring the demon out into the open as an active influence.[5] Still it was not quite possible for him to avoid altogether using Satan as an explanation, for the memoirs contain such remarks as this: '. . . in addition, as I have said, my love was almost mystical; and if the devil was deceiving me by making me consider as an insult the idea of any carnal admixture to it, this is something I could not yet realize . . .'[6] or: 'Since my adventure at Susa, to be sure, the Evil One had no further great victory to win over me.'[7]

Already during the dark years of the First World War, before composing those decisive revelations of *Si le Grain ne Meurt . . .*, Gide had come clearly to recognize the Devil's share in his tormented destiny. The whole of his 'Detached Pages' for 1916 is devoted to this subject; and it is surely significant that they were written simultaneously with the first part of the mystical outburst of *Numquid et tu . . .?*, which they immediately follow in the editions of the *Journals*. For, although he protests that it is not necessary to believe in God in order to believe in the Devil, such a remarkable coincidence of beliefs suggests that he might never have accepted Satan if he had not been spiritually prepared to do so. 'I had heard talk of the Evil One,' he writes there,

> 'but I had not made his acquaintance. He already inhabited me when I did not yet distinguish him. [. . .] I had invited him to take up his residence in me, as a challenge and because I did not believe in him, like the man in the legend who sells his soul to him in return for some exquisite advantage – and who continues not believing in him despite having received the advantage from him!'[8]

As he looks back on his life, Gide recognizes that many of the exhortations he had addressed to himself had contained a diabolic element, that in many a 'specious dialogue' with himself he had had an interlocutor. On the other hand, his conviction of a positive external force is not inflexible, for he adds: 'If someone should come along later and show me that he lives not in hell but in my blood, my loins, or my insomnia, does he believe that he can suppress him thus? When I say: the Evil One, I know what that expression designates just as clearly as I know what is designated by the word *God*. I draw his outline by the deficiency of each virtue.[9] And a brief dialogue with Satan concludes the meditation with Satan's flattering remarks:

'How well we know each other! You know, if you wanted to –'
'What?'
'What good friends we should be! . . .'[10]

That was in 1916, at the height of Gide's mystical crisis. Actually his conviction of the demon's existence did not become firmly established until then. Despite the early representation of Saul's temptations in the guise of a horde of little black demons and the occasional, rather perfunctory mention of the demon pushing Michel madly southward with the ailing Marceline in *L'Immoraliste*, it may fairly be said that the Devil plays no significant part in Gide's work until after the age of forty-five. In fact, he was just that age when in a decisive conversation at Cuverville, Jacques Raverat, a young French artist who had recently married the granddaughter of Charles Darwin and settled in England, confessed to believing in the Devil before believing in God. 'I told him,' says Gide, 'that what kept me from believing in the Devil was that I wasn't quite sure of hating him. Certainly there will be someone in my novel who believes in the devil.'[11] That conversation made a deep impression on Gide, for he was to refer to it often in the future and to remember it ten years later when writing *Les Faux-Monnayeurs*, where more than one character is tormented by such a belief.

Although Jacques Raverat's significant intervention in André Gide's life seems to be limited to that one crucial talk growing out of a reading of Milton, he left a profound mark by starting the writer on his absorbing identification of the demon. From then on, Gide's thought on the problem of evil was to burgeon and ramify rapidly, finding confirmation as it grew in his favourite writers. Less than two years later he describes himself as listening to the voice of the Devil despite himself. In the anguished spiritual autobiography of William Hale White, which Arnold Bennett wisely recommended to him in 1915, he found the sincere 'Mark Rutherford' deploring, in words that he himself might have written, the popular dismissal of the notion of a personal devil:

> No doubt there is no such thing existent; but the horror at evil which could find no other expression than in the creation of a devil is no subject for laughter, and if it do not in some shape or other survive, the race itself will not survive. No religion, so far as I know, has dwelt like Christianity with such profound earnestness on the bisection of man – on the distinction within him, vital to the very last degree, between the higher and the lower, heaven and hell. What utter folly is it because of an antique vesture to condemn as effete what the vesture clothes! Its doctrine and its sacred story are fixtures in concrete form of precious thoughts purchased by blood and tears.[12]

Mark Rutherford's thought here does not differ from Gide's apology for using such terms as 'the soul' and 'the Evil One' – implying, as he says, a certain mythology that 'is the most eloquent to explain an inner drama.'[13]

It was, however, in 1921–2 that Gide's reflections about the Devil received the most encouraging confirmation – and from two very different literary sources. The first in time was Dostoevsky, whom he had been voraciously rereading and on whom he delivered a series of penetrating lectures at just that moment. In them he confessed to having used the Russian novelist as a pretext to develop his own thoughts, always seeking, like the bees of which Montaigne speaks, what would suit his own honey.[14]

Gide consistently did this with his favourite writers – whether Virgil or Whitman, Goethe or Dante or Nietzsche, Browning or Blake or Shakespeare – lovingly finding himself already in them rather than espousing a foreign thought. Charles Du Bos speaks of Gide's unerring faculty for discovering in his predecessors 'that particle of virtual Gidism' which they contain.[15] When polishing his Dostoevsky lectures for publication, annoyed that they should still take so much of his time after their delivery and keep him from the massive, Dostoevskian novel he had already begun, he noted: 'But everything I find a means of saying through Dostoevsky and apropos of him is dear to me and I attach a great importance to it. It will be, just as much as a book of criticism, a book of confessions, to anyone who knows how to read; or rather: a profession of faith.'[16] He had already recognized himself in Dostoevsky before the war, when he wrote a long article on the Russian writer as he emerged from his correspondence. In that study of 1908, Gide had revealed an intimate knowledge of the novels as well as of the numerous collections of letters; and he obviously found a close spiritual relationship between Dostoevsky and himself, for he enjoyed stressing his familiar themes as handled by the Russian precursor.

Yet in *Dostoïevsky d'après sa correspondance* there is not a single mention of the demon – who looms so large in the later study. This simply proves that in 1908 André Gide was not yet ready to recognize the Devil; but in 1921–2 his own thought was so absorbed with that figure that he was pleased to discover what a place it occupied in Dostoevsky's work. He even granted that 'some will probably see a Manichean in him.'[17]

The second confirmation of Gide's thinking that came to him at this time lay in William Blake. In January 1922, doubtless inspired by the first of the lectures on Dostoevsky and by private conversations with Gide, the critic Charles Du Bos sent him a copy of Blake's *Marriage of Heaven and Hell*. With his customary perceptiveness, the half-American Du Bos, as conversant with English literature as with French, had justly sensed a deep affinity. From a journal-entry of 1914 we know that Gide had already read some Blake 'with amazement' in a borrowed volume of *Selections*. Now, after reading the little book he had just received, he noted: 'Like an astronomer calculating the existence of a star whose rays he does not yet perceive directly, I foresaw Blake, but did not yet suspect that he formed a constellation with Nietzsche, Browning and Dostoevsky. The most brilliant star, perhaps, of the group; certainly the strangest and most distant.'[18] Almost at once he must have begun translating *The Marriage of Heaven and Hell* – through a natural and already familiar desire to share his discovery with others – for his French version was finished by the beginning of June.[19]

But an even more immediate reaction to Blake's prophetic work than its translation was Gide's introduction of it into his lectures on Dostoevsky. It is almost as if, in his spontaneous assimilation of their thought to his own,

he had confused the English poet and the Russian novelist. In the fifth
lecture, in fact, he quotes this paragraph as the opening of *The Marriage of
Heaven and Hell* (it is not quite the opening) with the remark that
Dostoevsky seems to have unwittingly appropriated it: 'Without Contraries
is no progression. Attraction and Repulsion, Reason and Energy, Love and
Hate, are necessary to human existence.' One can readily see how this
statement, while justifying Gide's conflicts and the ambivalence he felt
within himself, must have delighted him by making his beloved progress
dependent on such contraries. This might be said to be the theme of Blake's
little book, as Gide showed by quoting in that same lecture at least six of its
'Proverbs of Hell':

'The road of excess leads to the palace of wisdom.'

'If the fool would persist in his folly he would become wise.'

'You never know what is enough unless you know what is more than
enough.'

'The roaring of lions, the howling of wolves, the raging of the stormy
sea, and the destructive sword, are portions of eternity too great for the eye
of man.'

'The cistern contains: the fountain overflows.'

'The tigers of wrath are wiser than the horses of instruction.'

And not content with quoting some of the best of Blake's subversive
proverbs, Gide adds two of his own devising: 'It is with fine sentiments
that bad literature is made'; and 'There is no work of art without
collaboration of the demon.'[20] In order to substantiate the latter, indeed, he
quotes further from *The Marriage of Heaven and Hell*: 'The reason Milton
wrote in fetters when he wrote of Angels & God, and at liberty when of
Devils & Hell, is because he was a true Poet and of the Devil's party
without knowing it.' From 1922 onward, in memory of Blake, Gide
occasionally entitles as 'Proverbs of Hell' some of the pithiest remarks in
his *Journals*, such as 'Descend to the bottom of the well if you wish to see
the stars.'[21] The form was a congenial one; many other examples can be
found in his work, without the label, even long before his encounter with
William Blake. *Paludes* and *Le Prométhée mal enchaîné*, for instance, abound
in them. Each reader could, in fact, make his own collection of infernal
maxims from Gide's writings.

During the composition of his *Dostoïevsky*, Gide was also writing what
he considered his only true novel, *Les Faux-Monnayeurs*; and from 1919
until 1925 he kept a special notebook in which he recorded 'inch by inch'
(as he said in English) the progress of the novel. It is not strange that in that
workbook, originally published in 1926 as *Journal des 'Faux-Monnayeurs'*
(*Journal of 'The Counterfeiters'* in America, and *Logbook of The Coiners* in
England) and appreciated chiefly for its fascinating insights into the
problems of literary creation, Satan should play a most important role. In
early January 1921 Gide noted there that the more we deny him the more

reality we give to the Devil, thus affirming him by our negation, and foresaw that this might become the central subject of his novel – 'in other words the invisible point about which everything gravitates.'[22] A few days later he expressed the desire to let the Devil 'circulate incognito throughout the entire book, his reality growing stronger the less the other characters believe in him. This is the distinguishing feature of the Devil, whose introductory motif is: "Why should you be afraid of me? You know very well I don't exist." '[23] It was then that he wrote a dialogue entitled 'Identification of the Demon' to explain that capital remark, which appeared to him as 'one of the catchwords of the book.'

From the fact that that dialogue did not find its way into the novel and the observation that the Devil hardly appears openly therein it has been assumed that Gide changed his mind on this point, as on so many others. But this conclusion overlooks the keywords 'invisible point' and 'incognito.' It never entered Gide's intentions to list the Devil in the cast of characters. To be sure, the Demon fairly frequently shows the tips of his horns throughout the novel in more than a merely metaphorical sense. On the first page he influences Bernard to violate his mother's secrets and on the last page he persuades old La Pérouse that the mysterious tapping on the wall is *his* infernal voice. Elsewhere he makes Bernard find a coin with which to withdraw Édouard's luggage, pushes Vincent to gamble the family savings and then smilingly watches him slip the little key into Lady Griffith's door, inhabits Olivier the night he receives Bernard's letter, and supplies Édouard with sophistries justifying his treatment of Boris.[24]

It is Vincent Molinier, however, who best embodies the character Gide promised himself in 1914 to put into his novel: the person who actively believes in the Devil. Although we are told that his scientific education kept him from believing in the supernatural and thus gave the Demon a great advantage over him, we later see him reappear in Africa as a madman, probably a murderer, who identifies himself with Satan.[25] Yet Vincent is himself a shadowy character at best whom we most often meet indirectly through Édouard's journal or the conversation of others; it is thus most appropriate that this last mention of him should occur in a letter written by a man who knows neither him nor his name and that the letter should be read by Vincent's brother, to whom it never occurs to identify him.

The key to Vincent lies in the *Journal des 'Faux-Monnayeurs,'* where his creator said of him more than four years before the novel was published: 'Vincent gradually lets himself be permeated by the diabolic spirit. He imagines he is becoming the Devil; it is when things go best for him that he feels the most damned. [. . .] In the end he believes in the existence of Satan *as in his own*; in other words, he eventually believes he is Satan.'[26] This, then, is the evolution of Vincent Molinier. But what Gide does not say is that he also stands as the *cause* of the novel's action. By leading Laura into adultery before the novel begins, he provokes Édouard's return from

England to save her, Bernard's meeting with Édouard and Laura, and all that ensues. By handing over his brother Olivier to the vicious Passavant, he further complicates the plot sufficiently so that he can then leave the stage altogether. There are other diabolic characters in *Les Faux-Monnayeurs* – notably the mysterious Strouvilhou, Passavant himself, and to a smaller degree Ghéridanisol and even Armand Vedel; but Vincent's satanic rôle is even more central than theirs. In all his behaviour one can hear echoes of that famous dialogue between Ivan Karamazov and the Devil which Gide so much admired. Is it not possible that it was in his person that Gide intended to make the Devil 'circulate incognito' throughout the novel?

The moment he had finished writing *Les Faux-Monnayeurs*, Gide himself set out for the Congo on a year-long voyage. Instead of there identifying himself with the Devil as the unbalanced Vincent had done in the same setting (and as some of his readers were beginning to identify him), he flatly stated once and for all his disbelief in the Demon. On 21 September 1925 he wrote in his travel diary apropos of Bossuet's *Traité de la Concupiscence*, which he had been reading:

> I know only too well for having often indulged in the practice myself: there is nothing in the life of a nation or in our individual life that is not susceptible of a mystical or teleological interpretation, in which cannot be seen, if one really wants to, the active opposition of God and the Demon. And that interpretation may even seem the most satisfactory simply because it is the most picturesque. My whole mind at present revolts against that complacent practice, which does not seem to me quite fair.[27]

In the case of Vincent Molinier, then, as in that of André Walter in his first book, André Gide had made his creature carry out to its logical extreme a tendency of his own nature, saving himself from the same fate, however, by that grain of common sense which he denied to his fictional character.

Over twenty years later Gide was to express no less categorically his mature attitude toward Satan by stating: 'As for me, I look upon the Devil as an invention, just like God himself. I do not believe in him; but I pretend to believe in him and gladly lend myself to this game. . .'.[28] Yet he wrote these words in his preface to *The Private Memoirs and Confessions of a Justified Sinner* by James Hogg, a book he wished to save from oblivion just because it contains so vivid a characterization of the Demon as 'the exteriorization of our own desires, of our pride, of our most secret thoughts.' In other words, to the very end of his life André Gide continued to play with the concept of a personal Devil, employing traditional terminology, half convincing himself that he believed, and going out of his way to adopt any literary work that personified the evil spirit.

In brief, Gide's contradictory attitudes on the subject can be summarized by stating simply that, whereas his conscious mind rejected the idea of the Devil together with the idea of God, he was constantly and obscurely drawn to posit both concepts as the extrapolation of an inner conflict. At the end of his 'Identification of the Demon' he formulated this theory: 'Just like the kingdom of God, hell is within us;' and a few years later he found the same thought admirably expressed by Milton in the line in which Satan says 'Which way I fly is Hell; myself am Hell.'[29]

It is dangerous to insist on the fact that evil is basic, for he who does so is generally thought to be very wicked himself. As Gide soon learned, the world has a tendency to think that by merely admitting the existence of evil we somehow create it. Perhaps none of Gide's provocative remarks has been more often discussed or used against him than the first two of his own 'Proverbs of Hell' boldly inserted into his *Dostoïevsky*. Certain critics, perhaps wilfully ignoring the fact that he was castigating merely so-called 'edifying literature,' interpreted his second proverb to mean that good literature is made only with bad sentiments.[30] Others reminded him that what he now called the demon's collaboration he had named otherwise in 1895 when he wrote in the Foreword to *Paludes* of 'that share of the unconscious that I should like to call God's share,' adding: 'A book is always a collaboration, and the more the book is worth the smaller the scribe's share is. . .'.[31] But to this Gide might have replied that he had only lately learned to identify his collaborator properly, and that, furthermore, as he says in the last of his 'Proverbs of Hell' in 1941:

> The promise of the caterpillar
> Binds not the butterfly.[32]

In any case, the very phrase 'collaboration of the demon' in this connection suggests some confusion in Gide's mind – it matters little whether it be intentional or unintentional – between the Christian concept of the Devil and the Greek view of the Daemon – that manifestation of divine energy, which may be good or evil, that element in man's fate which, according to Heraclitus, constitutes his character. It was this latter kind of demon (and a boundless confidence in his prompting) which Gide found early in Goethe and later felt had, in the comfort of Goethe's success, become rather stodgily middle class.[33] The principle is faithfully described by Stefan Zweig in words that Gide might have signed:

> The daemon is the incorporation of that tormenting leaven which impels our being (otherwise quiet and almost inert) towards danger, immoderation, ecstasy, renunciation, and even self-destruction. [. . .] Whatever strives to transcend the narrower boundaries of self, overleaping immediate personal interest to seek adventures in the dangerous realm of enquiry, is the outcome of the daemonic

constituent of our being. But the daemon is not a friendly and helpful power unless we can hold him in leash, can use him to promote a wholesome tension and to assist us on our upward path. [. . .] Restlessness of the blood, the nerves, the mind is always the herald of the daemonic tempest.[34]

So many of Zweig's expressions here correspond to favourite ideas of Gide – from the transcending of self to the upward path and from the value of renunciation to that of inquiry and unrest – that the passage almost seems to have been written by the French author. It was in just this sense that Gide quoted Goethe as saying: 'That a man's strength and his force of predestination were recognizable by the demoniacal element he had in him.'[35]

In Gide's case the slipping from a neutral Daemon with as much potentiality for good as for evil to a stimulating and yet frankly evil spirit can be most clearly seen in his letter of 22 November 1929 (his sixtieth birthday) to Montgomery Belgion:

I believe it to be ill-advised, unprofitable, uninstructive to judge human actions, or more exactly to evaluate them, solely on the plane of *good* and *evil*. The comforting and reassuring idea of *good*, which the middle-classes cherish, invites humanity to stagnation, to sleep. I believe that often what society and you yourself call *evil* (at least the evil that is not the result of a mere deficiency, but rather a manifestation of energy) possesses a greater educative and initiative virtue than what you call *good*, and is thus capable of indirectly leading humanity toward progress.[36]

But if this is the clearest statement of Gide's eventual fusion of pagan Daemon with Christian Devil, the most revealing indication of this tendency on his part – because wholly unconscious – lies half-hidden in his *Dostoïevsky*.

There, after stating that the intelligence always has a demoniacal role in Dostoevsky and that the novelist invariably links the Devil with the intellect, Gide goes on to say:

The great temptations that the Evil One offers us are, according to Dostoevsky, intellectual temptations, questions. And I do not think I am getting far from my subject by considering first the questions that so long summed up the constant anguish of humanity: "What is man? Whence does he come? Where is he going? What was he before his birth? What does he become after his death? To what truth can man lay claim?" and even more exactly: "What is truth?"[37]

It would seem, especially in view of the fact that Gide does not really consider these questions here beyond voicing them and does not develop the thought further, that he is indeed getting away from his subject. Yet if we remember that the questioning spirit is always a noble spirit to Gide, we shall recognize that first Dostoevsky, by insisting upon the interrogation, and then Gide, by attributing to him the questions that have forever haunted mankind, are ennobling Satan.

But even more significant is the fact that we have heard these very questions before in Gide's work. They are precisely the ones that Prometheus in vain asks his eagle. Gide seems to have been insufficiently aware, in fact, that Lucifer (the light-bearer) and Prometheus (the fire-giver) have much in common: both the archangel in revolt against God and the titan rebelling against Zeus are gravely punished for their pride in siding with man. Gide's interest in the Devil parallels his interest in Prometheus; more sophisticated and more subtle in its expression, it replaces that earlier interest. Perhaps because he had earlier traced a suggestive parallel between Prometheus and Christ, he hesitated to draw another one between Prometheus and Satan, those two arch-unsubmissive spirits who both symbolized progress in his mind. The Devil might be called a Christian counterpart of Prometheus, the greatest Daemon (both in the sense of demi-god and in that of energetic force) of them all. That at least once Gide nevertheless recognized the similarity between them is apparent from his words on Goethe written in 1928 in the outline of a lecture he was to give in Berlin:

> No, all is not calm, smiling, and peaceful in Goethe and that is indeed what makes him so great. There is in him something demoniacal, untamed, something Promethean that relates him to the Satan of Milton and Blake, something restive that we still question, that will never reveal its secret or pronounce its final word because that final word is itself an interrogation, a question indefinitely deferred.[38]

Clearly for Gide, as for Goethe, Nietzsche, Dostoevsky, and the other predecessors he admired, the daemonic spirit inhabited, in Zweig's phrase, the dangerous realm of inquiry. It made for progress precisely because it could not leave well enough alone. His own work is interrogative rather than affirmative in spirit, and this fact has contributed more than anything else to its deep and widespread influence.

Notes

1. *J*2, 189 ('Detached Pages,' 1916); and *Dostoïevsky, OC*, XI, 280.

2. Cf. ROUGEMONT: *La Part du diable* (N.Y.: La Maison Française, 1943), p. 91 and Magny: 'Satanism in Contemporary Literature,' in *Satan* (ed.) by Bruno de Jésus Marie (N.Y.: Sheed and Ward, 1952), p. 453.

3. Cf. MAGNY in ibid., p. 461.

4. Cf. *Si le Grain ne Meurt . . .* , *OC, X*, 345–6.

5. Cf. ROGER MARTIN DU GARD, *Notes sur André Gide*, pp. 18–19 (dated February 1920).

6. *OC, X*, 349.

7. Ibid., p. 411.

8. *J2*, 188 ('Detached Pages,' 1916).

9. Ibid., p. 189.

10. Ibid., p. 190.

11. *J2*, 84 (25 September 1914).

12. *The Deliverance of Mark Rutherford* quoted in *J2*, 120 (25 January 1916).

13. *J2*, 129 (16 February 1916).

14. Cf. *Dostoïevsky, OC, XI*, 282–3.

15. Cf. *Le Dialogue avec André Gide*, p. 305.

16. *J2*, 301 (22 April 1922).

17. *Dostoïevsky, OC, XI*, 266.

18. *J2*, 297–8 (16 January 1922). Cf. Ibid., p. 71 (25 August 1914).

19. Cf. *J2*, 302 (5 June 1922).

20. *Dostoïevsky, OC, XI*, 279–80.

21. *J3*, 277 (4 July 1933).

22. *Journal des Faux-Monnayeurs, OC, XIII*, 19.

23. Ibid., p. 21.

24. Cf. *OC, XII*, 21, 549, 125, 65, 87, 251 and 318.

25. Cf. *OC, XII*, 209 and 527.

26. *OC, XIII*, 44.

27. *Le Voyage au Congo, OC, XIII*, 130–1.

28. Preface to HOGG: *The Memoirs of a Justified Sinner* in *Préfaces* (Neuchâtel: Ides et Calendes, 1948), p. 141.

29. 'Pages retrouvées,' *N.R.F., XXXII*, 501–2 (April 1929); *J1*, 677; *J2*, 252.

30. Cf. *J4*, 44 (2 September 1940).

31. *OC, I*, 369.

32. *J4*, 60 (23 February 1941).

33. Cf. 'Préface au Théâtre de Goethe,' *Préfaces*, pp. 93 and 113.

34. *Master Builders: A Typology of the Spirit* (N.Y.: Viking Press, 1939), pp. 243–5.

35. *Journal des Faux-Monnayeurs*, OC, XIII, 82.

36. *OC, XV*, 553, Cf. *André Gide et notre temps*, p. 30.

37. *Dostoïevsky OC, XI*, 267.

38. 'Feuillets 1928,' *OC, XV*, 515–16.

2   Mischa Harry Fayer on Liberation from the existing social order*

In 1950, at the behest of his then secretary Yvonne Davet, Gide agreed to have certain of his texts collected and published in a volume under the title *Littérature engagée*. The aim was to show him as a precursor of the generation who, inspired by Sartre had coined the phrase in his *Qu'est-ce que la littérature?* of 1947, saw the intellectual as inescapably bound up with social and political questions. This subsequent generation did indeed consider Gide as a pioneer and a model in this regard, but the use of Sartre's phrase for Gide's so-called 'committed' work – speeches, letters, articles and other occasional texts representing interventions in ideological and political debate – tends to overstress the political features of the phase Gide went through in the 1930s. The consolidation of the Russian Revolution and the rise of European fascism gave rise to this material, but in fact it has its deeper origins in two personal sources. First was Gide's sexual option, which made of him an overt outsider seeking to create for himself a position in the social 'concert', to adumbrate a harmony that would incorporate his dissonance, as he put it. Second was his loyalty to protestant-inspired freedom of conscience, which made him an authentic and irredeemable individualist even in social questions. Coupled with these elements was his abiding allegiance to what he saw as the true spirit of the Gospels – which had caused him to attribute to Christ's teaching his doctrine of nomadism in *Les Nourritures Terrestres* and subsequently to ascribe evangelical roots to his Marxism.

Fayer's discussion, placing Gide's involvement in a cultural and ethical context, views it in an appropriate perspective. Needless to say there have been subsequent treatments of Gide's activity during this era (see addendum to note 5) but Fayer's remains useful – and carries the seal of Gide's approval in the form of a letter of congratulation he wrote to the author after reading this study.

---

*From *Gide, Freedom and Dostoevsky* (Burlington, Vermont, The Lane Press, 1946), pp. 133–41.

For years Gide believed that the moral question of remoulding human nature should be given precedence over social questions.[1] Like Dostoevsky, he thought it futile to change social institutions so long as human nature remained the same. In the 1930s, however, he reversed his stand. He became convinced that social reorganization must precede any attempt at spiritual regeneration, and that economic security must serve as the very foundation for genuine culture.[2] In a diary entry of 1935 he says explicitly:

> I had thought, until quite recently, that it was important first to change man, men, each man; and that this was where one had to begin. This is why I used to write that the ethical question was more important to me than the social question.
>
> Today I let myself be convinced that man himself cannot change unless social conditions first urge him and help him to do so – so that attention must first be paid to them.
>
> But attention must be paid to both.[3]

In view of this ideological change, Gide's tardy adherence to communism becomes comprehensible. So long as he believed that social problems could be solved on the moral plane, he remained, above all, a *moraliste*. After this change, the need for practical machinery to implement his philosophy of freedom became imperative, and rightly or wrongly, he pinned his hopes on communism – but a communism compatible with personal freedom and surrendering no intellectual prerogatives to Marxian dogma or the opportunism of the Party Line.

Gide's label for his new social philosophy proved extremely misleading. To the usual incomprehension and misunderstandings, new ones were added. His open adherence to communism in 1932; his declarations that the USSR was mankind's greatest hope;[4] his explanations that in embracing communism he remained consistent – all seemed incredible. His defection and denunciations of the Stalinist régime subsequent to his trip to the USSR in 1936 were again greeted with surprise and the well-known accusations of inconsistency. The prolonged controversy over Gide's communism in the 1930s, with its partisan charges and countercharges, did not help to clarify the matter.[5]

To establish the fact that Gide's social philosophy remained thoroughly consistent, because all his apparent contradictions were dictated by his primary concern for freedom, let us examine the nature of Gide's communism; his reasons for approving of the USSR; and his motives in subsequently denouncing the Stalinist régime.

In a diary entry of August 1933, Gide states that he can reconcile individualism and communism because he endows them with personal meaning. By communism he does not mean egalitarianism. He is willing to begin with equal opportunities for all providing they do not result in a 'uniformity of qualities'[6] which is as impossible as it is undesirable for the individual and the group. The same principle also applies to the question of internationalizing economic interests. Such process must leave racial and cultural peculiarities intact.[7]

Gide's communism, in a sense, is the fulfilment of Zossima's prophecy [in Dostoevsky's novel, *The Brothers Karamazov*] that the rich will become ashamed of their riches. He tells us repeatedly that his privileged status in society has become intolerable to him; and that he cannot be happy as long as there is unspeakable misery all around him.[8] In *Les Nouvelles Nourritures* he writes:

> Truly, I do not want a happiness that springs from wretchedness. Riches that leave another poor I do not want. If my clothes are stripped from others, I will go naked. Ah! Lord Christ, your table is open to all, and what makes the beauty of your banquet is that all are invited to it.[9]

Gide insists that Jesus, champion of the poor, and not Marx led him to communism.[10] He now needs no dialectic justifications in aligning himself with the underprivileged, for Christ's teaching has become an integral part of his being. The very idea of having to plead Christ's cause with the communists seems absurd to Gide. It is against religion, the church, and the priest that Christ should be defended; not against those who have the welfare of the disinherited at heart. Since communists deny Christ's divinity, they should judge Him on a purely human basis. They would then realize that Roman imperialism had condemned Him for causes they most fervently espouse.[11]

The spectacle of human misery receives special attention from the communist Gide. With the feeling of deepest compassion [. . .] he relates his encounters with three unfortunate humans: one, a Negro in tatters, looking as if all hope had left him, yet striving to maintain an appearance of dignity; the second, a poor wretch who can find no better way of eking out a living than by raising rare fish and selling them in the streets; and the third, a fourteen-year-old Italian girl so desperately unhappy that, from sheer pity, her would-be rescuer allows her to drown.[12]

Although Gide's communism is more emotional than rational, and stems from Christ rather than from Marx, he is by no means ready to content himself with [. . .] pity. The rich, he thinks, will never willingly surrender their prerogatives. The only means of bringing about social and economic justice is force. Speaking of the Spanish Revolution, he says:

> I should like to ask those who are shocked by such violences how a chick can get out of the egg without breaking the shell.[13]

And *à propos* of the social upheaval which preceded the Bolshevik experiment, he asks:

How could so novel a reorganization have been achieved without, first, a period of profound disorganization?[14]

To what extent is Gide's communism consistent with his previous views and attitudes? Gide himself claims that it represents no ideological deviation from the past:

> In heart as well as mind I have always been a communist; even while remaining a Christian; [. . .] I have always walked forward; I am continuing to do so; the great difference is that for a long time I saw nothing in front of me but space and the projection of my own fervour; at present I am going forward while orienting myself toward something; I know that somewhere my vague desires are being organized and that my dream is on the way to becoming reality.[15]

In the light of his general record it would seem impossible to deny that he was in many respects a communist long before he chose to label himself as such. Enough to recall his attacks on marriage and the family; on revealed religions, clericalism and the Church; or on bourgeois hypocrisy and Barresian regionalism. It is true that he was then more concerned with the demoralizing influence of capitalist institutions than with their political and economic implications. But even after assuming the label, he repeatedly acknowledged that he felt totally incompetent in such matters, and that the reading of Marx, for instance, left him confused and bewildered.[16] Nevertheless, the 'decomposing action'[17] of which André Rouveyre had accused him, was real and aimed at results desired by communists.

Particularly noteworthy was Gide's campaign against narrow nationalism fought in the name of cultural enrichment, but inseparable from the aims of communist internationalism. This naturally brought him in conflict with French traditionalists who favoured cultural exclusivism. Gide declared that intransigent resistance to foreign importations meant national ingrowth and eventual sterility:

> By only wishing to accept from abroad that which already resembles us, in which we may find our order, our logic, and, so to speak, our own image, we commit a grave error. . . . By only contemplating her own image, the image of her past, France puts herself in mortal danger.[18]

Gide recognized the soundness of nationalism which, in opposing foreign adaptations, served to safeguard the identity and continuity of French culture.[19] But he believed that foreign influences alone can vitalize this culture. History has shown that when used in moderation, they have often acted as a leaven in producing most remarkable results. Ronsard inspired by the Italians, Corneille under Spanish, and the Romantics under English and German influences, have created literary masterpieces which are thoroughly French. French literary creations of foreign inspiration have always retained their national stamp.[20] The cultural isolationists, who turn their gaze backward in rapt contemplation of 'la Terre et les Morts', and with a feeling of superiority boast of their ignorance of foreign countries, cannot adequately appreciate their own fatherland. Values are best understood and appraised on a comparative basis, and only he who knows foreign lands can best value his own.[21] As the world is constituted today cultural exclusivism without subsequent stagnation is inconceivable: '. . . henceforth no country in Europe can aspire to any real progress in its own culture by isolating itself . . .'[22] Cultural pluralism, on the other hand, is the only hope of Western civilization.[23] It means the synthesis of national cultures where each will play its own irreplaceable part and yet blend harmoniously with all the others as do the various instruments in a symphony. To achieve this, 'We must not tend towards uniformity, but towards harmony, which cannot be realized without mutual understanding.[24]

The man who would thus reconcile nationalism with internationalism was naturally annoyed with the writers who try to convince their French compatriots that they could never understand other nations. In order to support such spurious assertions they overemphasize national differences while ignoring those basic and universal human qualities which make all nations kin.[25] Speaking of Franco-German relations Gide said: 'It is absurd to reject anything, no matter what, from the European compact. It is absurd to imagine one could suppress something, anything, in the compact.'[26] And he later reiterates: 'There is no more fatal error today, both for nations and for individuals, than to believe that they can get along without one another.'[27]

In the attempt to reconcile nationalism with internationalism Gide reiterated many of Dostoevsky's arguments. Summing up his own ideas on the subject, he says:

> I have often expressed my view on intellectual protectionism. I believe that it presents grave dangers; but in my opinion any pretension to denationalize intelligence presents no less great a danger. In saying this, I am expressing once again the opinion of Dostoyevsky. There is no author who is at one and the same time more narrowly Russian and more universally European. It is by being so specifically Russian that he is able to be so generally human, and to touch each of us in so particular a manner.[28]

Gide has thus foreseen the future allies of fascism.[29] In exposing them he was helping the cause of freedom. But he also dealt in a practical way with some immediate social problems. In *Souvenirs de la cour d'Assises*, published in 1914, he vigorously attacked the jury system of France. In *Le Voyage au Congo* and in *Le Retour du Tchad*, which appeared in 1927 and 1929 respectively, he exposed the abuses of French colonial imperialism. With a feeling of infinite compassion for the African natives, but relying on sober eyewitness accounts and cold statistical data gathered in his travels, Gide painted a ghastly picture of greed, cruelty, mismanagement and exploitation amounting to wholesale murder. The chief offenders, according to his report, were the big stock companies, but the government itself was shown as guilty of complicity and flagrant violations. Gide did not, however, confine himself to mere accusations in the press. He brought about a governmental investigation which resulted in convictions and penalties.[30]

In the light of these activities, Gide's approval of the USSR is natural. It is also comprehensible because of his growing conviction that the capitalist system must end in utter barbarism and chaos if it is not soon destroyed, and the price he placed on every heroic effort 'toward the never-yet-attempted'.[31]

For years Gide felt that capitalism had become a serious menace to civilization; but never is he more apprehensive for the future than in the 1930s. Everywhere he sees the profit system wantonly sowing the seeds of another world catastrophe, while propaganda and religion blind the masses to the truth.[32] In 1932 he writes:

> I have come to wish most heartily for the upset of capitalism and everything that lurks in its shadow – abuses, injustices, lies and monstrosities.[33]

A few months later he exclaims:

> From top to bottom of our society I see nothing but iniquity, abuse of power, exploitation of others, deceit . . .[34]

In the early 1930s Gide sees in the Soviet experiment the only salvation from capitalism, the only hope for the future.

> Never have I bent over the future with a more passionate curiosity. My whole heart applauds that gigantic and yet entirely human undertaking.[35]

His devotion to the USSR, by his own admission, bears the nature of a creed; and if his life were required to insure the success of communism in Russia, he would cheerfully give it.[36] Such faith in the eventual outcome is essential, he thinks. That is why the supporters of the existing order are representing bolshevism as an unattainable dream, a failure and a threat. But it is impossible to make one fear a monster while persuading him at the same time that the monster is not real.[37]

Gide is aware that bolshevism is relying on coercion in order to carry out its programme, just as fascism is. The underlying motive, however, is what matters most. The latter seeks to restore the past; the former to do away with oppression, economic insecurity and racial persecutions.[38] For the sake of this glorious attempt Gide voluntarily surrenders his own artistic freedom. At the meeting of the 'Union pour la vérité' on 23 January 1935, he explains why he has not written for four years. Since he cannot conform to Marxist requirements, he prefers to keep silent. Marxist orthodoxy is as dangerous as any other, at least as far as artistic creation is concerned. But the building of a new social order is far more important than the sacrifice of a few works of art.[39]

For the same reasons Gide is willing to surrender individual freedom. This sacrifice is indispensable in an undertaking of such scope and magnitude, and because

> . . . man achieves nothing worthwhile without constraint and . . . very rare are those capable of finding that constraint in themselves.[40]

But the forfeit, whether in personal life or in art, must be temporary and for the sake of a greater freedom to come.

In a sense, the Soviet Union played the same part in Gide's communist creed that paradise plays in the faith of a religious believer.[41] [. . .] It was easy for him to believe that the new Russia offered the longed-for escape from the grim realities of the capitalist world; and to see it as the land of promise where, in a not-too-distant future, his dreams of a free man in a new society – a society without religion and the family[42] – will become a living reality.

But 'paradise' proved much easier to believe in from a distance. At close range it displayed, alongside remarkable technological achievements, many evils of the capitalist 'hell'; the same economic differentiations,[43] marginal existence of workers, systematic dissemination of falsehoods. Some of the Western evils, Gide found to his dismay, had here assumed unknown proportions and were undermining the very foundations of civilization. A growing uniformity in the modes of living was depersonalizing the Soviet citizen.[44] Rigid conformism in thinking, imposed through concentration camps and purges, was obliterating the revolutionary spirit.[45] Everywhere, in life and in art, intellectual cowardice,[46] servility and sycophancy[47] were rampant. Gide observes:

> . . . I doubt whether in any other country in the world, even Hitler's

Germany, thought be less free, more bowed down, more fearful (terrorized), more vassalized.[48]

The Stalinist régime had annexed the communist ideology and turned it into a weapon of reaction in much the same way that capitalism had annexed Christ.

Some have accused Gide of naïveté: he should have known better before going to Russia; he should have been better informed.[49] But how was he to disengage the truth from propaganda, or from the tangle of contradictory reports? And was it not precisely to see the truth with his own eyes that he had undertaken his trip?

He went to the USSR in the hope of finding a new man and a better society in the process of becoming.[50] He found magnificent parks of culture, streamlined factories, excellent schools, healthy children and a hopeful youth – amazing material and technological improvements. But the 'humbled and injured,' the meek, and the cowardly were still there. Dostoevsky's Russia was as alive as ever, except that the meek had become meeker and the cowardly more abject, while the 'self-willed' and 'demoniac' were being liquidated with an efficiency unknown to the autocracy.[51]

Gide's greatness again showed itself in his frankness: he had erred; let the world know it. He refused to save face or avoid the 'Communist Index' at the price of concealing the truth as he saw it.[52] He refused to imprison himself in a doctrine; or, what is worse, in an error. He would not remain the slave of his past. Gide spoke – not against communism as an ideal, only against the manner in which a group of fanatics and political careerists, led by an Asiatic despot, was translating mankind's greatest hope into reality. He denounced the Stalinist régime in the name of freedom and of culture just as he had in their name approved of a vision which seemed to have no counterpart in reality. Again Gide emerges the champion of freedom, true to his values and to himself.

Notes

1. Cf. *JI*, 93; *J1*, 76: 'Literature and Ethics', 1897: 'Social question? Yes indeed. But the ethical question is antecedent'.

2. See *André Gide et notre temps*, pp. 65–6.

3. *JI*, 1241; *J3*, 334: 30 October 1935. Cf. 'L'Avenir de l'Europe', *OC*, *XI*, 135 (1923).

4. Cf. 'In the abominable distress of the present world, new Russia's plan now seems to me salvation. There is nothing that does not persuade me of this! [. . .] And if my life were necessary to ensure the success of the USSR, I should give it at once' (*JI*, 1126; *J3*, 232: 23 April 1932).

5. The following more important works on Gide's communism indicate the repercussions in the press created by his adherence: In 1933 LUCIEN DURAN published a comprehensive article, 'André Gide et l'URSS', *Mercure de France*, 15 August 1933. In the same year RAMON FERNANDEZ contended in 'Notes sur l'évolution d'André Gide' that 'the evolution of Gide was leading him towards socialism', *Nouvelle Revue Française*, XLI, 1933, 132. In the following year Fernandez came out with a 'Lettre ouverte à Gide', in which he reproached him in amicable terms for submitting to Marxist orthodoxy at a time when it was the imperative duty of every intellectual to fight for freedom of thought. (See *Nouvelle Revue Française*, 1 April 1934, p. 703–8.) [These texts are reproduced in Ramon Fernandez, *Gide ou le courage de s'engager*, ed. Claude Martin, Publications de la Société des Amis d'André Gide, Paris, Klincksieck, 1985, pp. 127–35.] In the same issue of the magazine JEAN LOUVERNÉ sought to prove that Gide's communism went back as far as his *Le Roi Candaule* of 1901, presumably an anticapitalistic play; and that his humanism was perfectly compatible with communist ideology. (See 'Conversion? *Nouvelle Revue Française*, 1 April 1934, pp. 628–48.) In June of the same year ALBERT THIBAUDET tried to settle the polemics. According to him, Gide's adherence is more of a 'conclusion' than a 'conversion'. Gide concluded in favour of communism in much the same way that the royalist agnostic concludes in favour of Catholicism. But he warned that Gide was entering a narrow gate. (See 'Conversions et conclusions', *Nouvelle Revue Française*, 1 June 1934, p. 997–1003.) On January 23, 1935 the 'Union pour la Vérité' held a special meeting to discuss Gide's communism. Gide himself, and men of the literary calibre of François Mauriac, Henri Massis, Jacques Maritain, Jean Guéhenno and Ramon Fernandez participated. The meeting assumed the proportions of a major event. A stenographic account of the speeches, entitled *André Gide et notre temps*, appeared in 1935. An attempt to sum up the pros and cons of the question was made by CLAUDE NAVILLE in *André Gide et le communisme* in 1936.

[Addendum: For more recent studies of the question, see GEORGE I. BRACHFELD, *André Gide and the communist temptation*, Geneva, Droz, 1959; DAVID CAUTE, *The Fellow-Travellers*, London, Weidenfeld and Nicholson, 1973, pp. 95–9; W. J. MARSHALL, 'André Gide and the USSR: a re-appraisal', *Australian Journal of French Studies*, XX, 1 (1983), pp. 37–49; RUDOLF MAURER *André Gide et l'URSS*, Berne, Editions Tillier, 1983; DANIEL MOUTOTE, *André Gide: l'engagement (1926–1939)*, Paris, SEDES, 1991.]

6. *JI*, 1179; *J3*, 279: 12 August 1933.

7. Ibid.

8. See *JI*, 1178; *J3*, p. 278: 4 July 1933, and *André Gide et notre temps*, p. 61–2. Cf. 'My happiness is to increase other people's. To be happy myself I need the happiness of all', *Later Fruits of the Earth*, p. 167.

9. *Les Nouvelles Nourritures*, p. 58; *Later Fruits*, p. 166.

10. *JI*, 1176; *J3*, 276: June 1933.

11. *JI*, 1178; *J3*, 278: 4 July 1933.

12. *Les Nouvelles Nourritures*, p. 39–58; *Later Fruits*, pp. 157–66.

13. *JI*, 1044; *J3*, 160: 13 May 1931.

14. Ibid.

15. *JI*, 1132; *J3*, 237: 13 June 1932. Cf. Ibid., *JI*, 1118; *J3*, 225–6: 27 February 1932.

16. See *André Gide et notre temps*, p. 61. In 1933 Gide wrote: 'I have already said so: I know nothing about politics.' *JI*, 1175; *J3*, 275; June 1933. In 1937 he wrote, *a propos* of Marx's *Capital*: 'It is the Mass in Latin. When one does not understand, one bows down.' *JI*, 1289; *J3*, 376.

17. See A. Gide, 'Lettres' *OC, XII*, 559.

18. *Dostoïevsky, OC, XI*, 305. This idea is typical and is frequently reiterated. The following passage written almost a decade later bears this out: 'It might even be said that, given the Frenchman's virtues (of clarity, restatement, tact, and ability to perfect), no other nation has greater need of the foreign; and that without a contribution from outside he would run the risk of fatally whittling down his substance if he did not, on the other hand, also possess inventive powers – which he most often succeeds in exploiting only much later, behind other countries' (*JI*, 1024; *J3*, 143: 25 January 1931).

19. *Dostoïevsky*, op.cit., p. 305. See also 'Emile Verhaeren', *OC, X*, p. 6 (1920).

20. *JI*, 1023–4; *J3*, 142–3: 25 January 1931.

21. 'L'Avenir de l'Europe', *OC, XI*, 124–5 (1923). This idea that literature prospers through assimilation has also been expressed by MELCHIOR DE VOGÜÉ in *Le Roman russe*: 'Literature is an organism that lives from nutrition; it must ceaselessly assimilate foreign elements to transform them into its own substance.' See p. liii.

22. *OC, XI*, 134.

23. 'Feuillets. Projet de conférence pour Berlin (1928)', *OC, XV*, 507–8.

24. Ibid., 509.

25. *JI*, 780–1; *J2*, 346: 7 January 1924.

26. 'Réflexions sur l'Allemagne', *OC, IX*, 113.

27. *JI*, 673; *J2*, 248: 'Detached Pages'. See also 'L'Avenir de l'Europe', *OC, XI*, 135.

28. *Dostoïevsky*, op.cit., 306.

29. Gide contends, for instance, that Barrès would have approved of Hitlerism because it is 'a successful Boulangism'. JI, 1162; J3, 264: 5 April 1933. [General Boulanger, named Minister of War by Clémenceau in 1886, later became a royalist and threatened the Republic in 1888–9 as a popular dictator who might have seized power. Barrès was among his many admirers.]

30. See L. MARTIN-CHAUFFIER, 'Notices' in *OC, XIII*, viii.

31. *JI*, 1084; *J3*, 197: end October 1931.

32. *JI*, 1159; *J3*, 259: 1933.

33. *JI*, 1116; *J3*, 224: 21 February 1932.

34. *JI*, 1130; *J3*, 235: 8 June 1932. Cf. his words *a propos* of the First World War: 'One realises, in the hour of danger, that the entire edifice, from top to bottom, is worm-eaten, that the whole of society . . .' *OC, VIII*, 183.

35. *JI*, 1044; *J3*, 160: 13 May 1931.

36. *JI*, 1126; *J3*, 232: 23 April 1932.

37. *JI*, 1109–11, *J3*, 219. 30 January 1932.

38. *JI*, 1084; *J3*, 197: late October 1931.

39. *André Gide et notre temps*, p. 62.

40. *JI*, 1084; *J3*, 196: late October 1931.

41. Cf. 'Gide is a man for whom the problem of salvation exists.' A. Thibaudet, 'Conversions et conclusions', Nouvelle Revue Française, 1 June 1934, no. 249, p. 998.

42. *JI*, 1066; *J3*, 179–80: 27 July 1931.

43. Gide says in his *Back from the USSR*, 'There are no more classes in the USSR – granted. But there are poor. There are too many of them – far too many. I had hoped not to see any – or, to speak more accurately: it was in order *not* to see any that I had come to the USSR' (65; 60).

44. Ibid., 37, 47–8; 33, 43–4.

45. Ibid., 49; 45.

46. Ibid., 69–70; 64–5.

47. Ibid., 72; 67.

48. Ibid., 67; 62–3.

49. K. Mann, *André Gide and the Crisis of Modern Thought*, p. 249.

50. Cf. 'The important thing for me here is man – men – and what can be done with them, and what *has* been done.' *Back from the USSR*, 32; 31.

51. In his *Afterthoughts: a Sequel to Back from the USSR*, Gide says: '. . . soon, of this heroic and admirable people who so well deserved our love, none will be left but executioners, profiteers and victims' (34; 35).

52. *Back from the USSR*, 13; 13.

3 Germaine Brée, on Time sequences and consequences in the Gidian world*

Published in a commemorative issue of *Yale French Studies* following Gide's death in 1951, this article is in effect an extract-cum-synopsis of work in progress on Brée's epoch-making book published in French in 1953. Brée reflects on Gide's artistic standing in a world recovering from global catastrophe, still traumatized by ideological anxiety and menaced further by nuclear calamity. It is evident that the restricted universe of his fiction seems somewhat insubstantial in comparison. However, drawing together material she was to distribute throughout her book-length study, Brée provides an overview of certain thematic and structural concerns relating to the unfolding of time and its impact on human destiny, and shows nonetheless that Gide engages with a fundamental intellectual problem of the era: that of the interaction between chance, will and necessity in the workings of the universe created by human action. This is an age-old ethical problem too; and Gide's artistic ordering of its components is what constitutes the special quality of his work, which Brée highlights in accordance with Hytier's pioneering study (see below, Chapter 13). Though profoundly moral therefore, it can only be adequately approached from an aesthetic perspective. Comparing and contrasting the structures and workings of the *récits* and the *soties*, Brée shows how, despite Gide's conviction that accident interacts with motivation to turn erratic events into an ominously irrevocable destiny, his chief concern is not metaphysical revolt against this absurd universe – unlike Sartre or Camus – but rather the search for a harmonious sructuring of its elements. Hence the presence in all his narratives of a character or characters, whether or not they are explicitly novelists as such, who seek to shape life into a coherent sequence in time. The shortcomings of Gide's art, for Brée, stem from its tendency towards increasing abstractness as it extends the complexity of the situations in which this principle is played out.

---

*First published in *Yale French Studies*, 7, 1951, pp. 51–9.

(. . .) We now stand back from the Gidian world, it is true, looking into it from the outside, struck perhaps more by the luminosity which suffuses it than by any other aspect of it. Gide's world has something in common with a painting by Poussin: luminosity, harmony in structure, a few figures, taken out of time, out of any material space or social reality. All Gidian characters exist unhampered in what might be called a Gidian space. Not one evokes the bitter struggle for survival in our contemporary world, the restrictions and limitations it places on the individual; not one, with the possible exception of Theseus in his maturity, is concerned with any problem other than that of self-realization within the limits of the family circle, a family which is always a more or less distorted image of the Prodigal Son's. The family to which the Prodigal Son belongs lives in the Father's house, rich and securely established; the Father administers the estate wisely; the mother accepts the given order in loving self-effacement; the oldest son lives within the inherited material and moral comfort of the house; the Prodigal Son returns to the security of the house for shelter when he has squandered his inheritance. It does not occur to him, as he speeds his younger brother on the way, that the house itself might be menaced and about to crumble. He seems to us today something of a dilettante who plays safe even in his attempt at adventure. All Gidian characters tend, like the Prodigal Son, to 'return' within a traditional order. Their problems are problems of adjustment to a smoothly-running universe. At present they seem to us dated.

Many Gidian situations are clearly luxury products flowering in a hothouse atmosphere which has little in common with the present 'univers concentrationnaire'. Gide seems unable to transmit in his work all that part of human life which is conditioned by bodily and emotional participation in the multiple existence of a human community, all that part of 'la condition humaine' which is shaped by a sense of the precariousness, pathos and solidarity of human destiny as it appears today, heavily shrouded by uncertainty and the immediacy of pervasive suffering. There is a vital lack of humanity in Gide's world which is clearly apparent in the material he chose for elaboration in *Les Faux-Monnayeurs*, the novel which was intended to reflect his mature and complete vision of life. The whole world of *Les Faux-Monnayeurs* is flimsy, ineffectual and rather pointless as the characters wend their way through the futile cerebral-sentimental complications in which they have full leisure to indulge. It is startling to find Gide comparing his novel to Fielding's vigorous human universe, unable as he is to give any consistency to his effete Olivier, to the singularly dull Laura, or even to Édouard.

Yet, narrow as Gide's world seems, limited in many ways, its very texture and atmosphere arrest the attention of the reader and bring him, with definite aesthetic pleasure, an intricate and inexhaustible web of subtle problems, both ethic and aesthetic. One cannot approach Gide's world naively; even the most simple *récit* requires circumspection, an aesthetic sophistication which distinguishes between content and intent, an intent present only in the structure of a tale which never states it, but implies it merely. Perhaps the most tantalizing of the problems raised by the Gidian world lies in the discrepancy between the acuteness and seriousness of Gide's vision and the narrowness of range of the world he elaborates, however subtle, complex and self-sufficient a literary feat its elaboration may be.

Of the problems Gide's world raises, none recurs more persistently than the problem of time in relation to the shaping of a human destiny. All Gide's fictional works, *récits, soties*, novel, are carefully timed; they contain a definite chronology. The events related in *Les Faux-Monnayeurs*, for example, take place in just over a year, from Laura's wedding, one fall, recorded in Édouard's diary, to Boris' death in the fall of the next year. The novel starts with the events which take place in just over twenty-four hours – beginning on a certain Wednesday night a little before the July baccalaureate session – and ends with those which centre around the second baccalaureate session in October; Édouard's diary however goes back to the preceding October, and, for all the characters separately we can reestablish a chronology of the events which, in that year, lead up to the final 'dénouement', and it is a dénouement for each one of the separate developments which were set in movement the fall before. Though Gide may, on the surface, disrupt the time-scheme of his tales, the succession in time of the events themselves, or their relation in time is always clearly indicated. Past and present do not mingle in the Gidian world. In fact, the domain explored by Gide is conditioned by his constant meditations on what determines the ordering of a life time, and on what makes that ordering seem, like the passage of time itself, inevitable. He does not, like the ordinary novelist, merely accept as a fact that in a story the time sequence is like the river bed which sustains the flow of a life.

In every tale, time is that which reveals the fundamental value of the human experience described. In all Gidian situations, intelligence, moral intention – good or bad – always fall short in their appraisal of the present and their prevision of the future; time alone reveals the nature of their inadequacy. It reveals that inadequacy by the form the individual's relations with himself and others eventually take as the tale develops. Since that form is a result of some inadequacy in his grasp of the situation, the individual can in no way foresee its development nor understand it. What Gide sets up for his characters is a plausible development in time, the significance of which escapes them, but which they see clearly was not fatal, uniquely determined. He introduces into all his tales, whatever the form he chooses for his narrative, the question of a discrepancy between the human notion of moral consequence and the problem of chance action and retroaction which can affect a life. However simple a Gidian situation may be it always puts to the reader one and the same question: how can a being act in human situations in which no logical, preconceived, long-term rules are laid down, situations in which, as on a crowded billiard table, each move can set a dozen other balls rolling unexpectedly? Is a calculated, systematic human course of action any better in time than a set of shots made at random? Gide sets up the adventures of his characters consciously so that they, in some way, present tentative solutions to that problem. The discrepancy between the individual's evaluation of his adventure and what really happens to him is rigorously determined by Gide's point of view on the solution offered. That point of view quite arbitrarily – and always rather ferociously – is what, step by step, carries the character, in time, to his real destination. Gide is the Miglionnaire and the Prometheus – in the Gidian version – of his world.

The main significance of the amusing little tale *Paludes* lies in the relation of its harassed hero to the recurrent patterns which from Monday to Monday appear in his life. His struggle against stagnation is in itself a form of stagnation visible in the pattern it has imposed on time. He makes of the succession of days a small closed circle he is living which delimits his mental marsh. He is in the marsh of lost time. In the *récits* the question raised is that of movement in time, of orientation in time. It is one of destination. The characters move toward a destination which, retrospectively, when they see the path they have walked as a whole and as it were *a contretemps*, seems to them a predestination. Each moment of their lives appears, at the end, as consequent to the whole, not, however, as the inevitable consequence of the one before. Gide, in the *récits* deliberately dissociates the convenient assimilation of time sequence and consequence in the development of a human destiny. Like Jérome when he reads Alissa's diary, all the heroes of the *récits* discover retrospectively that the pattern of their lives could have come out differently in time. Yet, though the ordering of events in time could have been different, their succession is irreversible, and its outcome all the more baffling because no inescapable preordained pattern of destiny slowly reveals itself as fatal. Having, like Alissa deliberately chosen their destination, or like Michel been pushed toward it by a strong inner urge, all the characters of the *récits* find time then takes them to a strange unwanted destination. Life tricks them by deflecting the most carefully calculated shot, and then mocks them as they watch its devastating random effects. The character is, however, both a player – one of the players – and the ball played. He too can be deflected by some, to him, erratic outer shot. The characters in the *récits*, one might say, carefully calculate their shots as if they were outside the table. The characters in the *soties* move on the whole erratically, at random, as if someone else held the cue. André Walter, Michel, Alissa, the clergyman of *La Symphonie Pastorale*, all turn towards us faces as baffled as the young historian's when confronted with the real Isabelle, or Lafcadio's when, after the murder of Fleurissoire, he sees an incongruous, disconcerting, Protean aspect emerge from what had seemed, at first, a dull ordinary and reassuring assembly of people, widow, child, waiter and near-sighted professor.

In every Gidian tale the relation of the time sequence to the events narrated is the statement of a problem – a fundamental problem – the problem of the part played by chance, will, necessity, in the complex chain of consequences that any action initiates. The relation, within the tale, of time sequences to consequences raises the question of human freedom in decision and action, and of human logic in evaluating decision and action. It therefore also raises the problem of the individual's responsibility – in virtue or guilt – towards himself and others. The structural devices chosen by Gide for the narration of the tale – retrospective accounts, diaries, a combination of the two, or the juxtasposition, then sudden convergence in time, of unrelated series of events – all emphasize and highlight some aspect of the relation of time sequences to consequence. Gide's literary ordering of time opens into his world perspectives which are not those of the characters involved in the story. These perspectives are different in nature from those the ordering of time introduces into the world of Proust or Joyce. Gide's intellectual view of man's essential ethical problem – how to act in orderly sequence and with coherence in a life which encompasses time and yet for which no long-range laws can be laid down – is closely connected to one of the most general intellectual problems of our time. Gide's very particular brand of humour too, which emphazises the ironical incongruity of an inner coherence when it is transferred outwards and attributed to a world moving at random, is a statement of the same problem. Like the time-schemes in his tales it is the aesthetic statement of a really modern view of an age-old ethical problem. It envelops situations and characters alike and qualifies them. That is why Gide can assert with equal sincerity and equal truth that his work is profoundly moral and that the only approach to it is the aesthetic.

Les Faux Monnayeurs might be described as demonstrating through its time scheme, how many apparently irrelevant developments can converge to bring about the tragic death of one young boy, a boy whom no one, until the very end, intended to harm. There are, one might say, three main trends of development rooted in the unconnected events of the October days Édouard described in his diary: the events which concern his sentimental life – Laura's marriage, his interest in Olivier; the events which concern George's activities – the stolen book, the secret society; the interview with La Pérouse and the discovery that Boris exists. In the first set of events, Laura's adventures, for which her unhappy marriage is responsible, bring Édouard back, but the action of Bernard in leaving home has as its unforeseen random consequence Édouard's estrangement from Olivier. In June, estranged from Olivier, not quite knowing what to do with Laura and Bernard, Édouard decides, at random, to bring Boris back to La

Pérouse. It is therefore by chance that Édouard's path crosses the life of Boris. When Édouard comes back to Paris the main inner direction of his life reappears. It takes him in time to Olivier.

In June, the nature of George's activities is slowly becoming clearer. Profitendieu is on the track of the schoolboy delinquents who frequent the pension Azaïs. In October the schoolboy gang, warned by Édouard that they must stop their dealings in false coins, are at a loose end. The three separate sequences of events we had been following converge in time and at random. The spotlight falls on Boris. But if . . . if Bernard had not been obliged to leave the pension at that moment; if Bronja had not died; if La Pérouse had either not loaded the pistol or, the pistol loaded, committed suicide; if Azaïs, financially pressed, had not made use of old La Pérouse in the pension; if the young Passavant had been less self-centred; if Édouard had not been so preoccupied by Olivier; if Laura had not had to call Édouard back; if Vincent had not abandoned Laura; if Édouard had taken George's activities more seriously; if Profitendieu, desirous to save the reputation of their families, had not left the young deliquents both unreprimanded and unoccupied; if Azaïs, presuming they were innocent children had not encouraged their perversity; if Sophroniska had not given Strouvilhou the talisman . . . Though only Gherisandol intends to harm Boris, all the characters in the novel at some time helped to load the pistol which killed Boris; all, at some time, like Sophroniska, gave a talisman to the insidious Strouvilhou. All are, in fact, accomplices in the murder of Boris, including Boris himself. We are at the heart of the subject of *Les Faux-Monnayeurs*, and at the heart of the Gidian problem of responsibility.

When Boris steps into the circle at the pension Azaïs and kills himself, the reader, who can stop to think, can trace back retrospectively, step by step, the drama of Boris as, unknown to himself and to all concerned, it develops in time. Its progression is invisible and alogical. Instead of following the straight line of Boris' destiny, Gide follows all those which, cutting across it, have as an unforeseen, erratic consequence, by their action and retroaction in that one particular line of Boris' life, his tragic death. What then is the responsibility of each in that event?

The time-scheme of *Les Faux-Monnayeurs* transmits a problem which Gide's experimentation with the time structure of his tales in the *soties* had already stated. Gide is always concerned with the interplay of motivation and accident in the development of a human life. In the *soties*, however, he stresses that part of life which escapes all prevision, the 'devil's share' as he himself calls it. He engages his characters in a complex web of related situations which overlap and react one on the other, precipitating in time chains of reaction of which no one is master. The situation of the characters is presented as seen from outside relatively to more complex situations which they do not know. They are exactly in the position of Anthime Armand Dubois' experimental rats. Anthime's rats, by the chance coincidence of their capture and the interests of Anthime, are systematically starved, blinded and otherwise mutilated. By the chance passage in the room of Anthime's wife, they are one day, fed, a random gesture due to the kindness of her heart. Their destiny is again altered completely as a consequence of Anthime's conversion. The rats, however, establish no order to explain, from within and relatively to themselves only, the unforeseen development of their destiny in time. Not so Coclès and Damoclès. Involved by chance in Zeus' freakish act, Coclès and Damoclès carry it over into their lives, develop it as a relation with a moral content, draw from it consequences, ethical and social consequences, which satisfy the completely arbitrary and opposing logical demand they make on life. Caught in a random act, they prolong it in time and transform an erratic event into a destiny. The direction their two lives take in time after their accidental convergence – towards death for Damoclès, towards success for Coclès – shows the irrelevancy of their divergent points of view and consequent actions; and yet that point of view is what shapes their destiny, gives content to their lives, and reveals their character. Coclès and Damoclès are the forerunners of Theseus and Oedipus.

In *Les Caves du Vatican* Gide deliberately lays down a complex pattern of chance convergence in time, the 'miracle' pattern of the experimental rats' lives, of Anthime's conversion and de-conversion. With clocklike precision the separate lines of activity of the characters all lead to Rome and to the chance meeting of Fleurissoire and Lafcadio in the train. The carefully decentralized structure of the *sotie*, the precisely timed convergence of the separate sequences which make Lafcadio's act possible, its immediate random rebound and repercussion from sequence to sequence all qualify the characters' thoughts and acts. Not one dominates the situation; but all, within the partial situation that they grasp, make logical deductions and decisions, and carry out actions which then affect the whole. In time, these precipitate unforeseen changes in the situation, in the positions of one and all within the situation, as the situation itself is modified erratically, and for each separate character inexplicably; it may then appear to all that the strings are being pulled from the outside, as indeed they are, for Gide is doing the pulling, precisely to give his characters just that impression, to disconcert them.

In the last analysis, all Gide's characters, in the *récits* as in the *soties*, are rather like players who, in a football game, persist in playing basketball, with the conviction that that is the game being played. The *récit* is the tale of the basketball player as he sees the game; the *sotie* shows the basketball player in the middle of the football game. In both cases he is pathetic and absurd: explicitly pathetic and implicitly absurd in the *récit*; explicitly absurd and implicitly pathetic in the *sotie*. He does not know the rules of the game he is playing any more than a Kafka character; but unlike a Kafka character, he thinks he knows. With Lafcadio, Gide introduces into the human game the erratic player, who, like Zeus, acts without motivation, at random. Unlike Zeus, however, Lafcadio finds he cannot withdraw from the game. He finds his act has set in motion a complex web of relationships which it qualifies and modifies in time. He faces the consequences of his act in the relations its establishes between himself and others, relations which affect him, and which he may or may not be able to modify in time. Unlike Zeus, Lafcadio is engaged in the game being played. Time is the umpire which exacts from the Gidian player, consequential or inconsequential, penalties for which he is, like Lafcadio, unprepared. Time makes clear to the individual that his life is engaged, his and that of others. All Gide's tales imply that there is a certain sense to the game of life. To see none, or to mistake it is to err gravely. The game is arduous and complex but the rules cannot, in time, be bypassed. However cleverly a Gidian character counterfeits for his own benefit or for that of others, he never tricks life. Time inevitably reveals the counterfeit. One of the essential tasks of each individual, therefore, is to discern the real nature of the game, to compose his own part in it in harmony with the forces at play within and around him. But this he can only do in time, by trial and error, since even the most lucid cannot dominate the entire game, since the 'devil's share' in it is so large.

The *inner* life therefore of each individual within the game is like a journey over some uncharted land where little by little he charts his path. The journey is an essential Gidian symbol, and the adventures of the Gidian characters in time – like those of Bunyan's Pilgrim or of Ulysses – have an allegorical or symbolic value. For the Gidian explorer, however, there is no eventual heaven or Ithaca. If one follows each character as he plots his course, one clearly distinguishes the Gidian point of view on life which, implicitly only, shapes their destiny, by qualifying what they become as they journey in time.

Gide's characters often appear in pairs: André Walter and Michel; Alissa and Lafcadio; Coclès and Damoclès; the Prodigal Son and his elder brother; Strouvilhou and Azaïs; Édouard and Passavant; finally, the two great figures of Theseus and Oedipus, who confront us in the last Gidian *récit* like the enigmatic and inseparable harlequin and clown of Picasso. Gide is obviously preoccupied with the ambiguity of a human life, its double relation to Zeus and to Prometheus. Unlike Sartre or Camus he is unwilling to sacrifice Zeus. His work contains no metaphysical revolt. Man's journey in time, in its most healthy aspect, appears to him as a search for an equilibrium, a form of harmony which, if sincere, can over a period of time chart, in an erratic world, a coherent human path. Each man therefore is responsible for what, in time, he becomes. Life asks of him that he have the courage to realize his form in time progressively, making of no error a fatality, of no idea a destiny. Gide's ethical preoccupation here turns into the aesthetic problem of form. It is not by chance that in all Gidian tales the central character is an author who struggles to give an account of the events he has lived successively, who tries to 'relate' them, to order them coherently, to give them a shape in time. The Gidian author is not merely a projection of Gide himself, he is every man as Gide sees him. For each and all the problem in that ordering is essentially the problem of the novelist, the ordering of a life in a coherent sequence in time. It is no doubt Gide's modern view of the problem of time sequence and consequence which determined for him simultaneously the situations he chose to delimit and elaborate, and the nature of his search for an adequate form for the novel.

The time structures which he chose to establish, however, particularly as they grow more complex, tend to become abstract. They turn into a scheme, a device which is an end in itself, and destroys, to a certain extent, the complexity, unity and humanity of the characters themselves. That is why Gide's more complex works, *Les Caves du Vatican* and *Les Faux-Monnayeurs* are essentially schematic. That is why, perhaps, Gide never attempted to write a second novel. The outcome of Gide's search for a human pattern of movement within a world which moves at random may disconcert and even disappoint the reader. It is nonetheless both significant and challenging.

4 David Steel on Gide's Prodigal: Economics, Fiction and the *Acte Gratuit**

In addition to a doctoral thesis on the theme of childhood in Gide's work, David Steel is the author of numerous studies on Gide, several of which – among them articles on the conception of the bastard in Gide's fiction, on his anticipation of and reactions to the work of Freud – have proved seminal. In the essay reproduced here Steel treats a theme which had become too frequently appropriated by a crude marxist approach to literature: that of the relationship between a writer's economic status and his literary output. Steel adopts a perspective which acknowledges the socio-historical conditioning undergone by an artist whose writing was facilitated in part by a large inherited fortune, but stresses the fact that an awareness of his status actually drives him to seek a resolution through his writing to the unease this inspires in him. Steel also brings to bear insights deriving from Freud, Mauss and Bataille, whereby economic substance carries psychological, sexual and anthropological implications.

The key to his approach is the only partially translatable double sense contained in the French word *dépenser* and its derivatives, which refer to expenditure not only of material or financial reserves, but also, for example, of psychological resources. Thus Steel is able to demonstrate a significant thematic interdependence of the economic, the psychic and the moral in Gide's work. His analysis of Gide's writing shows the author moving readily between these spheres, producing texts in which the discourse of economics, facilitating numerous monetary metaphors, generates sets of themes and character types hinging on a contrast between avarice and prodigality. But while such an opposition plots points of reference for Gide's preoccupations, on the psychological and moral planes it gives way to dialectical subtleties and paradoxes which go beyond a simple polarization. Hence Alissa, who avoids transactions with everyday life and refuses to give of herself to Jérôme, is in fact

* A slightly modified version of an article which first appeared in French under the title 'Le Prodigue chez Gide; essai de critique économique de l'acte gratuit' in the André Gide special number of *Revue d'Histoire Littéraire de la France*, March-April, 1970, pp. 209–29. Translated and revised by the author.

practising a self-denial which is a displaced form of prodigality; while Lafcadio both keeps a rigorous account of his dealings with others and recklessly gives way to the urge to dissipate his accumulated psychic energy. Viewed from this angle, the term *acte gratuit*, developed in a number of fictional dialogues and applied to the murder Lafcadio commits, lends itself most tellingly to a pseudo-economic evaluation.

This preoccupation inevitably spreads to the notion of value in literary representation, foregrounded most notably in the title of *Les Faux-Monnayeurs*, the novel in which Gide develops the analogy between the fiduciary value of monetary currency, psychological authenticity, and the conventions governing the production and reception of realism in literature. Meanwhile, at the personal level, Gide's literary vocation can be seen as an attempt to liquidate his material as well as his cultural and psychological capital; nonetheless, it continues to bring in handsome returns, in accordance with the author's attachment to a key principle of the Gospels.

As Steel points out in this revised version of his original argument, the approach he adumbrated has lent itself to further development in several subsequent studies, by both himself and other Gide scholars.

> A père avare, dit-on, fils prodigue;
> à parents économes, enfant dépensier.
> Musset[1]

Like most serious writers of that system of literary exchange that is fiction, Gide, in his works, raises the issue of human values, implicitly or explicitly prioritizing them as he thinks fit. In doing so he of necessity establishes an attitude towards material values – commodities, property, money.

Money does not always make the fictional world go round and some novelists, Balzac being a case in point, pay more attention to it than do others, such as, for instance, Camus. To some degree, nonetheless, mimesis demands that fiction reflects the economic structures of social reality and Gide's work is of unusual interest in this respect.

In what follows I want to examine the idea of expenditure as the driving syndrome behind a number of Gide's prominent fictional figures, as a key to his concept of the *acte gratuit*, the motiveless act, and as an expression of his concern about his own great personal wealth. Highlighting the biblical figure of the Prodigal Son as a template for a series of spendthrift Gide characters, and seeing Lafcadio's motiveless act in *Les Caves du Vatican* as the act of a squanderer, will reveal a network of fictional themes and monetary metaphors centred around the notion of expense. It will also lead to an exploration of the links between the economic, psychological and moral aspects of human behaviour as illustrated by a number of his characters within the general contexts both of the protestant ethic and of potlatch.

The moral readings Gide made of botanical data are well-known. His equally ingenious moral translations from the discourse of economics have been less readily recognized. In addition, the role played in the development of Gide's thought by his uncle, Charles Gide, Professor at the Collège de France and the most celebrated French economist of his generation, has been neglected. To what extent, after the death of Paul Gide, the uncle became a surrogate father or intellectual guide to the boy Gide has not really been debated, nor will it be here. It is clear, however, that the writer learnt much from the economist. Gide knew his uncle's *Histoire des doctrines économiques* and successfully exploited his familiarity with it in his quarrel with Barrès. Playing on the 'double sense of the word culture' (which in French can mean both culture and cultivation) Gide assimilates certain principles of the English economist Ricardo's theory of ground rent to Barrès's nationalist premiss of 'the cult of the earth and the dead'. He opposes the American Carey's theory to that of Ricardo and suggests that Carey's economic argument is equally meaningful in the psychological domain and might even one day shed new light on the history of literature.[2] Gide also knew his uncle's *Traité d'économie politique* and quotes it in his *Journal* for 1904, again to draw a moral lesson from an economic formula.[3]

The following pages will deal with the psychological and moral relevance of economic concepts, but ones which are rather less technical than ground rent and which Gide scarcely needed to research in the works of his uncle. As he exploits a certain economic vocabulary for the purposes of enlarging his psychological understanding the nephew may quite naturally remind us of the uncle, but when the vocabulary in question is made up of terms as everyday as *dépense* (expenditure), *gratuit* (free), *compte* (account) and *calcul* (calculation) it might be an exaggeration to attribute it to the influence of Charles Gide alone. To measure the uncle's influence precisely is then, not easy, although no doubt his contribution was considerable. Familiarity with Charles Gide and with his work presented a field of imagery to the writer which he viewed with interest and which stimulated his gift for lateral thinking. Nothing, however, proves that he would not have pondered over similar notions without a knowledge of the work of his uncle.[4] Gide had, after all, like other educated persons, some grasp of the rudiments of economics and its language, if only because he had to, at least, oversee the management of the personal fortune which he had inherited. The influence of this wealth on his thinking and writing will be one of my contentions here and the starting-point of my analysis.

Gide was rich, so rich that Charles-Louis Philippe, on being introduced to Valery Larbaud, the heir to the Vichy spring-water fortune, expressed his delight at meeting someone besides whom his friend Gide seemed poor.[5] But the puritanically-educated Gide was equally imbued with the message of the Gospels, which preach the words of an austerely penniless

Christ that it is easier for a camel to pass through the eye of a needle than for a rich man to enter heaven.[6]

In the young Gide particularly then one may justifiably see, if not a guilt-ridden capitalist, certainly a bourgeois rentier with Christian qualms about his state of financial privilege. These misgivings surface in the very first pages of his *Journal* in 1893–94 in a remark all the more revealing for its brevity: 'Wealth considered solely as a permission to work freely' (*JI*,48; *J1*,34). It expresses the embarrassment his wealth represented for him and the intellectual strategy by which he chooses to justify it. Discretion demands that it is only in the answer he brings to it that the problem itself is expressed. Two solutions to the dilemma would seem to present themselves. Wealth can be accepted and justified by a number of ingenious arguments; alternatively it can be dispensed with either by giving or by a sort of frantic dispersal, both procedures being covered by the term prodigality. The justification or the dissipation of wealth are alternating attitudes in a number of characters in Gide's writings. It may happen that one character personifies the first tendency whilst another represents the second, but it is sometimes the case that a character evolves from one to the other or that consciously or unconsciously they are the battleground of the two conflicting simultaneous impulses.

The sentence from the *Journal* quoted above presents the solution of the casuist. Money should not be considered as the mere means for the obtaining of property, social privilege or a life of leisure. On the contrary, it would be an enablement to a life of work – that of the mind. Wealth would have no other justification but to afford the time necessary for the free creative play of the intellect. Confronted however as it is with the protestant integrity of Gide's early education, the speciousness of the argument could scarcely withstand the categorical morality of the Gospel. It is then that the second attitude comes into play – that of giving, spending, squandering.

It appears in *Les Nourritures Terrestres*, which are both a lyrical realization of the abundant sensuous resources of the world and an incitement to enjoy them: a call for the consumption of the fruits of the earth. Beyond the notion of the devouring tourist's gaze (albeit that of a sophisticated, sensitive tourist), itself a prelude to consumption, the text foregrounds the theme of garnering or stockpiling as a precedent to consuming. The third part of the Fifth Book is a paeon to the 'inestimable provision' of granaries and fruit-stores, the 'heaps of grain' and the 'piles of apples', but the sensuousness of the description works only to the extent that appetite is awakened: 'Will enough be left to outlast my hunger?' (87–8; 211–13), The properly destructive element of such consumption should be underscored – an attack on objects and, by extension, on property. The Ménalque of *Les Nourritures Terrestres* states his 'aversion [. . .] for any *possession* on earth' (183; 55). He nonetheless admits having worked to enrich himself: 'for fifteen years I accumulated wealth like a miser; I gathered riches with all my capacities', but simply so as to have the pleasure of selling everything off: 'When I was fifty, the hour having struck, I sold all my belongings [. . .] in a couple of days I realized a large fortune, which I invested in such a way as to have it always at my immediate disposal' (189; 61). Not only does Ménalque feel a dislike for personal possessions, he takes pleasure in the act of ridding himself of them, a pleasure he strives to sharpen by a greater accumulation of them beforehand. In a moment of munificent destruction he has the trees of his estate chopped down, the pleasure of it stemming from the abnegation (191; 63). For him, asceticism itself can be voluptuous.

Despite his strategy, however, Ménalque does not so much abolish his wealth as liquidate his possessions. He renounces the ownership of property but remains rich, having merely converted commodities into cash. The few possessions that find favour must be portable. By abstractifying his economic substance into a bank balance, creating a financial pool into which he can dip at will, he shapes the economic potential to fund his nomadic lifestyle. We recognize here the economic substructure of the Gidean notions of the *disponibilité* or the *mobilité* of the self. Ménalque spends, makes inroads into his reserves, but never seems to run the risk of exhausting them. He is prodigal, but without ever attaining the penniless pathos of the biblical paradigm. Diluting the ethos of *dénuement* (destitution), which is one of the strengths of the text, he remains very much a figure 'laden with insolent wealth', suspect in the eyes of the reader as ultimately of the author-narrator, who, in the last book of the work, remarks to his character 'If I am now at rest, it is not with riches like yours' (241; 125).[7]

Following the same paradoxical strategy as his Ménalque of the *Nourritures*, Gide moved to redeem himself by selling. In 1900 he divested himself of his Normandy manor-house of La Roque-Baignard, just as half a century later he auctioned off a large part of his personal library. Years afterwards, on a visit to his former property, now ringed with barbed wire, he declared in his *Feuillets d'Automne*: 'I have never had (the soul) of an owner. The very word property strikes me as both ridiculous and odious' (*JII*, 1087). Nonetheless the main thrust of his efforts towards self-impoverishment was to be expressed vicariously, that is to say on the literary level alone.

The burden of his own financial situation is the main psychic impetus in the protagonist of *Le Roi Candaule*, another figuration of the prodigal troubled by a rich man's guilt complex.[8] Candaule, who, the prologue tells us, is 'a giving nature', finds it difficult to bear being wealthy whilst surrounded by subjects less affluent: 'I seemed to myself a grasping hoarder' (60). He longs for poverty, the lot of his childhood friend Gygès. Driven by 'a kind of indecisive generosity' (48), Candaule proclaims he will not rest until he has raised Gygès to his own level of privilege: 'I shall be a prey to anxiety/As long as you remain unacquainted with/my fortune in all its complexity' (96). But a curious realignment occurs in the direction that the king's munificence takes – from the economic to the sexual. Candaule offers him what he holds most dear – his wife. In his preface to the first edition of the play Gide illuminates the conduct of his character by a quotation: ' "Generous to a fault," Nietzsche writes; and elsewhere: "It is a curious thing to note that excessive generosity is inseparable from the loss of a sense of modesty." Modesty is a form of reserve' (32).[9]

The prodigality shared by Ménalque and Candaule, as well as by Philoctète, the hero of the short traité of 1899 who presents his precious bow to Néoptolème, did not escape Jean Delay who compares the 'magnificent extravagances' of the three characters.[10] In *L'Immoraliste* we see another prodigal figure make inroads into both his moral reserve and his economic capital. Rather than generous, Michel is profligate to the point of vice, although, like Candaule, he too will make an offering of his wife . . . but to death. In him we see a new personification of the *rentier* in revolt against his own situation. He puts his estate of La Morinière up for sale, a transposition of Gide's sale of La Roque, encouraged in this by a new Ménalque figure, still as hostile to the ownership of property but still as rich: 'For a person who has not got the sense of property, you seem to possess a great deal. Isn't that rather serious?' says he to Michel, pinpointing the ambiguous position of his friend with disturbing accuracy (428; 82).

Michel in fact cares much for things and cares little for them. He lets his property be stolen, one way of getting rid of it. A closer look, however, reveals that it is his wife's property that he allows to be taken. The scissors (a symbolic figuration of the female form and condition) which he lets the boy Moktir steal are his wife's, willing collusion this, by Michel, in the invasion of female territory by the male adolescent. A budding Candaule, he voluptuously contemplates the dispossessing of his wife. At the same time he spends in order to acquire, to surround himself with an accumulation of beautiful things. As he settles in Paris for the winter he notes that:

> Marceline was a little uneasy, not only at the increased rent, but at all the other expenses we should certainly be led into. I countered all her fears by pretending I had a horror of anything temporary; I forced myself to believe in this feeling and deliberately exaggerated it [. . .]. In consequence, I stopped short at no expense, telling myself at each new one that here was another tie and thinking also that by these means I should suppress every vagabond inclination I felt – or feared I might feel – within me. (421–2; 73)

What transpires from these lines is more than just the desire to possess and Michel himself knows it. There is something desperate about his race to spend. Unbalanced by his growing inclination towards nomadism he looks to the object world as a prop. Property is a form of psychological insurance, a defence mechanism. It is as though he was trying to hold back the flood of his new desires behind a barrage of purchases. Ménalque has it that his friend suffers from 'moral agoraphobia' (432; 86). He abhors a vacuum. Frightened by the flux of his new being he looks for permanence and solidity in things, like the drowning man clutching at a straw. His strategy proves a vain one; the durability of objects is just as illusory, as he learns when he sees his friends negligently spoiling the *objets d'art* with which he has surrounded himself. His initial response, as he himself admits, is 'to save them, to lock them up in a cupboard for my own use alone' (430; 84). Nor is his reflex a purely egoistical one. For Michel things are preferable to people only if they are invulnerable. He is obsessed with the immaculate: 'The reason I suffer is that I want to preserve things' (430; 85), he says. Confronted with 'the horrible wear and tear of material objects' and that of persons he prefers to do without and to divest himself of them.[11]

Michel's frenzied race to spend begins here. When with his wife Marceline in the Alps, he says:

> Nothing seemed fine enough for me nor too expensive. [. . .] The rooms were extravagantly dear. But what do I care? I thought. It is true I no longer have my lectures, but I am selling La Morinière. And then we shall see. . . . Besides, what need have I of money? What need have I of all this? . . . I am strong now . . . A complete change of fortune, I think, must be as instructive as a complete change of health . . . Marceline, of course, requires luxury; she is weak . . . oh, for her sake, I will spend so much, so much that. . . . And I felt at one and the same time a horror of luxury and a craving for it. (456; 119–20)

His desperate need to spend intensifies.

> I did not allow Marceline to have any say in our expenses or attempt to moderate them. I knew of course that they were excessive and that they could not last. I could no longer count on any money from La Morinière. It had ceased to bring in anything, and Bocage wrote that he could not find a purchaser. But all thoughts of the future ended only in making me spend the more. What need should I have of so much money, once I was alone, I thought; and sick at heart, I watched Marceline's frail life as it ebbed away more quickly still than my fortune. (459; 124)

Level of expenditure has become the symptom and the thermometer of Michel's malaise, but it has undergone a shift of function. Expenditure it seems is no longer an exchange of values, he no longer spends to buy, it is an attack on values. Admittedly his attitude remains ambivalent. He both relishes and recoils from luxury. He rushes towards asceticism accompanied by eight trunks of luggage, but these are impedimenta of which he quickly feels the ridiculous encumbrance. Soon he no longer tries to check himself. His disgust with objects becomes ever more intense: a 'growing horror of luxury, of comfort, of all the things I was wrapped around with, of the protection that my newly restored health had made unnecessary, of all the precautions one takes to preserve one's body from the perilous contact of life' (463; 129). Marceline once dead he would like to squander the rest of his wealth.

His wife Marceline's death is yet another element in the theme of spending and prodigality. As illness undermines her, Michel, unconsciously, becomes less attached to her. It is when she needs him most that he neglects her. True, he spends on her account (and, we note, does not let her keep accounts) since, according to his new creed, spending is a sign of strength and, as the weak cannot expend themselves, one must spend for them. It is due to Michel that her life is spent, he hastens if not causes her death. Driven by his inner demon, he convinces her they should leave Switzerland, the country of clean air and health, the country of financial reserve, banks, honest thrift and economy, for the balmier but unhealthier lowlands of Italy.[12] It is as though, subconsciously, he wished her dead. Spoilt, worn, unwholesome, Marceline now belongs to the order of objects of which Michel is in a rush to dispossess himself. Slowly but surely he drains and damages his life companion. As with the stereotypically wasting romantic heroine, consumption is her fate . . . consumption, in a sense too, by her husband.

Does Michel, one wonders, comprehend the cruelty of his 'What need should I have of so much money, once I was alone?' It is a dual process of waste that he is engaged in, that of his inheritance and that of his wife: 'I watched Marceline's frail life as it ebbed away more quickly still than my fortune'. Some commentators see in Marceline a Christ figure – and it is true Christ's ultimate *consummatum est* would apply equally to her.[13]

There is contamination of meaning at work here, where the notion of expenditure is concerned. Gide is drawing an analogy between economic substance and the vital resources of being. The idea of the rich man thus coincides with that of a sort of Nietzschean overman whose internal dynamism is expressed in self-expenditure, but who, in his impetus, risks damaging others. In Gide's view the strong often act at the expense of the weak. Marceline is aware of this: 'I quite understand your doctrine', she says to her husband, '– for now it has become a doctrine. A fine one, perhaps [. . .] but it does away with the weak' (459–60; 124). Marceline will not be the last victim of the career of the Gidean prodigal-overman as will be seen later in the context of *Les Caves du Vatican*.

A further metaphorical shift is apparent here, one which is the linguistic reflection of a more generally valid psychological trend. Simultaneously with the dissipation of his wealth Michel indulges in dissipation in the sexual sense of the term. Already Candaule is evidence of the way in which the guilt feelings of the rich can find expression in sexual irregularity. It goes without saying that Gide is not the first to draw an analogy between sexuality and the attitude a person adopts towards money. Saint Augustine saw in avarice a symptom of repressed sexuality. Thomas Aquinas saw a parallel between avarice and incest, each representing emotional investment in family possessiveness.[14] Sexual activity is a sort of expenditure of one's being – witness Baudelaire's aside that 'there are only two places where one pays for the right to *dépenser*: the public toilets and women'.[15] In *L'Immoraliste* the two ideas overlap. In Biskra, Michel is attracted by the nudity of the boys; in Naples he gives himself up to 'vagabond debauch'; in Syracuse he frequents the demi-monde (463; 127–8). He finds his historical model in the Wisigoth figure of Athalaric, a boy-king and boy-prodigal who rejects the wise counsel of his mother, 'plunging for a few years into a life of violent and unbridled pleasures with rude companions of his own age' (407; 53). We have already seen another aspect of the intimate amalgam of pleasure and destruction in Ménalque's devastation of the grounds of his manor. A similar scene occurs in *L'Immoraliste* where an adolescent of ambiguous physical charm watches the felling of a plantation. The motif is present again in *Isabelle*, when Gérard, walking in the devastated parkland of La Quartfourche, says 'How strange it was that, by some over-abundance of life in me, the note of savage violence which all this devastation added to the beauty of the landscape only intensified my pleasure in it' (666; 160). These parallels might be less convincing if we didn't already know from a reading of *Si le grain ne meurt* of the sensual swooning feeling that the idea of destruction excited in the child Gide and if the terms that the autobiographical text chooses to express that childhood feeling weren't precisely those of expenditure and prodigality: 'If you find this astonishing you understand nothing about it; without an example to follow and without an end in view, what will become of voluptuousness? In a random manner it summons up in dreams excessive expenditures of energy, indulgence in inane luxuries, grotesque acts of prodigality (*JII*, 387). Through the notion of sexual dissipation and the connected idea of depredation we reconnect with the idea of 'over-abundance of life' which is the hallmark of the prodigal and which threatens the weaker individual. Despite Saint Augustine, must one then seek one of the wellsprings of this sort of excessive, violent self-expenditure in frustrated sexuality, in the repression of Michel's unconscious homosexuality or, where the biblical prodigal is concerned, in the family restrictions of cloistered adolescence?

It was from the Bible, the *vade mecum* of his childhood and adolescence, that Gide borrowed the paradigm of the prodigal, the spendthrift youth of *Le Retour de l'enfant prodigue* who claims his inheritance early and squanders it with wild munificence before returning, weary of penniless wandering, to his father's house. Gide's text, a palimpsest overwriting its biblical model, both venerates and subverts it. His prodigal reproaches brother and parents with being 'thrifty'; unlike them he prefers the practice of hectic consumption that will lead eventually to asceticism (476; 127. 479; 131). Forced, through his own weakness, to abandon his quest, he encourages the secret dawn departure of his younger brother who, without inheritance, leaves 'taking nothing'. It is with the invention of the younger brother, who attempts to succeed where the elder has failed, that Gide distorts the biblical original.

A further evolution in the model is apparent here. The new prodigal is poor at the outset. What he will squander is not riches or cash but values, those of his forbears. We have moved from the economic to the moral plane. Gide's new prodigal is the rebel. The beginnings of this dispensing with the old morality are there in *L'Immoraliste*. Michel jettisons the values of the French intellectual protestant middle class: ideas, chastity and property, and opts instead for African sensuality, pleasure and asceticism, a complete value reversal. His revolt, like those of all Gide's prodigals, mirrors that of Gide himself. In the *Journal* for 1902 one reads ' . . . And with that self-esteem which I had painfully acquired through pride, I was fed up and disgusted. I strained my ingenuity to lose it, and this was not hard. Acquisitions are worth amassing only for the sake of spending them easily later on. I gave myself up therefore to debauch; and indeed it did not displease me to introduce a bit of system into it; I meant to work hard at it. I envied ***, who got nothing but pleasure from it; I also gave myself a lot of trouble. (*JI*, 130–31; *JI*, 108: February 1902).[16] In an even more revealing passage of his *Journal* for 1923 the writer compares himself directly to the biblical figure:

> I was like the prodigal son who goes squandering his possessions. And that imponderable treasure which the slow virtue of my fathers, from generation to generation, had patiently accumulated on my head, no, I was not unaware of its value; but the unknown I could hope for by renouncing it seemed to me even more precious. The words of Christ rose up luminously before me like the column of fire [. . .] 'Sell all your goods and give them to the poor.' [. . .] And doubtless, pushing that relinquishment to the extreme, to the absurd, I should have ended up in complete impoverishment – for 'what have you that you have not received?' – but yet it was complete impoverishment that I coveted as the truest possession. (*JI* 778–79; *J2*, 344: 1923)

Just as fortune can be wasted on riotous living, so moral inheritance can be jettisoned, morality and money meeting in the combined notion of expenditure.

The compulsion to squander is a psychological attitude but, in the *Journal* for 1930, Gide indicates, as has already been suggested *à propos L'Immoraliste*, that it is linked to a physiological state which is none other than energy, the urgent drive towards extraversion, what he called in his own case 'that sort of inner pressure and ardor, that tormenting need to embrace, which as I sometimes feared, might have led me to crime, or to madness' (*JI*, 986; *J3*, 109: 6 June 1930). At the opposite pole to such fretful dynamism is lethargy, the depression of days, as he wrote the previous year, still using monetary imagery, 'on which one **feels has overestimated one's resources**; [one is] **in arrears**; in debt; showing a deficit (*JI*, 945; *J2*, 72: 20 October 1929) – Fleurissoire, in *Les Caves*, would have said 'in debt towards God' (817; 176). The excess of energy that needs to expend itself is a surplus of vital urge. Gide understands that this superfluity of being can transmute itself into moral excess, as, for example, in the case of Michel or of the murderer, Lafcadio. Excess is tantamount to luxury and there would seem then to be a case for considering the *acte gratuit* as a luxury act, an act of an overflowing excess of vitality.

All too often commentators on Lafcadio's *acte gratuit* in *Les Caves du Vatican* have forgotten the banal meaning of the adjective, '*gratuit*': 'free', that is 'not needing to be paid for'. In the light of such an understanding the entire concept of the gratuitous act lends itself to an economic interpretation. By his choice of vocabulary in *Les Caves* Gide moreover hints that the *acte gratuit* is intimately linked to the notion of wealth.

In *Les Caves* the writer Julius de Baraglioul imagines an *acte gratuit* perpetrated 'out of extravagance, – or the desire of a spendthrift, a gambler'. In his portrait of his intended fictional hero he continues to use the same financial terminology. From that catholic point of view, he says, 'the best-trained soul is the one that keeps the strictest accounts', then 'we may grant that [a man] may keep no accounts at all'; such a soul, he goes on to say, being 'free from [. . .] **calculation**' (817; 176). Not to keep account is the privilege of the rich man, especially of the rich spendthrift. Conversely, love of calculation, of accountability may be linked to avarice. Julius's fictional hero then, munificently rich, will be poles apart from avarice and the miserliness of old age. Unbeknown to him, of course, Julius is sketching the portrait of an ideal Lafcadio, of Lafcadio as he might wish to be and not as Gide presents him, a complex mixture of confidence and vulnerability.

It is Protos who gives us a description of his friend Lafcadio in the same monetary terms as Julius uses to describe his planned character, terms that evoke counting, figures, accounts and expenses. 'A youth, then, wished to escape from the social framework that hems us in [. . .] I don't suppose there was much calculation in what he did. . . . I remember, Cadio, in the old days, though you were a great dab at figures, you would never consent to keep an account of your own expenses' (857–8; 229–30).

From the 'account' Lafcadio gives of his childhood we know that he learnt 'calculation' from Baron Heldenbruck, one of the sequence of so-called uncles who gravitated around the lovely Wanda, his mother. 'He made me,' says Lafcadio, 'what he used laughingly to call his "cashier" – that is, he gave into my keeping a whole fortune of petty cash, and wherever we went together, it was I who had to do the paying' (738; 75). Lafcadio, then, learns to add, subtract and spend at an early age by the direct method. Another 'uncle', the Marquis de Gesvres, restrains the boy's appetite for accounting whilst accelerating his propensity to spend: 'The Marquis de Gesvres took a positively frenzied pleasure in spending money [. . .]. He taught me to spend money without keeping accounts and without taking thought beforehand as to whether I should have enough to satisfy my fancy, my desire or my hunger' (743; 81–2).

The prodigal is someone who does not keep accounts. Lafcadio aspires to that status and in part attains it. But Lafcadio's weakness is that he does not have the reserves of character to fund his major act of expenditure. The spending lessons of the Marquis never quite erase the accounting tuition of the Baron; the spendthrift Lafcadio is always haunted by the Lafcadio who keeps accounts. One of the first things that we learn about him is that he keeps a sort of account book in which *punte* are numbered. It was a present from a third 'uncle', Fabian Taylor, who had inscribed on the flyleaf 'For my trusty comrade Cadio from his old uncle, this book **for him to keep his accounts in**' and Lafcadio does indeed practice in it a mysterious accounting system which Julius, as he nosily leafs through it, dismisses as 'a childish and trifling computation of merits and rewards' (716–20; 47–51). Julius is hardly to blame for not having learnt from the teachings of Freud who invites us to look beyond the apparent triviality of a certain sort of accounting and himself saw in the harmless figures of Leonardo da Vinci's account book the hieroglyphs of his secret emotional life.[17] It is shortly afterwards that we discover that the *punte* of the notebook are masochistic markers on the painful path Lafcadio strives to climb towards that complete control of himself which, in his eyes, represents the superiority of the 'slim'.

Interestingly the practice of keeping a moral account book, in which sins and temptations were entered against worthy thoughts and good deeds, was part of the moral method that puritan divines recommended to their faithful. Such a book reinforced the preoccupation with the moral rectitude and self-control necessary for ultimate salvation in the after-life. The young Gide owned just such a book and the agenda kept by the narrator of *Paludes* represents a parodied version of it; 'My agenda is divided into two parts: on one page I write what I am going to do, and on the opposite page I write every evening what I have done. Then I compare the two; I subtract one from the other, and what I have not done, or the deficit, becomes what I ought to have done' (96; 22).

In more serious vein old Azaïs of *Les Faux-Monnayeurs* remembers the practice from his childhood: ' The President of the society gave us each a notebook, in which we set down with absolute frankness our failures and our shortcomings' (1017; 99). Lafcadio then, in his ambition to control his emotions and in the account-book he uses, is not exempt from puritanical influences.

The relationship between puritanism and notions of counting and control will be looked at later. Suffice it to say for the moment that Lafcadio is obsessed with counting and numbers, as was Gide who writes in his *Journal* for 1943: 'Without at all believing in the mystic virtue of numbers, I always and regularly *count*' (*JII*, 190; *J4*, 170: 9 February 1943). Jean Delay, quoting this text and analysing his subject's obsession with numbers as expressed in *Les Cahiers d'André Walter*, links it to a childhood character trait of Gide:

> For the anxious child, numbers had a magical value, and the obsessive need to count was a subterfuge, and refuge against anxiety, the search for a formula that will ward it off, but which, no sooner hoped for, reveals itself as ineffectual and becomes in turn a source of unease [. . .]. An obsession with numbers and the uncontrollable, compulsive need to count were to reappear in André Gide during periods of depression and of overwork.[18]

Before addressing his father Lafcadio forces himself to count up to twelve. Later, on the brink of his supposed climactic spontaneous act, he conditions the deed with an identical set of figures. Reminiscences of Stendhal's *Le Rouge et le Noir*, in which Julien Sorel steels himself by the figures of the clock, are perhaps also at work here in Gide's imagination. Like Julien, Lafcadio is both iron-willed and sensitive as an anemone, full too of other contradictions. A self-styled 'creature of inconsequence' (744; 83) he himself admits, in pillow-talk, 'the idea of impunity is odious to me' (871; 248). By all means let us imagine, with Julius, a man who 'may keep no accounts at all' but let us not make the mistake of seeing Lafcadio as such. Prodigal he may be, but with the soul and reflexes of an accountant.

Whilst feelings of inferiority and cold-blooded calculation enter into Lafcadio's so-called *acte gratuit* this does not invalidate the interpretation of the theoretical free act as Julius or even Lafcadio imagine it might be. Such a hypothetical act is characterized by its disinterestedness. It is an act motivated neither by profit nor acquisitiveness. To acquire is to gain or to win; to act gratuitously is to lose or to expend. It is the concept of expending which characterizes the *acte gratuit*, futile, disinterested expenditure. It is the act through which an excess of energy is expended. It follows then that it is the act of a person who is in surplus, a luxury act of someone possessed of a superfluity of wherewithal, be it money or whatever, for expenditure is the privilege of the haves. It is no coincidence that one of the first perpetrators of the free act in Gide's fiction is the millionaire Zeus of *Le Prométhée mal enchaîné* (where the circulation of a 500 franc note plays a crucial role) or that the most notorious is the affluent Lafcadio of the later *Caves* and not the impecunious bohemian of the early chapters. But it is the act too of a certain type of wealthy person, the rich prodigal who keeps no accounts. Before his act Lafcadio takes no account of orthodox morality; afterwards he hopes to have to account to no one for it. The ideal author of an ideal *acte gratuit* would not weigh the pros and cons. It would not be the mean gesture of a careful man, rather the act of a carefree prodigal. The act should be alien to any idea of counting or calculating, removed from any idea of moderation or measure (latin: *ratio*). On the contrary, it is immoderate and irrational.

The extreme of the 'careful' man, obsessed with profit or interest, is the miser. For Gide, who was himself often accused of meanness where money is concerned, avarice is an attribute of old age.[19] Himself then in old age, in his *Journal* for 1941, he notes the 'tendency of the aged towards avarice' (*JII*, 100; *J4*, 88: 30 September 1941) and, in that for 1944, 'the need that the old feel to hoard' (*JII*, 262; *J4*, 233: 6 February 1944). In *Les Caves* it is noteworthy that the *acte gratuit* is undertaken by an adolescent and that, like young love in traditional comedy, it occurs at the expense of an old man. One is reminded of the crime of another young murderer, Raskolnikoff, of the age of his victim Ivanovna and of her profession . . . based on interest *par excellence*: userer.[20]

Variations on the profiteering Aliona Ivanovna figure are not rare in Gide's work. In his two most complex books *Les Caves du Vatican* and *Les Faux-Monnayeurs* central roles are played by two gangs of crooks, motivated purely by the money nexus, confidence tricksters in the *sotie* and forgers in the novel, both therefore, in their ways, issuers of counterfeit values. Whilst it is true the title of *Les Caves* could well have been *La Monnaie du pape* it is only in *Les Faux-Monnayeurs* that the monetary metaphor which, until now, has merely appeared in filigree in the fabric of consecutive texts, governs the title itself. The metaphor is at last promoted to overriding nominative symbol. Of Édouard, the central figure in the novel, himself author of a novel entitled *Les Faux-Monnayeurs*, we learn the following:

> In reality, Edouard had in the first place been thinking of certain of his fellow novelists when he began to think of *The Counterfeiters*, and in particular of the Comte de Passavant. But this attribution had been considerably widened. [. . .] If he allowed his mind to follow its bent, it soon tumbled headlong into abstractions, where it was as comfortable as a fish in water. Ideas of exchange, of depreciation, of inflation, etc., gradually invaded his book (like the theory of clothes in Carlyle's *Sartor Resartus*) and usurped the place of the characters. (1085; 172)

What is the case for Édouard's novel is equally so for Gide's.[21]

One of the focal issues raised by *Les Faux-Monnayeurs* is that of authenticity, the coiner characters representing persons who attempt to substitute false or dubious values for genuine ones. Such a dichotomy is rather simplistic for, as Gide sees, values are not absolute but are subject to forces such as inflation or devaluation. As it is, few, if any, characters are untainted by a propensity for counterfeiting. Some, nonetheless, stand in opposition to the profiteers Strouvilhou, Passavant and Lady Griffiths.

Édouard, for example, is well aware in himself of that 'anti-egotistical force of decentralization [which] disintegrates my sense of property – and, as a consequence, of responsibility' (987; 68). Olivier Molinier recognizes in himself a similar need to give, but one which takes a rather different direction, ultimate gratuitous self-expenditure in suicide: 'Do you know the act which I sometimes think would express me best? [. . .] I understand Dmitri Karamazof perfectly when he asks his brother if he understands a person killing himself out of enthusiasm, out of sheer excess of life . . . just *bursting*' (1151; 242). In its sense of excess Olivier's impulse is close to that of Michel and Lafcadio. It is more internalized however, more introverted, and tends towards suicide rather than towards the death or the killing of the other. To the category of persons 'who feel impelled to act against their interest' (1228; 324) belong characters as various as old La Pérouse, who, whilst a member of the genteel poor, is only interested in offering free piano lessons: 'the only lessons I really care about . . . giving' (1025; 108), or Cob-Lafleur, disgusted by the luxury life of Passavant (1025; 108. 1228; 324).

At the head of this list of more disinterested characters comes, surname notwithstanding, Bernard Profitendieu. With him Gide further develops the literary figure of the poor prodigal on the model of the younger brother he had imagined for the biblical Prodigal Son. Lafcadio, in this context, had been an ambiguous figure with Gide vacillating between the impecunious youth of the early chapters and the affluent heir of the later pages. Once he has left the family home with no fortune but his energy, initiative and generous heart, Bernard is, of his own choosing, resolutely poor, and prodigal with it. Gide underlines the generosity of his character. Whilst climbing above cloud-level in the Alps, Bernard sees avarice as the main attribute of invisible mankind below him. It is in part the luxury and comfort of his middle-class home that has made him flee it (1069; 155. 1093; 180). He rebels against such bourgeois values and wishes to substitute for them other more personal ones. The false gold coin that he finds in the Saas-Fée grocer's interests but does not satisfy him. It is to the moral equivalent of the genuine value of a gold napoléon that he aspires rather: 'Oh, Laura! I should like all my life long, at the very smallest shock, to ring true, with a pure, authentic sound. Nearly all the people I have known ring false. To be worth exactly what one seems to be worth; not to try to seem to be worth more' (1093; 180).[22]

Admittedly Bernard lives at the expense of Édouard, but he aims to repay his debt as soon as he can 'bring to mint the uncoined riches whose abundance he felt in his heart' (1078; 64). The reader follows Bernard's repeated efforts to find the person or the cause worthy of becoming the object of his 'lover's longing for giving, for sacrifice' (1209; 303). He pursues his quest fruitlessly, disappointed in turn by his parents, Laura, Édouard, God and *Action Française* until his guardian angel (there is also a calculating devil in the novel, taking account of what goes on (973; 53)) tells him 'the time has come to do your accounts' (1209; 304). Yet another prodigal who, like Lafcadio, is well advised to keep accounts! What should be inferred from this? Perhaps that there is a time for spending and a time for saving, a time for squandering and a time for taking stock. No one, least of all the prodigal, should be denied the chance to return. Bernard, wiser, reinvested with experience, will do just that.[23]

It is clear to what degree economic metaphors have coloured the notion Gide has of his characters in *Les Faux-Monnayeurs* and even of marginal ones such as the professor who develops a theory of sleep as a careful saving-up of the psyche the action of which compensates for the 'expenditure and the traffic of exchanges in which life consists' (1089; 175). In a *tour de force* conceit the diabolical Strouvilhou proclaims his monetary theory of literature:

> We live upon nothing but feelings which have been taken for granted once and for all and which the reader imagines he experiences, because he believes everything he sees in print; the author **speculates on these** as he does on the conventions which he believes to be the foundations of his art. These feelings ring as false as counters, but they pass current. And as everyone knows that 'bad money drives out good', a man who should offer the public real coins would seem to be defrauding us. In a world in which everyone cheats, it's the honest man who passes for a charlatan. I give you fair warning – if I edit a review, it will be in order to prick bladders – in order to demonetize fine feelings, and those promissory notes which go by the name of *words*. (1198; 291)[24]

Édouard in turn expounds his economic theory of literature, more modest but just as paradoxical as Strouvilhou's: ' "A plague upon the economical [. . .] In art they turn into the prolix." "Why?" "Because they can't bear to lose anything" ' (1140; 230). Whether open-handedness does lead to litotes is a moot point. Édouard also discriminates between two types of person; the generous, those who give without reckoning, and the parsimonious, those who take everything, including themselves, into account. Laura's husband Douviers belongs to the second category:

> He never forgets himself in what he feels, so that he never feels anything great. Don't push me too hard. I have my own ideas; but they

don't lend themselves to the yard measure, and I don't care to measure them. Paul-Ambroise is in the habit of saying that he refuses to take count of anything that can't be put down in figures; I think he is playing on the words 'take count'; for if that were the case, we should be obliged to leave God out of 'the account'. (1184; 277)[25]

Indeed the more one considers *Les Faux-Monnayeurs*, the more clearly-defined the outlines of its economic structures become, as I have argued elsewhere.[26] Not only is it rife with references to a range of financial instruments and transactions as the economic status and actions of each of the characters unfold and mesh one with the other, thus offering a view of an orthodox system of economic exchange that is duplicated with a parallel illicit one, that of the coiners, but its economy is fed by two wealthy, homosexual capitalist writers, Édouard and Passavant, the one largely genuine, the other largely an egotistical sham, though each, in various fashions, funding a network of their more needy acquaintances. Throughout the novel, moreover, Gide plays on his awareness of a correspondence between the printed paper page of fiction and minted money – both constituting issued systems of credit which rely on suspension of disbelief in the reader-user and both of which can be subverted by inauthentic substitutes, shoddy literature on the one hand, counterfeit notes on the other. For one set of characters Édouard is thus the banker-writer distributor of, up to a point, sound values; for another set Passavant, with his links to Strouvilhou and the coiners, is the banker-writer distributor of false values. One becomes aware too that Édouard's character typology applies to the novel itself, most of the characters of which fall into the categories of, in a broad sense, generous givers or parsimonious takers. The generous givers – Laura, Bernard, Georges, Sarah, Olivier and Armand – headed by Édouard, but not all of whom are affluent, are all in their way prodigals, making the novel a sort of multiple modern version of the biblical parable.

Since the first publication of the present article and its sequel, Jean-Joseph Goux has extended the economic analysis of *Les Faux-Monnayeurs*, seeing it as a fictional illustration of a cultural crisis engendered by the European move from the gold standard to non-convertible paper money.[27] The shift from a value exchange system based on gold he sees as a metaphor for a contemporaneous shift in the linguistic exchange system away from a literary language based on realism and a painterly language based on representation. With its play on real and false coinage and its preoccupation with fictional form, Gide's complex and perspicacious novel thus makes itself the arena for a crisis in the mimetic values of art. Like non-convertible paper money, literature loses its real-world *signifié*, its gold, becomes aware of its non-sense and resorts to specularity and self-reflection.

If we return to Édouard's hypothesis on character-types, might one claim that a similar theory of character would apply to Gide's fiction as a whole? Were the analogy that has been established above, between the economic and the moral attitudes of particular characters, to be developed, may one not see two character types emerge, the prodigal and the thrifty, whose economic, moral and psychological characteristics would be determined by their basic typology? Thus the prodigal would be defined by an inclination to expenditure, amoralism and extraverted lack of inhibition; the thrifty by an inclination to save, puritanical moral austerity and sexual repression.

The character type of the thrifty puritan leads to perspectives which, while they temporarily distract our view from the literary domain towards those of economic history and the sociology of religion, are interesting to the extent that they support the connection between puritanism and thrift. In the *The Protestant Ethic and the Spirit of Capitalism* (*Die Protestantische Ethik und der Geist des Kapitalismus*, 1904–5) Max Weber analyses what, in the moral attitudes of ascetic protestantism of the sixteenth and seventeenth centuries, might have contributed to the growth of capitalism, both as ethical and economic mode, amongst the lower and middle middle classes. Quoting ample documentary evidence he identifies a powerful pro-capitalist force in a religion which, whilst condemning the love of money, luxury and the cult of acquisition, simultaneously advocated a life of sober and continuous industry as proof and practice of a faith without which there was no divine salvation. When strict moral limits on consumption go hand in hand with the fervent encouragement of lucrative activity there ensues, through the ascetic emphasis on saving-up for the future (and being saved in the future) a production of wealth which takes the form of an unspent intangible accumulation of capital.[28] As will be seen, the psychology of *La Porte Étroite* confirms, on an individual character level, the broader thesis elaborated by Weber.

If, returning to the thrifty character type whom we saw as accumulative, repressed and puritanical, we take Alissa as illustration (Rachel, in *Les Faux-Monnayeurs*, would be another) what can be deduced? Firstly she shows no inclination to spend or to consume; she practises sexual abstinence, the traumatic origin of which is the example of her adulterous mother, absolutely; she is an increasingly strict protestant to the point of extreme austerity and, like Lafcadio, makes use of the protestant's instrument of self-perfection, the account book – in her case, her private diary. Rather than a giver, Alissa is a withholder and a reserver, sexual reticence, as the preface to *Candaule* reminded us, being a reserve. Saving up her being she reserves herself for God and the afterlife. As has been argued elsewhere, such is Alissa's growing abhorrence of consumption that she espouses abstinence and a policy of self-wastage that is anorexic in its practice.[29] But one of the readings of the novel is that Alissa is mistaken because 'Whosoever will save his life will lose it', a Christian gospel paradox in which, in the various guises in which it manifested itself, such as *'Si le gain ne meurt/*unless it die', Gide sincerely believed.[30] The moral, thrift-driven Alissa of *La Porte Étroite* is the opposite of the prodigal Michel of *L'Immoraliste*. He spends and expends himself; he squanders his economic reserves; he loses his sexual inhibitions (as well as his less and less closeted homosexuality, one thinks of the late consummation of his marriage); he becomes the immoralist of the novel's title.

An over-rigorous approach to character typology scarcely allows, however, for the subtleties of human psychology. In Gide's work there is no prodigal or thrifty type which is absolute. Alissa, after all, gives herself to God with a will and a passion that are a form of self-expenditure and which set her apart from, say, the Passavant of *Les Faux-Monnayeurs* or the Protos of *Les Caves du Vatican* who are profiteers working for their own sexual or material ends. She acts not from the profit motive in the material sense but out of desire for the salvation she seeks (together with that of Jérôme) in the renunciation of the pleasures of the senses. In her case scales of disinterestedness are imprecise. Michel too is equally complex. He is a prodigal who has been thrifty and his prodigality is defined by reaction against what he formerly was. The pleasure of expenditure is multiplied if one has formerly lived by thrift. It is noteworthy too that both Michel and Alissa are motivated by a similar dislike of luxury and both practice (even take pleasure in?) an asceticism that borders on masochism. Michel says: 'My abstemiousness had gone to my head and I was drunk with thirst as others are with wine. My thrift of life had been admirable' (459; 123). Opposites though they may be, Alissa and Michel, each in a way as selfish as the other, follow the same path to material abstinence, one in the name of a transcendental religious value, the other in the name of a more human, individual self-invented creed. Prodigality and thrift ultimately meet in asceticism. In Lafcadio too we see an unsettling mixture of the thrifty and the prodigal, of accounting and expenditure, whilst even the generous Bernard of *Les Faux-Monnayeurs* eventually takes stock and . . . returns home. Perhaps only Gide's invented younger brother in his reinscription of the Scriptures, the *Retour de l'Enfant prodigue*, is a model of departure towards dissipation and pure prodigality, since his fate remains unknown to the reader.

It would seem that the Prodigal, he (and it is rarely a she, though the Laura and Sarah of *Les Faux-Monnayeurs* and the Geneviève of *L'Ecole des Femmes* are possible embodiments) who, through successive literary reincarnations indulges in expense in the multiple senses that we have outlined, represents the Gidean paradigm hero, protagonist of a dramatic scenario, as the novelist himself wrote in his *Journal* for 1930, 'to which I continually return; I should like it to be glimpsed also in the third act of my *Oedipe*. The sacrifice of the best. But it is in this gift of himself, this holocaust, that the best affirms himself and convinces himself of his own excellence' (*JI*, 1006; *J3*, 126: 10 August 1930).

Imprinted from continual early readings of the Bible it would seem then that the figure of the Prodigal owes its pride of place in Gide's personal mythology (and for him mythology was a pattern of psychological truths) to the deep inner conflict which opposed Gide the capitalist to Gide the Christian, a conflict which his sympathy for communism in the 1930s was, in part, an attempt to resolve. The development of such a character in its various guises allowed the writer to speculate in opposition to both capitalist and puritan morality, that is to say, against the Gide family morality from which Gide the prodigal son wished to escape.

It is no easy thing, however, to divest oneself of one's upbringing and youth. Gide never lost a puritanical admiration for abnegation. Indeed, in manhood, it remained a constant value for him, in dialectical opposition to equally admirable indulgence. His mature thinking oscillated between the two poles of economy and prodigality, the latter, for him, tinged with puritanism, because of its biblical connotations and because it rejected luxury and adopted, ultimately, sparseness. The prodigal abhors moral renunciation whilst espousing material renunciation. But, unlike the practitioner of thrift, asceticism is attained through expenditure and giving rather than through investment and saving.

Interest in the properly capitalist economic sense of the term is the motive for saving. Gide however, in his *Journal* for 1932, writes:

> Art, science and philosophy are worth something only when disinterested [. . .]. And I have no need of not being myself a *rentier* to judge a social system that creates and protects *rentiers*, to judge it most lamentable. (*JI*, 1140; *J3*, 244: July 1932)

The money of the *rentier* Gide accumulated in the form of interest-bearing shares, a share in French, being *une action*. Action however – and the previous quotation and indeed the whole tenor of the present article invites us to pass from the economic to the moral sphere – action, art and science, for Gide, were only valid if disinterested. He was thus led to evolve a fictional ethic of giving, spending and squandering, to seek an action unmotivated by interest or profit. With the *acte gratuit* Gide made an imaginary attempt to transcend a system of values all too susceptible to fraud, inflation, devaluation or crash, to escape a psychology à la Rochefoucauld, based on self-interest.[31] Gratuitousness and contingency are substituted for interest and planning. By developing his idea of an integral self-suspended act, devoid of connotations of profit, Gide experimented with a psychology that, whilst ironically it involved murder, was, in its way, both christian and marxist.

The *acte gratuit* thus inserts itself into an economic thematic which is itself the expression of an attempt to reevaluate human action. In terms borrowed from the field of finance, systematically transposed into the moral order, Gide develops an ethics of expenditure which, through the notion of prodigality, leads to self-giving. The process represents too a quest after a psychology of self-denial, the equivalent, on the literary level, of the more material effort that the guilt-ridden Gide made to distance himself by self-dispossession from a Ménalque 'laden with insolent wealth' or a Candaule the 'grasping hoarder'.

The strength of the impetus to self-divestment can sometimes border on violence. After all abolishing a part of one's being is tantamount to destroying it. Giving can be aggressive. Michel neglects his wife to death; Lafcadio murders; Olivier attempts suicide; Oedipe and Candaule are driven to a 'holocaust' of their being. There comes to mind the disturbingly dramatic statement of *Le Prométhée mal enchaîné*, 'I do not love men: I love what devours them' (322; 136).

Contemporaneously with the appearance of *Les Faux-Monnayeurs* there was published in *L'Année Sociologique* for 1925, an article by the anthropologist Marcel Mauss entitled '*Essai sur le don, forme archaïque de l'échange*' ('An essay on giving as an archaic form of exchange'). In this seminal study Mauss described and analysed for the first time the early tribal economic system known as potlatch. The practice of potlatch consists in the organization either of an ostentatory gift of wealth, in the form of valuable objects, or of a public ceremonial destruction of the same in order to defy or display superiority over a social rival. In his '*La Notion de dépense*' ('The notion of expenditure'), published in *La Critique Sociale* of January 1933, Georges Bataille used the notion of potlatch as the crux of his criticism of modern bourgeois society's hostility to unproductive expenditure, one of the manifestations of the latter being literature, defined as 'symbolic expenditure'. Later, in *La Part maudite*,[32] he developed his thinking on *dépense*, seeing it not just as an economic phenomenon, but as a biological and cosmic law. Similarly Roger Caillois in *L'Homme et le sacré*,[33] defined festival in tribal societies as governed by the dual attitude of expenditure and consumption, including that of action and words.

There is no doubt that Gide too conceived of writing as an act of expenditure, perhaps even, in defiance of the protestant-gotten fortune of his forbear-rivals, as an act of potlatch, though it is doubtful he knew that term or its meaning. Prometheus may let his vulture pick at his innards but he later kills the bird and writes a novel with a quill from its finest feather. The devouring element has become a writing instrument. In 1893 Gide wrote in his diary 'Christ's saying is just as true in art: "Whosoever will save his life (his personality) will lose it" ' (*JI*, 49; *J1*, 37: 1893). A later entry of 1912, substituting economic language for christian quotation, expresses the same sentiment more tellingly, a propos an anonymous writer colleague: 'He lives on an income **from investments**, and in literature I like only those who eat up their capital' (*JI*, 356; *JI*, 310; 14 January 1912).[34]

In *Corydon*, his treatise on homosexuality, first published in its entirety in 1924, Gide underwrote the idea of an interlinkage between sexuality, prodigality and art. It being observed that in primitive biological organisms there is a superabundance of forms of the male sex, he quotes Edmond Perrier as saying, can be understood as a case of 'extravagant but unproductive expenditure' (75; 56), since great numbers of superfluous males are left without a useful biological role in the reproduction of the species. Deprived of their utilitarian function, this 'substance not spent to the advantage of the species' is equated with 'extravagance (*luxe*) and superfluity (*gratuité*)' for the male 'finds himself at a loose end, richly endowed with an energy which he will soon try to work off' (68; 52). Biological prodigality, of which Gide, in this context, offers the definition 'I call prodigality all expenditure which is out of proportion to the result achieved' (77; 57), can thus be construed as waste, but waste that is favourable to free play and on the human level to creativity and art: 'prodigality (. . .) thoughtless expenditure (. . .) waste (. . .) but it is from this waste that art and thought and recreation will be able to flourish' (104–5; 70). Although we may deplore the scientific sexism of such an analysis it corroborates the view that it was Gide's homosexuality which was the wellspring of his creativity – while doing nothing to explain why all 'superfluous' males are not creative. Gide's writing then can be seen as an intimate act of self-expenditure, an indiscreet dissipation of his being, undertaken as an act of excess or superabundant luxury: 'It is only where there is life in superabundance (. . .) that art has a chance of beginning. Art arises from increase, from superabundance.'[35] He was a writer who expended himself in his characters who, he said, 'live powerfully within me, I would even say that they live at my expense'.[36]

It was precisely by this cultural ethic of *dépense* that Sartre, in the context of the insights afforded by Mauss, Bataille and Caillois, defined the historicity of the writer in the nineteenth century. For Sartre, the writer, a pure consumer, a parasite in a working society, producing art which is 'pure consumption', can only give by writing: 'To write is to give. In this way he accepted and excused what was unacceptable in his situation as a parasite in an industrious society; this was also how he became conscious of that absolute freedom, that gratuity, which characterize literary creation'. The nineteenth-century writer 'made himself the martyr of pure consumption. (. . .) He saw no objection to using the goods of the bourgeoisie, but on condition that he was to spend them, that is, transform them into unproductive and useless objects.' The cultivation of the instant, death and nothingness is the end point of such culture, of which Sartre sees Gide as a paradigm: 'When one considers the work of Gide in this perspective, once cannot help seeing in it an ethic strictly reserved for the writer-consumer. What is his gratuitous act if not the culmination of a century of bourgeois comedy and the imperative of the author-gentleman?

It is striking that the examples of it are all taken from the sphere of consumption: Philoctète gives away his bow, the millionaire squanders his banknotes, Bernard steals, Lafcadio kills and Ménalque sells his belongings.'[37]
In the analysis that has been offered in the present article there is much to support Sartre's view of Gide the consumer at the sumptuous feast of French nineteenth-century literature, but there is much also that gainsays that view. Gide hardly belonged to a category of writers who were 'the good conscience of an oppressing class'.[38] On the contrary it is arguable and argued here that his attitude towards expenditure stems from a precisely opposite troubled conscience *vis-a-vis* his own wealth, just as his substitution of a psychology of gratuitousness for a psychology of profit is an attempt to subvert the capitalist behavioural assumptions that Sartre also found unacceptable. The Gide whose role was to disturb, the uneasy bourgeois, the uncomfortable homosexual, the distressed believer whom Sartre himself affirmed had lived the death of God, was just as at odds with his historical social class as he was a part of it. The figure of the prodigal in his work is a major expression of his discomfort with that milieu and of his attempt to undo its economic and puritanical values which he could not accept.

NOTES

1. MUSSET, *Les Deux Maîtresses* in *Nouvelles*, Paris, Garnier, 1948, p. 3. This essay should be read in conjunction with my later article, 'Lettres et argent: l'économie des *Faux-Monnayeurs*', in *André Gide 5*, 'Sur *Les Faux-Monnayeurs*', Minard, 1975, pp. 61–79 and with the ensuing study by Jean-Joseph Goux (which eschews bibliographical reference to prior Gide studies on the topic) *Les Monnayeurs du langage*, Eds Galilée, 1984, pp. 228. The theme, first adumbrated by SARTRE in *Qu'est-ce que la littérature?*, Gallimard, 1948, Coll. 'Idées', pp. 158–65 [*What is Literature?*, tr. Bernard Frechtman, London, Methuen, 1950, pp. 94–9], has since become a topos of Gide criticism, especially of *Les Caves du Vatican* and *Les Faux-Monnayeurs*, notably and excellently by A. GOULET, see for instance the chapter 'La gratuité contre le système d'argent' in his '*Les Caves du Vatican' d'André Gide*, Larousse, coll. Thèmes et Textes, 1972; his *Fiction et Vie sociale dans l'oeuvre d'André Gide*, Minard, Publications de l'Association des Amis d'André Gide 1984–5, 1986; and his *André Gide, 'Les Faux-Monnayeurs', mode d'emploi*, SEDES, 1990. (Unless stated all books referred to are published in Paris.)

2. 'Nationalisme et Littérature II', in *NRF*, Nov. 1909, later collected in *Nouveaux Prétextes*, Mercure de France, 1911, pp. 74–84. In Gide's *Journal* for 1934 we read 'The young Czech communist who comes to see me congratulates me on certain pages of *Prétextes* (*Nationalisme et littérature*, concerning Ricardo's theories) which, he says, "are impregnated with a pure Marxist spirit." – So much the better! But, I beg of you, if I am a Marxist, let me be so without knowing it' (*JI*, 1213; *J3*, 308; 1 August 1934).
   In his article Gide refers only to the title of his uncle's book. The words quoted are on pp. 397–8 of the 4th edn. of *Histoire des doctrines économiques* by Charles Gide and Charles Rist. Gide would have read an earlier edition. The book gives extensive coverage to Ricardo's theories.

On publication of Gide's article in 1909 Christian Beck wrote to him and received in reply 'Pleased that Carey's theory was of interest to you; it is readers like yourself that one counts on; isn't it full of splendid meaning?', 'Lettres à Christian Beck', *Mercure de France*, 1 Aug. 1949, p. 630. Something of Gide's application of Carey to literature is hinted at in 'Feuillets' quoted in RRS, 1552, 'I believe that those of my books which were quickest to attract readers (albeit in small numbers) were those which were least original. *La Symphonie Pastorale* and *La Porte Étroite* spring to mind in particular. In *Pretexts* I wrote of Carey's theory which I consider to be applicable too in a figurative manner; the richest soils are those reached last and with greatest difficulty'.

3. The quotation given is the following: ' "The maximum of satisfaction is reached when the final uses of the last objects consumed are equal."

   Sentence by (?) that my uncle comments on excellently in his *Traité d'économie politique* (latest edition).

   Formulated in this way it is not very clear.

   An equilibrium must be established; and the sensual pleasure derived from the object must be at the same degree of dulling and wear' (*JI*, 140; *J1*, 118: 1904).

4. There are numerous mentions of Charles Gide in the *Journal* and in *Si le grain ne meurt*. The autobiography presents a somewhat critical picture for which the diary entries compensate, see *Si le grain ne meurt*, *JII*, pp. 371, 427, 580 and *JI* 1045, 1103–4, 1112; *J3*, 161, 213–4, 220. For a verbal portrait of the uncle that remained unpublished during the nephew's lifetime, see 'Un portrait inédit: "Charles Gide", par André Gide', *Bulletin des Amis d'André Gide*, no. 35, July 1977, pp. 35–42. Consultable also is A. LAVONDÈS, *Charles Gide*, Uzès, 1953, who writes of the admiration of the uncle for his nephew (p. 196), whilst, in a postface, CHARLES TEISSIER writes of the 'obvious relationship between the two minds' (p. 247).

5. Gide himself recounts the episode, appreciatively, in *JI*, 269; *JI*, 234.

6. Matthew XIX: 24, Luke XVIII: 25. In *Divers*, NRF, 1931, pp. 100–1 Gide writes: ' "It is easier for a camel to go through the eye of a needle, than for a rich man to enter into the kingdom of God." This means quite simply: it is *impossible*, for ever impossible, and among impossible things there is none more impossible than this: a rich man in the Kingdom of God. The Kingdom of God is made up of the abandonment of such riches.

   Nothing is more weighty, more significant than this: the necessity of the choice between the temporal and the spiritual. The possession of the world hereafter is constituted by the renunciation of this world.' See also Note 7 below.

7. In 1935, Gide regretted the ambiguity in the character of Ménalque: 'Jef Last finds fault with Ménalque's ethics. He is right. I too disapprove of it and, even at that time, presenting it only with reservation, took care to ascribe it to someone else. [. . .] The figure of Ménalque is better drawn in *L'Immoraliste*. Here, in *Les Nourritures*, being confused with mine in certain regards, it might distort my intention and infringes on what remains most valuable in the work: the apology of destitution. I felt this so keenly that I tried to return to that intention in various assertions of Ménalque along the way: "my heart has remained poor", etc. – but which today strike me as comparable to those sophistries by which some rich people, who want to remain Christians, try to enlarge slightly the eye of the needle, whereby, without losing too much of their wealth, to enter all the same the kingdom of God' (*JI* 1223; *J3*, 317: 24 March 1935).

8. For *Le Roi Candaule* references are to André Gide, *Théâtre Complet*, Neuchâtel, Ides et Calendes, 1947, vol. II.

9. Gide gives no reference and the origin of the quotations remains unlocated.

10. Jean Delay, *La Jeunesse d'André Gide*, vol. II, Gallimard, 1957, p. 630.

11. A similar obsession with 'the horrible wear and tear of material objects' (*l'horrible usure des choses*) can be seen in Gide at the same period. In the early years of the diary *usure* is a word that reoccurs frequently, see *JI*, 42, 57, 140, 176; *J1*, 30, 44, 118, 150. See also *Les Nourritures* pp. 155–7, 243–4; 18–20, 128. Of the two meanings that the French term covers (*wear* and *usury*) we shall return to the second. As to the first, one of the traditional responses to the wear and tear of the world has been to enjoy things while they last. *Carpe diem* is one formulation of the *dépensez* that Michel will adopt as a motto.

12. Gide saw, in Protestant Switzerland, with its secretive banks, and restraining dams, the country of moral, financial and technological reserve: 'Here I am again in this land "that God created to be horrible" (Montesquieu). The admiration of mountains is an invention of Protestantism. Strange confusion on the part of brains incapable of art, between the lofty and the beautiful. Switzerland: a wonderful reservoir of energy; one has to go down how far? to find abandon and grace, laziness and voluptuousness again, without which neither art nor wine is possible. If of the tree the mountains make a fir, you can imagine what they can do with man. Aesthetics and ethics of conifers.
    The fir and the palm: those two extremes' (*JI*, 367; *J1*, 314: 27 January 1912). These lines, written in Andermatt, admirably express the feelings of Michel who cannot wait to find himself in lowland country where neither nature nor man are forced into economies but can freely indulge in self-expenditure.

13. See for example R. GOODHAND, 'The Religious Leitmotif in *L'Immoraliste*', *Romanic Review*, vol. LVII, no. 4, December 1966 and B. T. WILKINS, *L'Immoraliste*. Revisited', *Romanic Review*, vol. LIII, April, 1962.

14. Where avarice and repressed sexuality are concerned the comedy which governs Act V Sc. 3, of *L'Avare* – the misunderstanding between Harpagon who is speaking of his moneybox and Valère who is speaking of his lover – has hidden depths.

15. BAUDELAIRE, *Oeuvres Complètes*, Gallimard, Bibliothèque de la Pléiade, 1959, p. 1199.

16. And in the *Journal* for 1906 one reads (Gide is speaking here of another): 'I am too keenly aware of the use he might derive from practising certain maxims of the Gospels, and I cannot restrain a *profound* indignation on seeing him squander without beauty a moral patrimony that generations have striven, *with abnegation*, to build up for him' (*JI*, 204; *J1*, 176: 28 March 1906). For the puritan debauchery may not be easy, but for the esthete it must be engaged in beautifully.

17. FREUD, *Un Sovenir d'enfance de Léonard de Vinci*, N.R.F., 1927, pp. 120–33.

18. JEAN DELAY, *La Jeunesse d'André Gide*, I, Gallimard, 1956, pp. 564–65.

19. Some of his best friends, notably Pierre Herbart, accused Gide of stinginess, though even Herbart also recognized that 'this miser has been known to be generous'. The same critic also held a view quite opposed to the thrust of the present article: 'It is on a superficial assessment (because of Lafcadio, a purely incidental character in his work) that Gide was made the father of the gratuitous act. Nothing was more alien to his nature. Gratuitousness has no part in the Gidian universe. Impressions, books read, things and beings are

classified, judged as a function of one sole criterion: their usefulness', see his *A la Recherche d'André Gide*, Gallimard, 1952, pp. 77 and 55. Herbart may be right in part but discounts Gide's tendency towards dialectical reasoning.

20. It is recognized that Raskolnikof, in DOSTOIEVSKY's *Crime and Punishment*, was one amongst a number of models for Lafcadio. See ALBERT SONNENFELD, 'De Dostoïevski à Gide', *Cahiers André Gide 3*, Le Centenaire, Gallimard, 1972, pp. 341–351.
     In *Primitive Rebels*, Manchester, 1959, p. 22, E. J. HOBSBAWM notes that the usurer was one of the traditional victims of the social bandit.

21. Carlyle-like clothing metaphors are also a feature of Gide's novels. In *Paludes* we read: 'Destinies made to measure. Necessity of bursting one's clothes, just as the plane-tree or eucalyptus, as they grow, burst their bark' (107;37). In *L'Immoraliste* the metaphor occurs in a conversation between Ménalque and Michel, who protests that like his mentor he eschewed a ready-made happiness and cut out one made to measure, but comments, 'I have grown [. . .] I think it is strangling me' (435;91). In *Les Caves*, where disguise and dandyism play large parts, the theme and symbolism of clothing are very important. In *Les Faux-Monnayeurs* Passavant says: 'I cut out my filial love according to the pattern I had in my heart; but I soon saw that my measurements had been too ample, and was obliged to take it in' (964;43–4). In the same special number of the review in which the present article first appeared Germaine Brée published a searching study on this theme: 'Rencontre avec Carlyle', *Revue d'Histoire Littéraire de France*, March-April 1970, pp. 286–95.

22. On more than one occasion in *Les Faux-Monnayeurs* Gide refers to a much more ancient unit of value, salt (source of the word salary) as an image representing fundamental worth. He points to the 'moral tragedy' of the gospel words 'If the salt have lost its savour wherewith shall it be salted' (1031; 113). In parallel to the idea of devaluation he develops the connected notion of desalination and decrystallization, both of which form leitmotifs in the text, desalination in the talk of the biologist Vincent Molinier who states that 'there are certain kinds of fish which die according as the water becomes more salt or less, and that there are others, on the contrary, which can live in any degree of salt water; and that they swim about on the edge of the currents, where the water becomes less salt, so as to prey on the others when their strength fails them' (969;49); decrystallisation in the post-Stendhalian reflections of Édouard on the slow disintegration of the crystals of conjugal love (pp. 988–89;69. 1052;137). For a further study of the topic see J. GRIEVE, 'Love in the Work of A. Gide', *Australian Journal of French Studies* vol. III, no 2, 1966.
     A prodigal in his own fashion, Vincent seems to be the only example in Gide's work of a gambler proper, though Lafcadio is very given to letting a throw of the dice make his decisions for him (or not, as the whim takes him). In the *Journal* for 1929 one reads 'I cannot resist the appeal of a risky move; attraction of the unexpected, which, in some very rare cases, can lead to the most fecund discoveries. Annex to the psychology of the gambler' (*J1*, 932–3; *J2*, 60: 2 September 1929). One could develop the undoubted affinity which exists between the psychology of the gambler and that of prodigal.

23. '. . . *puisqu'il ne faut jamais ôter le retour à personne*' is a quotation from Retz that Gide puts as an epigraph at the head of Book 2 of *Les Caves* (707;35).

24. Strouvilhou's manifesto is reminiscent of a humorous incident recounted in the *Journal sans dates*: 'I had been reading *L'Action Française* before falling asleep; I had a frightful nightmare: the Odéon, ill defended by Antoine, taken over by

Jews, rebuilt along the lines of the Stock Exchange, became the exclusive home of financiers who made art and literature the object of their speculations. On every prominent author they were gambling as to whether his value would go up or down', *Nouveaux Prétextes*, Mercure de France, 1951, pp. 243–6. By way of explanation one should add that bookstalls occupied the arcades of the Odéon theatre whose director was Antoine. Humorous as it is, Gide's dream is not without significance – he spent much time reflecting on what value would be ascribed to his work by posterity and by circulating his own, often controversial, values on paper, claimed to write with a view to future values rather than to his own contemporary ones.

25. Paul-Ambroise is an allusion to the mathematically-minded Paul Valéry.

26. In 'Lettres et argent: l'économie des *Faux-Monnayeurs*', loc. cit.

27. See *Les Monnayeurs du langage*, op. cit.

28. MAX WEBER, *The Protestant Ethic and the Spirit of Capitalism* (first published in German 1904–5, English translation 1930). Weber's classic study was developed by R. H. Tawney in his equally classic *Religion and the Rise of Capitalism* (The Holland Memorial Lectures, 1922; first published 1926; Harmondsworth, Pelican Books, 1938).

29. See D. A. Steel, 'Alissa-Anorexia? Self-Starvation, Salvation and Sexuality in *La Porte Étroite*', French Studies Bulletin, no. 50, Spring 1994, pp. 5–8.

30. John, XII, 25, Luke XVII, 33 and *Journal, JI*, 49; *J1*, 37: 1893. *JI*, 590–604; *J2*, 169–187: *Numquid et tu. . . . ?*. In 'Classicisme', an article collected in *Morceaux Choisis*, Gallimard, 1921, p. 93, Gide writes: 'The great artist has only one concern: to become as human as possible [. . .] he who flees humanity to be himself succeeds only in becoming peculiar, bizarre, defective . . . . Should I quote the phrase from the Gospel? – Yes, for I don't think I am diverting it from its meaning: Whosoever shall seek to save his life (his personal life) shall lose it; but whosoever shall lose his life shall preserve it (or, to translate the Greek text more exactly: shall render it truly alive).'

31. Although he later modified his position somewhat, Gide was frequently critical of La Rochefoucald [1613–1680] who, in his *Maximes* [1665], all too often reduces human motivation to egoism and self-interest; see *JI*, 698; *J2*, 271: 1921 and *JI*, 835; *J2*, 398: 1927.

32. Minuit, 1949.

33. Presses Universitaires de France, 1939.

34. That being said, there is a way in which Gide remained in his writing a capitalist entrepreneur in that he let his characters act for him, experimented vicariously with their fictional doings in ways which, in real life, for him and others, would have been too dangerous, or prohibited. See his 'Conversation avec un Allemand' of 1904 in *Morceaux Choisis* (*OC, IX*, 141–2) and the 'I don't act on my own – I cause others to act' spoken by Protos in *Les Caves du Vatican* (858;231).

35. *Prétextes*, 1947, p. 105.

36. *Journal des Faux-Monnayeurs*, p. 64.

37. JEAN-PAUL SARTRE, *Qu'est-ce que la littérature?*, op. cit., pp. 160, 137, 159, 164; *What is Literature?* op. cit. pp. 96, 80–1, 95, 98–9.

38. Ibid., p. 141, p. 83.

5   Philippe Lejeune on Gide and Autobiography*

Philippe Lejeune inaugurated a new era of critical study devoted to autobiography with his *L'Autobiographie en France* (1971) and *Le Pacte autobiographique* (1975), in which he sought to define the criteria whereby a text could be characterized as autobiographical. Since then the writing and the study of autobiography have become a field rich in fertile problematics, as scholars have deepened and widened Lejeune's investigations, and creative authors have been drawn to the genre, seeking to elude classification by testing its forms and techniques, in turn prompting new labels such as *autofiction*.

Though Lejeune himself has moved on with these developments and beyond them, it is worth recalling that early in his work on autobiography is his *Exercices d'ambiguïté: lectures de 'Si le Grain ne Meurt'* (1974) followed by the study reproduced below. These analyses constitute eloquent testimony to the subtle and productive ways in which Gide sought to go beyond the simple retrospective recreation of a life and a subjective viewpoint which form the basis of autobiographical writing. Having dedicated himself to the creative construction of an artistic identity through his literary vocation, Gide sought and found methods for subjecting his personal experience to intense moral and psychological scrutiny, whilst at the same time making it available, in the methods he adopted for displaying it, to productive examination by the reader.

As Lejeune amply demonstrates, Gide does not restrict his projected autobiography to the confines of a personal testimony of the conventional narrative kind. He opens up his entire literary output to manifestations of his inner being; his works – diary, fiction, correspondences, critical essays – form a self-regulating, endlessly self-reflecting system of texts which merely hint

* Extract from an article originally published as 'Gide et l'autobiographie', *André Gide 4*, *Méthodes de lecture*, *Revue des lettres modernes*, nos 374–79, Paris, Minard, 1973, pp. 31–69, and in *Le Pacte autobiographique*, Paris, Seuil, 1975, pp. 165–96. Abridged, translated and annotated by Jane Lee.

at the parameters of an identity forever in flux, unable or unwilling to be defined.

This strategy problematizes the distinction between the life and the fiction of the author, and revives important questions about the relation between the man and the literary work. While a traditional simplistic view tended to consider the writing as a transposition of experiences the author had lived, through the example of Gide it becomes evident that writing is itself a form of experience and a mode of exploration of the self. However, in the elaborate and subtly structured system of textual interaction that Gide set up, self-knowledge is deliberately deferred in the interest of continuing uncertainty, speculation and ambiguity as to the individual's potential.

Gide's position in relation to the autobiography can seem a paradoxical one.

On the one hand, the whole of his life and work seems to be a concerted effort to construct and produce an image of his self. It is not that Gide's oeuvre is what can broadly be termed 'autobiographical', the writer using material taken from his own life, but rather it is grounded on a strategy which aims to reconstitute the author's personality through the most diverse techniques of writing. Indeed it seems necessary to invent a new word to characterize Gide's general approach to writing, and to what is normally understood by 'autobiography' in its strictest sense, that is the retrospective narration of the evolution of the personality which the author acknowledges as his.[1]

On the other hand, the great autobiographical text of Gide's maturity, *Si le Grain ne Meurt*, may disappoint or intrigue the reader who expected to find precisely this type of coherent and all-embracing explanation of the author's life, for which the author assumes responsibility within the autobiographical pact,[2] or who tries to understand the narrative by reference to the archetype of the confessional autobiographical genre, Rousseau's *Confessions*. This ambiguous and inconclusive narrative – which does not seem to be written from one fixed viewpoint, at a moment where the cards are already on the table, but rather to be composed in a moving perspective which leaves room for further play, cannot fail to puzzle, nor to fascinate.

I shall refer later to the criticisms which Gide himself levelled at what he saw as the limitations of the autobiographical narrative. To create the contradictory image of the 'creature of dialogue' that he was, Gide wished that image to be the end-product of all the texts which he would write, which, when taken separately, make no claim to autobiographical accuracy, but which, when each reflects and is reflected in the next, define his image without either reducing or fixing it, in the *space* which between them they create. Read thus, these texts create a picture which is not his likeness, but what could be called his 'unlikeness'. The 'autobiographical space' which is formed by this process offers a picture of some complexity, through the variety of the forms in which it is expressed. But more importantly it produces, in that which is expressed, an effect of ambiguity.[3]

Complexity and ambiguity are not the same thing. Complexity is merely the state of a system in which a large number of elements stand in a multiplicity of relations to each other. It is the opposite of simplicity, but by no means excludes clarity. It may simply pose an obstacle to clarity, and introduce an element of mystery. Thus the narrator of *Si le Grain ne Meurt* often uses the ploy of giving several possible explanations of the same action, thereby obtaining effects carefully calculated to give the impression of a subtle psychological portrait, and then justifying the confusion of the analysis by the complexity of the object being studied (. . .). Ambiguity is something quite different. Operating on the level of what is said, it is where no decision is made as to the meaning of the text, that is, it is the reader's uncertainty as to the position of the author in relation to the story he is telling. In a complex text, different explanations can be offered to account for a character's behaviour; they may very well not be mutually exclusive, thus creating an effect of psychological mystery which attracts the reader. Ambiguity is situated at the base stratum of the values on which the work is founded or of the author's world picture, where normally we would expect a choice to have to be made, and where a system based on indecision cannot fail to disconcert. This fundamental indecision can affect a simple text just as much as a complex one (. . .).

Gidean ambiguity supposes that in the end, the reader will not be able to simplify or fix the position of the author, despite the desire that he will inevitably have to do so, given the ethical problems which almost all of Gide's works raise. This ambiguity may be implicit or explicit, according to whether the author hides his presence or whether he declares himself. If he hides, the case of fiction, the author leaves the problems open, rather than opting for a solution, by a systematic refusal to make any explicit judgement. The preface of *L'Immoraliste* offers a clear example of this strategy.[4] If the author declares himself, where he speaks in his own name, it is on the contrary by an overabundance of contradictory pronouncements that Gide obtains the same result. In this case he seeks, to borrow the phrase which he uses at the beginning of *Le Retour de l'enfant prodigue*, to leave 'indistinct and unravelled the two-fold inspiration that moves (him)' (475; 125). Even if personal commitment to a text has other advantages which we shall see later, it is clearly the fictional genre which is most propitious to the free development of contrasts and 'unlikenesses'. In fiction, Gide feels at liberty, in a sort of experiment conducted on himself, to pursue to its extreme each in turn of the potentialities inherent in his nature – at liberty regarding the reader, but also as a sort of liberation from himself. Fiction becomes at once personal confidence (the germ which produces the attitudes he depicts) and a depersonalization of experience (in the full realization – excessive or exclusive – of that particular trait); at once recollection and experimentation, narcissism and self-critique. The practice of fiction is often presented by Gide as a sanitary exercise, as a cleansing which enables him at once to fulfil himself and to be rid of himself.[5]

He revels in these exercises which allow him to say 'I' in the mode of hypothesis, of potentiality, without falling into the autobiographical 'myself'.[6]

This fictional method is not, though, simply sanitary. Gide is seeking at the same time through this method to set in place the components of a more complex system. It is a way of flirting with autobiography. If each work contains its share of personal confidence, it would of course be a mistake to see these texts as confessions. But taken together, Gide's works make up a system whose excesses and self-critiques balance each other out, and compensate for each other. It is at this level that we can find the image of the author's self, and although this image is a virtual one, it is *necessary to suppose* its existence in order to unify the field of Gide's fiction. The autobiographical space that this type of fiction implies is clearly presented by Gide in a text in which he defines two sorts of 'ways of looking at and portraying life' which in certain novels are combined: one, objective, based on observation of acts and events, the other subjective, described below. Doubtless he wished to see both combined in his work, as in that of Dostoevsky. Nevertheless the second alone seems truly to define it:

> The second, which begins by paying attention to emotions and thoughts and runs the risk of being powerless to depict anything that the author has not first felt himself. The resources of the author, his complexity, the antagonism of his too diverse possibilities, will permit the greatest diversity of his creations. But everything derives from him. He is the only one to vouch for the truth he reveals, and the only judge. All the heaven and hell of his characters is in him. It is not himself that he depicts, but he could have become what he depicts if he had not become everything himself. (*JI*, 829; *J2*, 392: 8 February 1927)

But this self which is everything is realized through the texts without being fixed in any single one of them: to the reader it will seem ungraspable. Moreover, in his complicated relationship with his public, Gide tried every possible trick to escape from being pinned down too easily; he happily lays traps, lets readers and critics go astray, even if it means having to guide them subsequently . . . . Fiction is fertile ground for misunderstandings such as these. The author is not to be identified with the narrator: yet the reader will always try to guess at the nature of the former through the latter. It is a bad habit, which is encouraged both by the ethical nature of Gide's narratives (the reader is always looking to find the author's 'position') and by the use of the first-person narrative. Critical and ironic, and only partially 'confessional', each fictional work gives rise to confusion and leaves the reader at a loss as to the position the author is taking. If error is possible within an individual book, the succession of such contradictory texts must inevitably leave the reader puzzled: what is the identity, and the moral stance, of the man who is capable of writing all of these? (. . .) This is the stumbling block of every biography of Gide: the biographer is reduced to talking very clearly *about* ambiguity, whereas Gide talked in an ambiguous manner. When it becomes the object which must be expressed, the Gidean mode of expression loses all its power of ambiguity: we gain control of it, whereas it had control over us. But is it then still itself? Gide was acutely aware of this problem. It is largely this which seems to have held him back for so long from becoming an autobiographer himself, that is, the author of a narrative aiming to give a coherent overall vision, and written within the autobiographical pact.

However, personal writings, where the author takes responsibility for his 'I', can take other forms than this: the diary and correspondence, which Gide kept regularly and abundantly from his adolescence on, and which he knew were destined to be published one day, would provide an additional angle on his work, or rather would be the backdrop against which the more stylized 'motifs' of his fictions would stand out. This 'I' of the confidences belonging to the diary and correspondence does not present the same disadvantages as that of the autobiographical narrative. A certain number of constraints arising from the circumstances in which they are written prevents these confidences from acquiring the same weight and solidity, and enables them to fit more readily into the system of ambiguity. These limitations are due to temporality and destination. Diary and letters, written in the heat of the moment, commit and fix nothing but that moment. Despite the tendency to recreate an imitation of the self which is inherent to personal writings, nothing prevents these texts from contradicting themselves, from varying, evolving and expressing contrary opinions (. . .).

Gide himself considered his most personal writing (for example his letters to Madeleine) as an element in a global play of texts: not only were they texts that he fully intended to have published one day, but he could even foresee the place they were to occupy, the role they were to play in the overall scheme: each text defined itself by its location and its function within a textual whole to which Gide entrusted the mission of producing his *image*. Gide never envisaged this idea of the *image of the self*, in a simplistically narcissistic sense, in the form of a 'copy', nor even of an 'autoportrait': it was not a matter of constructing an object, but of producing a certain effect, of setting up a 'system'. If a certain element in the system should go missing, it was not that the image was not 'incomplete', but that the system as a whole was *skewed*, because the other elements, deprived of that relationship or counterpart, would no longer be able to function in the same way. Whence Gide's anguish on the destruction of his letters to Madeleine: 'Henceforth my work will merely be like a symphony from which the sweetest chord is lacking, like an unfinished building' (*JII*, 1150; *Et nunc manet in te*, 66: 20 January 1919), or at the idea of a premature death which would prevent him from composing certain of the most important elements in the system: 'If I were to die right now I should leave only a one-eyed image of myself, or an eyeless one' (*JI*, 420; *J2*, 24: 15 June 1914).

Thus Gide's *goal* is to produce (in the double sense of to invent and to bring before an audience) an image of the self, that of a living being with all its complexity and its history. But the means by which he intends to attain this goal is not the use of autobiographical narrative in the strictest sense. It is the creation of an architectonic structure of texts, some of them fictional, others critical, others indeed personal, to which Gide assigns the task of rendering his image. It is as if his task were not to write what he was, but to be it by writing it. The image of the self has nothing to do with what is said, but is an effect of the act of saying. To be produced, autobiographical ambiguity does not need autobiography as a vehicle – quite the contrary. This effect of ambiguity does not seem to be a discovery made progressively, but the fundamental element of the Gidian literary *project*: Gide recounted several times how he had had, from the outset, the vision of his Complete Works in the form of a certain number of blank volumes, which already existed as *having to be written*, forming a ready-made system of contradiction and especially of alternation (*JI*, 436; *J2*, 38–9: 12 July 1914). (. . .) In compiling his *Morceaux Choisis*, it seems that Gide wished to counter the very pertinent objection made to him by Jacques Raverat on the way the narratives and the autobiography itself simplified his 'outline': ' "In order to have a somewhat lifelike portrait of you", he told me very correctly, "one would have to be able to read them all at once" ' (*JI*, 684; *J2*, 257: 5 October 1920). 'Read them all at once' is exactly what the volume of *Morceaux Choisis* proposes. The key which Gide offers here is not the secret of a message, but of a structure.[7] He thereby designates the *play of texts* which is his *œuvre*, extending the principle of ambiguity to the totality of his writing. [. . .]

The Place of Autobiography

All this is familiar: the importance of repeating it is to show that the production of an image of the self, which is apparently Gide's ultimate goal, sits very ill with autobiographical narrative in its traditional form, the archetype of which is Rousseau's *Confessions*. In this type of narrative, the author is necessarily identified with the narrator, and the author must reveal himself completely; the narrative must embrace his life in its entirety and proceed, in one way or another, to a form of synthesizing interpretation. These two requirements, of total revelation and explicit synthesis, are in fact impossible for Gide, and would destroy, in its very principles, the whole method by which he seeks to create his image. (. . .) Indeed, Gide's autobiography has only a tangential role to play in the construction of his autobiography: far from being a complete picture, it is one viewpoint to be added to others. It may be a privileged one, in that it reveals the existence of the autobiographical space, but it is nevertheless restricted, one might even say intentionally restricted.

If Gide chose to write an autobiographical narrative, when that is so contrary to his project, it is, above all, because it was the only way of laying to rest the lies or hypocrisies on one point in particular: his sexual life. What he appreciates in the autobiographical pact is that it forces him to commit himself. The writing and the publication of his autobiography had in Gide's eyes the value of an act as much as of a literary work. It meant breaking through the screen of the fictions and telling the truth, as a confession or as a challenge. Telling this truth presupposed both the identification of narrator and author – I, Gide, am this homosexual – and the telling of a story, in that it was only the telling of the story that could explain, or make acceptable, his sexual choice. (. . .)

The only form which could possibly provide this particular slant was the retrospective narrative for which the author clearly acknowledged responsibility. However, the autobiographical pact can only be accepted as a whole: the author cannot claim responsibility for his life without in some way fixing its sense, nor present it in coherent form without providing a synthetic interpretation; he cannot explain who he is without saying who he is. Apart from the obligation to commit himself, all these aspects of the autobiography are profoundly repugnant to Gide. The idea of 'self knowledge' seems to him to be a trap: it implies restriction and artifice.[8] He is unable to resolve whether to reveal himself, or to depict his present self, or to choose, or draw conclusions, or, quite simply, to tell all. It would be wrong to see this as moral evasiveness or as an aesthetic failure: quite simply, Gide's project is a different one. *Si le Grain ne Meurt* is the paradoxical product of two conflicting demands, an attempt to reconcile the advantages of the confession with the refusal of the structures of person and discourse which the traditional autobiography presupposes. (. . .)

It would be possible to compile a small critical anthology on the traditional genre of autobiography, drawing either on texts of a more general significance, or on reflections made during the writing of *Si le grain ne meurt*, to be found in the *Journal* or in the narrative itself.[9]

Reading these latter passages, which concern for the most part the writing of the first part of *Si le Grain ne Meurt*, and the essential of which is summed up in the final 'Note' of that first part, we might be hearing the

Flaubert of the *Correspondance* bewailing the torture inflicted on him by his *Bovary* – with the same amount of 'pose' – the aridity of his subject (his sullen childhood for which he feels considerable distaste), the tortuous style, the difficulties of the composition, and of course, on another level, the religious, emotional and sexual drama which the narrator was reliving between 1916 and 1919, at the very moment that he was retracing the story of its origins. The commentaries on the composition of the second part are less numerous, and more lighthearted. Curiously, in these laments, whilst he deplores the limitations of the 'autobiography' (the cumbersome need for detail, the impossibility of saying what is most important, the necessity to simplify and impoverish), Gide does not appear to look for any solution to these problems. Gide, who for the novel will explore both a new mode of theoretical reflection and an inquisitive and inventive way of experimenting with the form – to which the *Journal des Faux-Monnayeurs* and *Les Faux-Monnayeurs* testify – seems here to be resigned from the outset. The criticisms he makes of the autobiographical genre are relatively commonplace, and he makes no attempt at experimentation. In fact, it seems that the limitations of the autobiography actually serve Gide's purpose: it suits him rather well to succeed on certain counts (the confession) and to fail brilliantly on all the others, preventing the narrative from being a 'complete' work, which in any case he believes to be impossible – and undesirable. He seems to have played a pretty lucid game of making the most of a bad lot, sheltering behind the shortcomings and limits of the genre which he himself has been quite deliberately underlining. Gide is playing a strategy of failure, a sort of ruse of ill will. At the same time as succeeding in presenting his confession, and in purging his past, he sets out to prove that the autobiographical narrative is incapable, on its own, of producing the same effect of ambiguity as the convergence of several deliberately fictional linear narratives: in a word, in isolation, autobiography cannot produce an image of the self, whereas the 'novel' can. The (relative) failure of *Si le Grain ne Meurt* is a step towards the success of *Les Faux-Monnayeurs*.[10]

This statement requires some qualification: the first part constitutes the concerted failure of a narrative which should be complex but in reality is confused; the second part constitutes the success of a narrative which is perfectly ambiguous, but which only corresponds to a limited phase of the story. Gide has used all the means in his power at once to recreate within the autobiography an effect of ambiguity which this form seems to exclude *a priori*, and to force the autobiography into being incomprehensible except in the light of the whole of the rest of his work. Essentially, he has a policy of *throwing the narrator into indecision*, be it in the manipulation of the time-scale, the levels of narration, or the meaning of the story that he tells.

1) Time-scale.

The division of the narrative completely masks the subsequent story of the adult (what will happen after the engagement) and the present story of the narrator: where has the narrator got to *at the moment that he writes* in this drama, which he tells us 'N'a pas achevé de se jouer' ('is not yet played out') *JII*, 430)? It is quite impossible to guess by reading *Si le Grain ne Meurt*. This omission can of course be explained by the necessity for discretion. From the engagement onwards, André's story is indissociable from that of Madeleine, and *cannot* be delivered into the hands of the public. Consequently, the suspended ending is utterly mysterious.[11] Only one brief allusion, and that entirely incomprehensible, is made to the present difficulties of the narrator, at the beginning of the second part (*JII*, 549). It would be scarcely an exaggeration to say essentially, we do not really know 'whose' story *Si le Grain ne Meurt* actually tells. . . . As for the portrayal of the narrator as an adult, numerous elements are given, and he does not hide in order to proceed with his narrative: but nowhere do these elements take on the consistency or the unity of a portrait: or rather, when they do coincide, they simply serve to confound the reader utterly (see below, Section 3. Meaning). The continuation of the narrative is missing,[12] for which twenty years later *Et nunc manet in te* will only partially compensate. Certain areas of Gide's life remain in shadow, and principally the practice and the problems of homosexuality.[13] *Si le Grain ne Meurt* tells only of Gide's discovery of homosexuality. For anything more, we are forced to fall back on the scattered indications in the *Journal*. To have some idea of the relations between Gide and Marc Allegret, we must read certain pages of the diary, or decipher the 'transpositions' in *La Symphonie Pastorale* or *Les Faux-Monnayeurs*: no trace of them can be found in the autobiography. And when in *Et nunc manet in te* Gide finally reveals the drama of his marriage, it is by hiding another part of his life, the birth of his daughter Catherine in 1923.[14]

This can once again be put down to the necessity for discretion: Gide had proved himself as eager to compromise himself, as he had been to protect from curiosity those he loved. However, if that had been so, he could very well have conceived of a posthumous work, and taken precautions like those of his friend Roger Martin du Gard, who only authorized the publication of certain writings fifty years after his death. Why did Gide not do the same? Gide's horror of the posthumous work is known. His autobiography serves firstly to testify, as a confession or a challenge, – in any case it had to provoke a scandal. (. . .) He feared above all that after his death, his testimony might be stifled or falsified, as had happened to Rimbaud and Whitman, and as was to happen under his very eyes to Jacques Rivière.[15] Hence the necessity to publish during his lifetime – and during that of Madeleine. That was impossible in 1916 when he began to write his narrative, since Madeleine still knew nothing of his homosexuality. It was only to become possible from the moment that by chance Madeleine discovered the secret, in 1916, and after the crisis of 1918.[16]

Even then affection and caution were to restrain his desire to publish for a long time. He resorted to the compromise of publishing the work confidentially in twelve copies, which assured the survival of the text and protected it from misuse by literary executors, whilst shielding Madeleine from a public scandal. But the compromise was to be provisional only. Gide deeply wished to publish, be it simply to 'passer outre' ['go further'],[17] to perform the act of the living being which is in direct opposition to the notion of an act from 'beyond the tomb'.[18]

Whence, from 1920 to 1926, the procrastination over *Corydon* no less than *Si le grain ne meurt*, Gide's exasperation in the face of his friends who sought to restrain him, and despite everything his own disquiet, overcome by the desire to have done with the business, the hesitations and calculations concerning the order in which to publish, the best time to publish, etc.[19] From this horror of the posthumous publication, the most important point to remember is that *Si le Grain ne Meurt* was *written for immediate publication*, with all the restrictions to its scope and all the precautions surrounding its meaning necessitated by its immediate recipients: the rejection of the posthumous work in fact corresponds to a renouncing of the principal demands of the autobiographical genre, that is complete revelation and synthetic perspective. This renunciation was in no way a sacrifice or a mistake, but a deliberate choice. Gide was not *unfortunately* prevented by the imperatives of discretion from writing a complete autobiography: he chose these limits, and used them cunningly in order to make his autobiography a particular sort of text where the confession is made without the story being attached to it.

2) Levels of Narration.

Here we shall deal with the composition of the first part.

Rarely has there been a failure in composition which is so deliberate and so deft. *It is all as if there were two stories, artfully juxtaposed.* One, taking up nine-tenths of the text, made up of wonderfully retold childhood memories, which gives, through the serene elegance and the ease of the writing, the image of a childhood without problems – of a 'normal' childhood. The other, made up of a series of very specific, highly dramatized incidents, retraces in terms which are as yet mysterious, the origins of the drama to come, a 'drama which has not yet played itself out' (*JII*, 430). These two levels do not seem to intercommunicate: the profane story and the sacred drama coexist like oil and water without mixing, in sections of text which do not link or overlap, and which often contradict each other. Consequently, it takes a great deal of good will on the part of the reader as he reads the first four chapters to conciliate these luminous tales of childhood games, country residences, and family life, of the awakening to the fruits of the earth in all their forms, with the hypothesis put forward at the beginning of Chapter I, and brutally recalled at the end of Chapters I, II, and IV, of the dark, withdrawn childhood, cooked up by the Devil. In what follows, the few sequences devoted to Madeleine will similarly be thrown into the middle of a narrative to which they seem to bear no relation whatsoever. Gide, who readily attributes all these weaknesses in composition to the autobiographical genre (cf. the note at the end of the first part), knew very well that these difficulties in fact arose from his inner conflicts and from his contradictions:[20] far from trying to surmount them, he used these evident weaknesses of the genre to draw from them an artistic effect in the overall structure of the work, to form a contrast with the second part. [. . .]

The sacred drama is concentrated in a series of fairly short texts which constitute, through the first part, the equivalent of what Rousseau called a 'chain of secret affinities': but unlike Rousseau, Gide never in this first part explains clearly and comprehensively the structure and the ultimate end of this chain; on the contrary, he uses extremely veiled allusions, wrapped in a language abounding in images, lyrical or dramatic: the drama of the second part, with its ambiguous light, is thus placed between two zones of shadow: the narrative of the life of the child and the adolescent with its premonitions and allusions, and the silence over the life of the adult following the engagement.

Whilst it is allusive, the sacred drama has at the same time a floating coherence: the link to be made between the most dramatic episodes remains uncertain in its *nature*. The principal links in the chain are the theme of the dark childhood (up to the beginning of Chapter V), the hypothesis of the Devil (from the end of Chapter IV), the very ambiguous chain of *Schaudern* which represents a panicking anxiety, the love for Madeleine, the dionysiac ecstasy, and finally the dialectic of light and shadow. Gide is faithful to his project: he wants to *represent*, not to explain, resolve or reduce: by resorting to a mixture of different mythological discourses, he reproduces the tonality of the drama and its complexity, and leaves the explanation open. The end of the first part, where the tension is released, and which is invaded by the chronicle of Gide's literary life,[21] accentuates this uncertainty, which the final Note deftly underlines by throwing responsibility onto the autobiographical genre. This relative confusion throws into relief the clarity of the second part; and Gide will, at the same time, and despite everything, have *told* the story of his childhood, and *kept silent* about his life in its totality. The reader will thus have been prepared for the existence of a drama, reassured as to the humanity and normality of his hero, lulled by the charms of a bourgeois childhood and a mystical and literary adolescence. This long andante will prepare him to appreciate the presto of the second part. But he will not be very clear as to who is writing. The dissimulation and the long, insidious suspense of the first part serve to prepare the second part in a strategy of seduction aimed at a very specific audience. In a posthumous perspective where we look for a synthesis, it might be thought that Gide could have gone beyond these effects of staging, to pursue his line of research and to establish an interpretation, which in a certain way would have forced him into making choices which he had always disliked.

3) Meaning.

This particularly applies to the second part. Rarely has a narrative been more ambiguous. It is all as if there were two different narrators, speaking in turn, or sometimes both together. We are no longer concerned with the story which is being told, which unfolds briskly with a fairly simple story line, but with the meaning of this story for which two different interpretations are given, and where neither can be overlooked in the course of reading, nor discarded at the end. Although we the readers find it hard to accept, it would indeed seem that this ambiguity is not simply a trick played at the expense of the recipient of the text, but in fact corresponds to a contradiction lived by Gide at the moment of the events themselves, and still active in him when he tells of them. Is homosexuality a natural and healthy inclination, and an authentic way of living discovered beyond the puritan lie and the double interdict which weighs on sexuality (repression of sexuality in general; definition of heterosexuality as the norm)? A whole triumphant, victorious and sunny side of of the second part convinces us of this. But the shadow of the Devil, of his tricks and his temptations, of his multiple incarnations, floats over the whole of the narrative, particularly at the beginning and at the end. It is not so much the too overtly diabolical figure of Wilde, as the idea of a sort of 'blinding by happiness' – of internal division, illusion and unconsciousness which someone is taking advantage of, and which can only lead to conflicts: precisely those which are announced by the final image of the marriage of Heaven and Hell – that is, the drama which since 1916 had entered its most acute stage and was moving towards its denouement. The double narration reflects the inner conflicts of the narrator – of the man who retelling this drama in 1918 could say within the space of five sentences both: 'I have been hateful' and 'I'm not convinced that I'm wrong'.[22] A reading of many other texts will be needed to grasp the sense of the narrator's indecision, the function of the ambiguity, the usefulness for Gide of the abrupt ending that leaves the story in suspense (a technique which, indeed, he often uses in his narratives).

Far from encapsulating Gide's life, the autobiographical narrative acquires in its turn the value of a witness to one moment in that life; it is a step whose function is to bring about an objective understanding of, and to go beyond, an essential conflict. This is therefore not at all a synthesis in the manner of Rousseau: rather it is a 'transitional autobiography', which while it is an act of unveiling in relation to society, also has about it those properties of 'catharsis' and 'retroaction' which Gide attributed to his fictions.

So, in order to grasp the significance of these limitations of the narrative, and the function of its ambiguity, we must locate *Si le Grain ne Meurt* within the 'autobiographical space' by means of a series of reference points:

a) In order for the system to function as a whole, there had to exist at least one published text clearly founded on the autobiographical pact and which presented the perspective in which all the other texts should thereafter be read. Such is the role of this autobiography, where the courageous sexual admission is the gauge of the author's commitment. But at the same time as opening up this perspective, it was also necessary that the text should be incapable of filling it, that is of obstructing it, so that it should leave the reader puzzled and the author free.[23] In 1939, with the publication of his *Journal* (albeit truncated), Gide would be conforming to a similar preoccupation.

b) Technically, *Si le Grain ne Meurt* represents a doubtless necessary step forward in the search for polyphony. Since 1911, Gide had been dreaming of the "novel", a complex structure, the struggle between conflicting viewpoints by means of which he could express himself entirely, and without simplification. This novel, which he had at first thought he was writing in *Les Caves du Vatican*, would come to fruition between 1919 and 1925 with *Les Faux-Monnayeurs*. But *Si le Grain ne Meurt* was written and *Morceaux Choisis* was compiled with the same aim of the synthetic and simultaneous expression of ambiguity: they were attempts to produce in a single volume the effect resulting from the accumulation of texts which were separate, varied and contradictory. Hence the multiple subjects in the first part, or the double viewpoint of the second. In this attempt, Gide was to know relative failure (the confusion of the first part) or a too limited success (the second part), and he emerged from the experience convinced that the autobiographical 'I' was ill equipped to express the 'self'. The creation of *Les Faux-Monnayeurs* is fed by the experience of this technical failure, just as it is abundantly fed by the material drawn from, and the problems raised by, the autobiography. The autobiographical experiment no doubt played a not inconsiderable role in the passage from the practice of the narrative ("récit") to that of the "novel".

c) In its ethical standpoint, *Si le Grain ne Meurt*, with its strategy of ambiguity, cannot readily be understood without a broader vision of the crisis undergone by the narrator between 1916 and 1921, as it is reflected in the *Journal*, in *Numquid et tu . . .? and in La Symphonie Pastorale*, and as recalled in *Et nunc manet in te*. It is not only that on the level of the biography the contemporary story of the author must be reconstructed in the margin of each chapter, but also on the level of the texts the reader must follow, across ten or so years, the process which I shall call 'the work of the Devil'. Gidean ambiguity is not a state of static oscillation, repetitive and sterile: the oscillation produces an advance. This movement will see Gide pass from a Christian universe to a Humanist one. *Si le Grain ne Meurt* is but one step in this slow process, the outcome of which cannot be read in the text. Here, the theme of the Devil is incomprehensible unless we reconstruct it from the pages of the *Journal* of 1916, from *Les Faux-Monnayeurs*, and the *Voyage au Congo*. Far from providing an overall perspective on Gide's life the autobiographical narrative testifies in an obscure way to a process which is still working to change the course of that whole life.

Thus replaced in these contexts, the place of *Si le Grain ne Meurt* in the interplay of Gide's works can be seen to be an important one, but also a limited one. (. . .) The only truly synthetic work which Gide wrote is, of course, *Les Faux-Monnayeurs*, not simply because of Gide's 'conflicting viewpoints', nor yet because Gide projects himself on the work at all levels of its structure, managing to confront simultaneously the problems of the different ages of his life (Boris, Bernard, Édouard). It deserves this status above all for being the only work which, through the *Journal des Faux-Monnayeurs*, brings together in the same entity autobiography and fiction, and places at its centre the problematic figure of the writer so sorely missing from *Si le Grain ne Meurt*.

And yet *Les Faux-Monnayeurs* cannot be considered a complete Gidean 'synthesis': the fruit of a serene maturity, this ironic book cannot offer an image which comes close to the man that was Gide. (. . .) There is no complete picture of the man other than his writings taken together as a whole.

The Autobiographical Space and the Reader

The definition of this 'autobiographical space', and the use to which he puts it, probably constitutes Gide's most original invention regarding literary forms. This 'form' is perhaps less readily recognizable than, for example, the interplay of techniques and viewpoints of *Les Faux-Monnayeurs*, since it embraces the whole œuvre and is created by the interacting of relations between elements and by an ambiguous combination of what could be called 'reading contracts'. But this 'invention' is of the same order as the formal inventions in *Les Faux-Monnayeurs*. Just as he does in the novel, Gide only uses elements and techniques which are perfectly classical and thus stays enclosed within the traditional ideology and world vision of the text that these techniques imply; all his art lies in the combining of elements, in the virtuosity with which he uses simultaneously that which before had been used separately – and of using them entirely consciously. *Les Faux-Monnayeurs* has been called a sort of carnival of the traditional novel, far more than the inauguration of the modern novel (as opposed to the work of Proust, Joyce, Kafka or Faulkner); by the same token it could be said that Gide's entire œuvre, taken as the deliberate construction of an 'autobiographical space', is a sort of closing ceremony for traditional forms of personal writing, an exemplary construction which, with diabolical thoroughness, articulates within one system lyrical writings, fiction, essays and autobiography. It is at this very general level that Gide's originality is situated, far more than in a specific and restricted work such as *Si le Grain ne Meurt*, whose very classic style and construction can disappoint the modern reader, who will be more interested in the experiments of a writer like Leiris or all that contemporary literature which questions the very nature of the notion of the person through its narrative techniques and manner of writing.

This self-consciousness which organizes the autobiographical space is at once the evident strength but also the hidden weakness of Gide's work.

The 'autobiographical space' has in fact existed since the end of the eighteenth century, and has been the object of experiment by numerous authors. To project the self, to confess oneself, to dream of the self, to purge the self, to express the self through a fiction – this has been possible for anyone to do, more or less consciously, since Rousseau first did so in his *Confessions*. (. . .) But it is also reading habits that have made the autobiographical space a reality, albeit with a certain delay: from Sainte-Beuve onwards, a certain number of critics have tended to make the study of the author a principle by which to understand the œuvre. However, whilst for authors this procedure existed as a fact – but was not articulated as a theory – for critics, it was an interpretation which they discovered after the work was completed. What is particular to Gide is to have made the system explicit, to have seen all its possibilities, and to have transformed unthought-out procedures into a strategy. He has turned an incidental effect into a goal to be aimed at from the outset and pursued quite consciously: it is as if his work had already been read.

To construct a theory of the Gidean 'autobiographical space' as I have tried to do here, the critic need look no further than the countless texts in which Gide sets out this theory (prefaces, letters, diaries, etc.): these are not necessarily texts from the years of maturity, with the author discovering the unity of this space and its function after its creation – on the contrary, Gide's discovery is made in advance of his writing. (. . .) But whilst this theoretical lucidity and the creative decision made from the start may well fascinate the reader, they may equally well get in his way. By succeeding too well in this ploy and in its orchestration, Gide seems, despite all his precautions, to lose a part of what makes up the 'autobiographical space', that part of the subject which can only be apprehended by another, which I shall call the 'reader's share', and which is slight in Gide's œuvre – the only place which is set aside for the reader being that of error or of incomprehension of the game to which Gide holds the key. Gide has also, it seems, let slip the possibility for his fiction to express a part of himself not already known, and which might not immediately and clearly be attributed to him. Hence a certain bewilderment on the part of the reader. How can he escape the impression that the construction of the autobiographical space determines in advance any reading, that it is a reading which has already been established, and that he can do no more than repeat? Is there really any place for a reader in this system?

Here a distinction should doubtless be made between two generations of readers: we no longer stand in the same relation to the texts as did Gide's contemporaries. Thanks to the publication of personal texts and correspondances we now know all the pieces which make up the network of Gide's writing. For his contemporaries, this was not so: each book appeared as a surprise, in relation to the previous one, and also as an enigma, in that the 'ironic' sense could pass the reader by , and where, even if it were perceived, its sense did not permit the author to be fixed in a defined and definitive position. The books were perceived to offer a 'confidence', but without it being possible to explain the nature of that confidence. The simplest solution still remained, that of reading the books without reference to the author, drawing directly from them the moral that the reader wished to see: this procedure, whilst entirely legitimate, became difficult to uphold as soon as the reader read *several* Gidean narratives. The author, a virtual point which the reader tried to locate by triangulation, would inevitably hold on to his secret, the unity of the œuvre, a unity which could then only be seen in the light of the autobiography. Our unease, today, is the reverse: the publication of the diaries, correspondences, and contemporary reminiscences, the efforts of Gide's biographers and of university researchers have had the result of throwing a livid light on Gide's face, with his history and his contradictions, and of moving his works back into a sort of penumbra, so that we end up by wondering how any of them can have been read for themselves seriously, by people who did not know what we know.

L'Immoraliste, La Porte Étroite, La Symphonie Pastorale, Les Faux-Monnayeurs can appear today as mere fantasies and projections onto the Gidean autobiographical space, rather than as fictions to be read or texts to be analysed. [. . .] If his contemporary readers registered unease when faced with the author's indecision, today's readers feel unease at the evanescence of his work: this sort of contradiction or bewilderment at the level of the reading of the work is precisely the effect of Gide's 'autobiographical space', which excludes at once a purely novelistic reading of the texts and their reduction to pure biography. Claude Martin has shown in his study of *La Symphonie Pastorale* that the only possible reading of the work is an ambiguous one:[24] and it may be doubted whether many readers are capable of such an understanding, and there may be doubt, too, as to the value of an exercise requiring such subtlety. But, by necessitating this ambiguous reading, Gide also succeeds in ensnaring the attentive reader in what one might call his 'autobiographical field', as we talk of an electric field or a magnetic field – with its poles, its vibrations and its oscillations. He thus recreates, within his work itself, the impression that in life he gave to those close to him, of being 'richer than his work';[25] and by this vertiginous game, he creates himself, in the eyes of his reader, as a transcendant consciousness.

NOTES

1. This might be a word such as 'auto-graphy', or a word formed from 'ego', such as 'egology' or 'egography'.
   In the cases where this system of texts also includes an autobiographical narrative in the strictest sense, I have chosen to designate this by the term 'autobiographical space', an ambiguous expression to designate an ambiguous reality (on this problem, see my study of 'The Autobiographical Pact', *Poétique*, no. 14).

2. [In his introductory study to *Le Pacte autobiographique* (Paris, Seuil, 1975), Lejeune looks for defining characteristics of the autobiographiy, as opposed to the autobiographical novel, and comes to the conclusion that the only distinguishing feature of the genre is the 'pact' that the author makes with the reader. This pact is that the character who is placed before the reader is one whom the author is prepared to recognize as himself. Lejeune offers the following definition: 'The autobiographical pact is the affirmation in the text of this identity (the identity of the name (author-narrator-character)), which in the last resort can be taken to correspond to the name on the cover' (p. 26).]

3. To avoid cluttering this analysis with quotations, I have chosen to refer in these notes to the major texts by Gide on the questions being treated. On ambiguity and the refusal to choose between contrary viewpoints, see for example, *JI*, 31; J1, 20–1 [1892] *JI*, 777; J2, 343, the essential text on the 'état de dialogue' ('state of dialogue'); *J1*, 801; *J2*, 366 on the fertile ground offered by contradiction.

4. In the preface, Gide argues that the work is intended neither as an act of accusation, nor an apology for the actions of the protagonist, but rather aims to paint a realistic portrait. 'For the rest, I have not tried to prove anything, but only to paint my picture well and to set it in a good light' (368; viii). Any such 'problems' posed by a work of art, he claims, find sufficient answer in the work of art, and not in any external judgement.

5. This double aspect of autobiography and self-critique is very clear in the necessarily allusive words with which Gede offered Claudel his *La Porte Étroite*, where he invites him at once to divine 'the secret share of confidence', and to understand that 'the idea of the work bears within itself its own critique'(*Correspondance Claudel-Gide* (Paris, Gallimard, 1949), p. 90); see also the explanation of the 'law of retroaction' in *JI*, 40–1; *J1* 29–30 [1893]; for *L'Immoraliste*, Gide needed to explain to Jammes the dynamic of his fictions, and offers some very striking formulae in which he defines his whole novelistic "equilibrium" (purging, clearing, alternation, complexity. . . .) *Correspondance Jammes- Gide* (Paris, Gallimard, 1948), pp. 199–200; see also, on *La Porte Étroite*: JI, 275–6; J1, 240, JI, 365; J1 318 on *Les Caves du Vatican*: JI 436–7; J2, 38–9.

6. On "depersonalisation", see *JI*, 759; *J2* 323 [1923]; *Journal des Faux-Monnayeurs*, 86–7 and 94; in the *Cahiers de la Petite Dame* Vol I, (Paris Gallimard, 1973) [Hereafter CAG4], p. 25, speaking of *La Symphonie Pastorale*, Gide distinguishes between the 'I' of the novel and the 'I' of autobiography; see also *JI*, 829–30; *J2*, 392–3 ([1927]).

7. Gide's deep-seated intention is clearly analysed by Maria Van Rysselberghe and confirmed by Gide (CAG4, p. 78, 19 April 1921): to her remarks, Gide replies: 'Yes [. . . .] this is the thread of Ariadne, the key. The composition of this book is very important to me. Through my choice, I wish to sketch my personality; it is time. I would like everything to be of the best and to organise itself'.

8. 'Why should I attempt to form, by artificially imitating myself, the artificial unity of my life?' (*JI*, 174; *J1*, 148: 24 August 1905); or echoing the opening of Stendhal's autobiography *Vie de Henry Brulard*: 'In two days I shall be fifty-one, and I still do not know myself! I seem to myself to be the most incomprehensible of mixtures. However, I do not try much to analyse myself' (*Cahiers de la Petite Dame*, CAG 4, 59–60 [20 November, 1920]); 'I am loathe to sum up my impressions.' (ibid., p. 75 [16 April 1921]).

9. In the text of *Si le grain ne meurt* the lamentations on the inadequacies of the autobiographical narrative are part of the act played by the narrator (see *JII*, 429, 436, 438, 463, 492, 500–1) and each time have a very precise function at the place where they occur in the text – as has the final note of the first part, which serves to join the two parts.

10. This hierarchy of the two narratives appears clearly in the *Journal des Faux-Monnayeurs* or in various observations by Gide (*Cahiers de la Petite Dame*, CAG 4, 92 [9 August 1921]; Letter to André Rouveyre of 22 November 1924, in *Correspondance Gide-Rouveyre* (Paris, Mercure de France, 1967), p. 90.

11. The choice of the final word of the book 'we became engaged' contains at once a suspension and a veiled form of confession. By leaving the marriage in shadow (why did Gide not write 'we were married'?), at the same time as removing the conjugal drama from the curious gaze of the public, he refers to it in an indirect way: the very nature of the 'marriage blanc' is to make the engagement into a permanent state. As for the explanations which precede this suspended ending, they appeared mysterious to those close to Gide who actually knew how the story was to continue (cf. CAG 4, 92).

12. On two occasions in *Si le Grain ne Meurt*, Gide seems to announce a continuation (*JII*, 547 and 607). But reading Gide's direct declarations it would indeed seem that to prolong the narrative beyond the engagement was no more

than a highly improbable hypothesis. 'I doubt whether I shall be able to pursue further the writing of those Memoirs. And yet what interest they would have!' (*JI*, 696; *J1*, 269: 14 July 1921) or a passing temptation ('Despite myself, I can already glimpse the sequel to be written'), *Cahiers de la Petite Dame*, CAG 4, 92 [10 August 1921]). There will be no further talk of it.

13.   On these limitations of the autobiography, see the analysis by HENRI RAMBAUD in FRANÇOIS DERAIS and HENRI RAMBAUD, *L'Envers du journal de Gide et les secrets de la sincérité*, éd. augmentée (Paris, le Nouveau Portique, 1952), pp. 63–6.

14.   This other side of Gide's life appears in *Et nunc. . . .* only in the form of an allusion which is mysterious and casual at the same time (*JII* 1130). Gide was fully aware of the deformations that these restrictions gave to his portrait. He notes, with sorrow, about the *Journal* published by him in 1939 after the censoring of all the passages concerning Madeleine:

> The few allusions to the secret drama of my life become incomprehensible through the absence of what would throw light on them; incomprehensible or inadmissible, the image of this mutilated me that I give there, which presents, in the ardent place of my heart, but a hole. (*JI*, 1331; *J3*, 413: 26 January 1939)

This statement could also apply, though to a lesser extent, to *Si le grain ne meurt*.

15.   Gide affirmed on several occasions that from before 1900 he had intended not only to write his Memoirs, but to publish them during his lifetime (see letter to François Porché, in C, 191–2). He explains very clearly the reasons for this in a letter to Edmund Gosse, *The Correspondence of André Gide and Edmund Gosse* (New York, New York University Press, 1959) pp. 189–90, letter of 16 January 1927) and in the *Projet de préface* for the *Œuvres complètes* (vol. X, 1936, pp. 453–4): his horror of the 'conventional camouflage', 'the devotion of relatives and friends which is intended to camouflage the dead'. In August 1922, he announces to the Petite Dame: 'I do not believe in posthumous publications; I find no peace of mind in the thought of them.' (CAG 4, 147). In 1925, the attitude of Isabelle Rivière will reinforce him in his distrust (ibid., 229 and 249).

16.   Thus in 1916 he will call his autobiography an 'œuvre posthume' – in that its publication will only be possible in an indiscernable future (the term used in a letter to Edmund Gosse, op. cit., p. 130, 3 July 1916). It is the crisis of 1918 which makes publication a possibility, not simply because Madeleine is from now on informed, but because by burning all Gide's letters, she herself had broken the tacit contract which bound them on this point. To understand the limits and precautions of Gide's confession, it needs to be seen that Gide never took the initiative with Madeleine: he left to circumstances and to chance the task of revealing the truth to Madeleine, rather than confronting it openly in a painful discussion which she had to open herself. It is exactly the same attitude that Gide took with his mother in 1894: an unfortunate chance, which he neither provoked nor tried to prevent, revealed to Madame Gide the emancipation of her son, who then claimed his right to freedom. But whereas in 1894 he finished by giving in, the crisis of 1918 will lead him to gain his liberty.

17.   [For Gide, the phrase has a specific personalized sense. It designates the action of the individual of pushing himself beyond his immediate situation, and confronting new challenges. It is frequently used in a context in which the individual is contravening the rules of conventional morality – Lafcadio's gratuitous murder of Fleurissoire, Thésée's abandoning of Ariane; however, for

Gide the ability to 'passer outre' is both a gauge of his character's liberation and of his strength.]

18. [Lejeune is here implicitly contrasting Gide's project of writing a work to be published during his lifetime, and to affect the course of that life, with Chateaubriand's project to leave a picture of himself after his death which would resurrect his image, in his *Mémoires d'outre-tombe*.]

19. It is in the *Cahiers de la Petite Dame* that one can follow most easily in its details, its nuances and its complexities Gide's conduct between 1920 and 1926, up to 19 October 1926 when he announces to the 'Petite Dame' (Maria Van Rysselberghe): 'I'm definitely going to release *Si le grain ne meurt*, open the cage' (CAG 4, 290).

20. Cf. '. . . I have not even approached my subject, and one cannot even yet glimpse the introduction, or foresee the approach, of what was to fill the whole book, of that for which I am writing it' (*JI*, 572; *J2*, 156: 13 October 1916); and 'Perhaps I shall tarry excessively over these trifles in the vestibule [. . .] it seems to me that *everything* remains to be said and that up to now I have merely prepared the way' (*JI*, 615; *J2*, 195: 21 January 1917).

21. We know that the last two chapters were written some time after the rest, in the winter of 1920–21, to weld it to the second part. The final chapter (X) with the myth of the 'selve obscure' and its interminable portrait gallery (from which the principal portrait is missing, that of Paul Valéry) gives the impression of a languid and imprecise padding out of the characterization of the narrator, of whom we learn almost nothing whatsoever.

22. *Cahiers de la Petite Dame*, CAG 4, 10.

23. To a certain extent he needed to avoid the problem pointed out by Valéry in 1917: 'I see simply that this work will inevitably be the key to your whole work; readers will look for you in it, and will always find in it the explanation of all that you will have written. You must not lose sight of this. In a certain sense you are doing in this book what you have already done and everything that you will ever be able to do. It is a book which *will have written* your other books.' (*Correspondance André Gide-Paul Valéry*, Paris, Gallimard, 1955, p. 454, letter from Valéry, 27 July 1917.)

24. *La Symphonie pastorale*, édition établie et présentée par Claude MARTIN, Paris, Lettres Modernes, 1970, p. xcviii. Martin's analysis of *Les Faux-Monnayers* in *André Gide par lui-même* (Paris, Seuil, 1963) comes to the same conclusion: the novel 'only reveals all its richness when it is closely attached to the person of its author' (p. 149).

25. *Correspondance Gide-Roger Martin du Gard* (Paris, Gallimard, 2 vols, 1968), vol I, p. 153.

Part Two:

Approaches to the Texts

6 Lucien Dällenbach on André Gide's shields*

In the 1960s and 1970s, as writers such as the *nouveaux romanciers* questioned the methods and structures of the traditional novel, the device known as *mise en abyme* underwent a remarkable revival. Named by Gide in a phrase he attributed to the terminology of heraldry, it denotes a technique whereby an element in the novel acts as a mirror for the text as a whole. Hence, in certain of Gide's novels, such as *Les Cahiers d'André Walter, Paludes, Les Caves du Vatican* and *Les Faux-Monnayeurs*, the characters include a novelist writing a book very like the one in which he features. Elsewhere, a component of the text sums up in miniature its overall subject or theme: metaphorically, as in the palimpsest Michel evokes in *L'Immoraliste* to convey his discovery of an authentic self beneath the person he had been conditioned to become; or literally, as when in the same novel the character of Ménalque embodies and expounds the new ideals which Michel is pursuing. Gide scholars had contented themselves with the already rich stock of reflections this conception gave rise to: about the internal structure of a novel, about the relationship between the representation and the reality it purported to depict, and so on.

With the exception of the English writer Aldous Huxley in *Point Counterpoint* (1928), relatively few other novelists seemed to have employed the technique to any resounding effect until Robbe-Grillet, Simon, Sarraute and Butor produced texts in which the *mise en abyme* appeared to proliferate and take on an ever more complex set of functions and significations. This in turn led critics to explore its implications, and to follow Gide scholars in puzzling over its origins – which immediately became less than clear. Gide had only referred to the technique in one brief passage of his diary, and the more this passage was subjected to scrutiny, the less satisfactory it appeared as the founding text of a device with what some saw as profound metaphysical overtones. Lucien Dällenbach emerged as the leading expert on the subject.

---

* First published in *Le Récit Spéculaire: essai sur la mise en abyme*, (Paris, Seuil, 1977); English text from *The Mirror in the Text*, translated from the French by Jeremy Whiteley with Emma Hughes (Cambridge, Polity Press, in association with Basil Blackwell, 1989).

Having explored the workings of the *mise en abyme* in articles on *avant-garde* novels by Butor, Simon and others, he looked back to Gide and beyond and drew together his findings in his major book from whose introductory chapter the following text is taken. His work has established the importance of the device as a universal and virtually essential feature of literary production.

Dällenbach offers a careful re-reading of Gide's 'theoretical' pronouncement, clearing away certain misconceptions and illustrating thereby the avenues of reflection the device has opened up – but highlighting also a number of neglected details which prove productive when properly examined. In particular, this analysis stresses the role of the writing process in the author's construction of his own identity. Signalling the psychoanalytical dimension of Gide's writing strategy and relating it to Lacan's theories on the evolution of the subject, the critic shows how, in *La Tentative Amoureuse*, the author achieves the 'second degree' of reflective activity necessary to avoid the twin pitfalls of excessive narcissistic self-contemplation, and alienation of a self that dreams of autonomy.

The First Reference

In order to clarify what should be understood by *mise en abyme*, it is most appropriate to return quickly to the sources and to reproduce the text in which the *mise en abyme* is mentioned for the first time. Gide wrote in 1893:

> In a work of art, I rather like to find thus transposed, at the level of the characters, the subject of the work itself. Nothing sheds more light on the work or displays the proportions of the whole work more accurately. Thus, in paintings by Memling or Quentin Metzys, a small dark convex mirror reflects, in its turn, the interior of the room in which the action of the painting takes place. Thus, in a slightly different way, in Velasquez's *Las Meniñas*. Finally, in literature, there is the scene in which a play is acted in *Hamlet*; this also happens in many other plays. In *Wilhelm Meister*, there are the puppet shows and festivities in the castle. In *The Fall of the House of Usher*, there is the piece that is read to Roderick, etc. None of these examples is absolutely accurate. What would be more accurate, and what would explain better what I'd wanted to do in my *Cahiers*, in *Narcisse* and in *La Tentative*, would be a comparison with the device from heraldry that involves putting a second representation of the original shield 'en abyme' within it.[1]

This text, which is more often quoted than interpreted by critics inclined to think that Gide is speaking about himself,[2] is more complex than it appears at first sight. Although it is more correct and concise than the passage from Hugo that it is perhaps recalling,[3] its apparent clarity becomes blurred if one reads it carefully; despite its straightforward appearance, it is so enigmatic that one starts to wonder whether this 'charter', which gives the *mise en abyme* its status in literature, is not responsible, to a certain extent, for the uncertainty surrounding it today. Before coming to a conclusion on this question, by considering at source the subtle ambiguities of the passage, let us try to note some basic points from it:

1   the *mise en abyme*, as a means by which the work turns back on itself, appears to be a kind of *reflection*;
2   its essential property is that it brings out the meaning and form of the work;
3   as demonstrated by examples taken from different fields, it is a structural device that is not the prerogative either of the literary narrative or indeed of literature itself;[4] and
4   it gets its name from a heraldic device that Gide no doubt discovered in 1891.[5]

The last point leads to some further remarks:

(a)   The word *abyme* here is a technical term. I shall not therefore speculate on its many connotations[6] or hasten to give it a metaphysical meaning: instead of invoking Pascal's 'gouffre', the abyss of the Mystics, Heidegger's 'Abgrund', Ponge's 'objeu' or Derrida's 'différance', I shall rather refer to a treatise on heraldry: ' "Abyss" ("Abîme") – the heart of the shield. A figure is said to be "en abîme" when it is combined with other figures in the centre of the shield, but does not touch any of these figures.'[7]
(b)   Although the word still remains allusive, we can now understand what Gide had in mind: what fascinated him must have been *the image of a shield containing, in its centre, a miniature replica of itself.*
(c)   Rather than worrying about whether heraldry contains such a device, or whether it is simply a product of Gide's imagination,[8] I shall take the analogy on its own terms, in other words, as an attempt to explain a structure that could be defined as follows: *a mise en abyme is any aspect enclosed within a work that shows a similarity with the work that contains it.* [. . .]

The passage is truncated and the 'thus' of its first sentence refers to *La Tentative Amoureuse*, mentioned at the end of the text as an example of the *mise en abyme*. So the first important conclusion we reach is that the text has a circular structure. It starts off implicitly with the *mise en abyme* and ends up explicitly with it.

The second point to consider is that the ambiguity of this circular text lies in the three successive 'thus'es and in the 'finally' that follows on from these. The argument slides from *La Tentative Amoureuse*, which is definitely referred to, from one adverb to another ('thus ... thus ... thus ... finally') weaving the various examples interchangeably together, until the slide is halted by the unexpected phrase 'none of these examples is absolutely accurate', which puts them into perspective.

From this fact alone, one initial conclusion is clear; one cannot do justice to Gide's fundamental intentions by purely and simply assimilating the *mise en abyme* to the pictorial and literary examples that prefigure it. In the final analysis, the only thing the heraldic metaphor does – and it does this better than any other metaphor – is to express what Gide 'wanted to do' in some of his books. [. . .] To understand what he really did want to do, we must put our text back into its context:

> *I wanted to indicate*, in *La Tentative Amoureuse*, the influence the book has on the author while he is writing it. For, as we give birth to it, it changes us and alters the course of our life; in the same way that in physics, when liquid is poured out of filled floating containers in one direction, the containers move in the opposite direction, our actions have a retroactive effect on us. 'Our actions act upon us as much as we act upon them', said George Eliot.
>
> So I was sad because a dream of unattainable joy torments me. I tell of this dream, and, dissociating the joy from the dream, make it mine. The dream thus loses its mystique and I am joyful as a result.
>
> A subject cannot act on an object without retroaction by the object on the subject that is acting. It is this reciprocity that *I wanted to indicate* – not one's relationship with other people, but with oneself. The active subject is oneself. The retroactive thing is a subject one imagines. So it's a kind of indirect action on oneself that I conveyed in *La Tentative Amoureuse*; it's also just a tale.
>
> Luc and Rachel too want to achieve their desire; but whereas in writing of mine, I achieved it in an ideal way, they dream of the park of which they can only see the gates and which they want to go inside in reality: so they feel no joy. In a work of art, I rather like to find thus transposed ... the device from heraldry that involves putting a second representation of the original shield 'en abyme' within it.
>
> The retroaction of the subject on itself has always appealed to me. It's typical of the psychological novel. An angry man tells a story – this is the subject of the book. A man telling a story is not enough – it must be an angry man and there must always be a continuing relationship between the man's anger and the story he's telling.[6]

These comments pave the way for a productive line of enquiry. [. . .] I shall [. . .] consider the phenomenon that it is the *mise en abyme*'s function to bring to light – the way in which the writer constructs the writing, and vice versa.

Twinning

This reciprocity, as Gide presents it in his *Journal*, seems to be clarified by what psychoanalysis tells us about linguistic communication (and this is perhaps not entirely coincidental): namely that the 'sender gets back from the receiver his/her own message in inverse form',[7] and that, mediated through the desire of the other, my words construct me by anticipating the response they seek. Gide, years before Lacan, observed this on many occasions, and it would not be impossible for his whole œuvre to be understood in terms of a methodical attempt to create according to this law. To use this law in order to give solidity to a being who was receptive, fluid and existed *ad libitum*,[8] and at the same time to avoid the aspects of this law that alienate a spirit who dreams of self-sufficiency (the inevitable recourse to the other, who, by constructing me, falsifies me) – this is, at its most basic level, the unavoidable requirement of Gide's wish for *sincerity*. Can one ever hope to satisfy it? All of Gide's work aims to enable him to do so. The choice of the medium of writing is itself part of this strategy. By writing, Gide becomes his own interlocutor. But unless this introspection is combined with one particular condition, it still only provides a precarious solution: for although it excludes the (de-)formative personality of the other, it replaces it with the captivating and no less specious character in the novel. In order to derive a real benefit from the transaction, one has to contrive to ward off the very otherness of the fictive character, and, in order to do so, to impose sufficient constraints on oneself: in other words to create it in one's own image, or, better still, to make it engage in the very activity that one is oneself undertaking in creating it – the writing of a novel (*The Notebooks of André Walter*) or the telling of a story (*La Tentative Amoureuse*).

It is tempting to compare this narcissistic doubling with the creative experience, which Lacan calls the 'mirror stage' or 'mirror phase',[9] since this strategy of auto-generation through writing reveals a perversion on the symbolic level that results in an even worse lapse into the imaginary. Thus we know, through a fortuitous note in the *Journal*, that Gide sometimes wrote in front of a mirror so as to get inspiration from talking and listening to his reflection:

> I am writing on the small piece of furniture of Anna Shackleton's that was in my bedroom in the rue de Commailles. That's where I worked; I liked it because I could see myself writing in the double mirror of the

desk above the block I was writing on. I looked at myself after each
sentence; my reflection spoke and listened to me, kept me company
and sustained my enthusiasm.[10]

The reflexive language of writing, exalted by the reflected image of the
writer; the mirror of his early years recalling the first fusion of body and
language: what we have here is doubtless a typical reappropriation
scenario, which only a psychoanalyst could interpret fully. For my part I
shall only take two points from it: the first is that this reflection through
writing is based on an imaginary reflection, which allows the writer
obsessively to enjoy the image of himself as he wants to see himself – as a
writer; the second point is that the imaginary reflection that aims to restore
the immediate and continuous relationship between self and self comes up
in this scenario against the discontinuity and the shift caused by the very
activity of writing itself! Gide may well imagine himself a writer by means
of this narcissistic image, but he can no more see himself writing than one
can stop and watch oneself walking. 'I could see myself writing', he
states.[11] But as soon as it is uttered, this statement is belied by the detail that
follows: 'I looked at myself after each sentence.' No doubt this means that
the reappropriation cannot be complete, but also that while the two
reflections are dependent on each other, they remain distinct: whereas the
visual experience of looking in a mirror is instantaneous, the writer and his
reflection can only speak to, and answer, each other *in turn*.

However, we must not infer that the mere acceptance of this diachronic
constraint can alone create a work 'en abyme' as Gide conceives of it. In
order to achieve this form, another condition must be met: the work itself
must *point up* the reflection that is taking place; or, more precisely, the
reflection must become the subject of the reflection. *La Tentative Amoureuse*
provides a better example of this 'second-degree' activity than do the
Notebooks,[12] and since it is in the context of this latter text that Gide refers
metaphorically to heraldry, a concise analysis of this work may be
sufficient to enable us to define fairly precisely what Gide's own version of
the *mise en abyme* was.

The author who writes the 'Envoi' is tormented by a dream of happiness
he knows is unattainable, but he achieves it by proxy: he makes a narrator
(with whom he identifies) tell a (fictive) lady the story of Luc and Rachel's
happy love affair. From the beginning of this experimental tale, a certain
complicity is apparent between the two couples. Their respective situations
are similar, apart from the fact that Luc and Rachel are happy. Rachel
corresponds to the woman who is listening to the narrator, and Luc is such
a perfect extension of the narrator that from time to time Luc takes on his
role when he is with his companion: he tells stories. He does not ramble: he
transposes his own love life in the same way that the narrator transposes as
he creates Luc's: Luc's narratives go beyond their immediate addressee

(Rachel) to affect the subject and the object of the narration – the 'narrateur' and the 'narrataire'[13] – whose destiny they recapitulate and anticipate, and it is through this fluctuation between the two narrative levels that the retroaction can occur.

Initially, there is a contrast between the narrator's sadness and the lovers' happiness (' "Madame, I shall tell this story to you. You know that our sad love affair lost its way on the moor" '),[14] but soon the balance changes and Luc and Rachel's boredom (which overtakes the narrator – ' "Madame, this story bores me", p. 54) is followed by the triumphant realization that his ill-fated desire should not distract him from his more ambitious plans (' "I am happy; I am alive, I have great things in mind. I've finished telling this boring story: great things now await us" ', p. 58). So the imaginary identification that the narrator himself contrived finally has a great therapeutic value for the storyteller. Restored by his fictional work, he can devote himself to more real adventures with a joyful heart.[15]

The example of *La Tentative Amoureuse*. is clear enough to enable us to try to formulate what the structure of Gide's *mise en abyme* is. What distinguishes it from everything else is that it attributes to a character in the narrative the very *activity* of the narrator in charge of the narration. This is what is achieved when the 'je' of *La Tentative Amoureuse* is taken over by Luc. If this taking over of the narrative is different from that initiated in *The Arabian Nights*, and used, for example, in *Le Roman comique* or the picaresque novel, this is because the secondary narrative in Gide reflects the primary one in so far as the process of retroaction requires an analogy between the situation of the character and that of the narrator, in other words between the thematic content of the main story and that of the story contained within it. One can therefore define Gide's *mise en abyme* as a coupling or a twinning of activities related to a similar object; or as a relationship of relationships, the relation of the narrator N to his/her story S being the same as that of the narrator/character n to his/her story s.

From this, it is possible to understand a certain number of key facts; first among these is that the 'charter' owes part of its ambiguity to a word whose sense is not made clear: the word 'subject'. As soon as we realize that the 'subject of the work itself', for Gide, is *relational* (the relationship between the work and the person writing it) – and is in other words duplicated as soon as the work begins – we can see why *Heinrich von Ofterdingen* was neglected and *The Fall of the House of Usher* challenged as examples. Since Novalis's novel and Poe's tale tell stories and do not contain the reciprocal construction of a story and a narrator, the duplication they provide only comprises two of the four terms required (N:S::n:s), and so could not satisfy a writer who had chosen, as a problematic subject, the problematic of the subject.[16]

What is less easy to understand in this context is why Gide came to give a privileged position to a metaphor that, because it was not able to designate simultaneously the reflection of a narrator, of a story and of the dialectic between them, doubtless applied to his own work, but even more accurately to his other examples. It may well be that this comment reveals that it is impossible to explain fully a choice, the basis of which is not entirely evident, but in both sets of examples the image of the 'shield within the shield' does represent the duplication of the 'subject' (which is 'simple' in Novalis and Poe, and relational in Gide) of the work within the work; it is therefore appropriate as an image of *all works* that use the *mise en abyme*, and, all in all, this device is now sufficiently defined by the preliminary statement of the 'charter'. In other words, as long as the nature of the reflected subject is irrelevant, we can return, after many a detour, to our initial belief – namely, that when the expression *mise en abyme* first appeared, it unequivocally designated what other authors call 'the work within the work'[17] or 'internal duplication'.[18]

Notes

1. *JI*, p. 41, cf. *Journals 1889–1949*, translated by J. O'BRIEN (London, Penguin, 1984), pp. 30–1. [Unless otherwise stated, all translations from foreign texts are mine. I have used some standard translations, but where necessary (e.g. to convey Dällenbach's precise point) I provide a new translation, while referring the reader to a published source (as here). *Tr.*]

2. The only commentary that has ever been given of it is the short one by B. MORRISSETTE in 'Un Héritage d'André Gide: la duplication intérieure', *Comparative Literature Studies*, 8. 2(1971), 125ff.

3. In *Le Nouveau Roman* (Paris, Seuil, 1973), p. 49. J. RICARDOU quotes a passage from Hugo's *William Shakespeare* that seems curiously to herald the passage from Gide: 'All Shakespeare's plays except two (*Macbeth* and *Romeo and Juliet*) – that is, thirty-four out of thirty-six plays – show one characteristic that seems hitherto to have escaped even the most eminent commentators and critics, . . . a duplicate of the action, which runs through the play and reflects it in miniature. Alongside the storm in the Atlantic, there is the storm in a teacup. Thus Hamlet fathers another Hamlet; he kills Polonius, Laertes's father, and so puts Laertes in exactly the same situation in relation to him as he is in relation to Claudius. He has two fathers to avenge, and there could be two ghosts. Thus, in *King Lear*, Lear, in despair because of his daughters Goneril and Regan, and consoled by his daughter Cordelia, is paralleled in Gloucester who is betrayed by his son Edgar. The divided, self-enclosing idea, the subplot that imitates and runs alongside the main drama, the action and its satellite, the minor version of the action – the divided unity – this is most certainly a strange phenomenon. . . . These double plots are pure Shakespeare. They are also characteristic of the sixteenth century . . . The spirit of the sixteenth century was fond of mirrors; all Renaissance ideas had two levels. Look at altar screens in churches: the Renaissance, with its strange and exquisite art, always reflects the Old Testament in the New. The double plot is everywhere.'
   Ricardou sees evidence that Gide's text echoes Hugo's in the repetition at the beginning of the passage, of the adverb 'thus' ('ainsi'), which introduces the

examples in both texts. Be that as it may, what is certain is Hugo's opportune memory of this characteristic feature of Shakespeare's plays when he wrote *L'Homme qui rit*. Cf. below, pp. 58ff.

4. On the subject of the *mise en abyme* outside literature, see, e.g. J. Voigt, *Das Spiel im Spiel. Versuch einer Formbestimmung an Beispielen aus dem deutschen, englischen und spanischen Dramas*, Dissertation (Göttingen, 1955); R. J. Nelson, *Play within the Play (The Dramatist's Conception of his Art: Shakespeare to Anouilh)* (New Haven, Yale University Press, 1958); M.-J. Lefebve, 'La Mise en abyme mallarméenne et la preuve par X', *Synthèses*, 258–9 (1967–8), 81–5; V. Anker and L. Dällenbach, 'La Réflexion spéculaire dans la peinture et la littérature récentes', *Art International*, 19/2 (February 1975), 28–32 and 45–8; and C. Metz, 'La Construction "en abyme" dans *Huit et demi* de Fellini', in *Essais sur la signification au cinéma* (Paris, Klinksieck, 1968), pp. 223–8.

5. Gide's passion for heraldic art, which was contemporary with his writing of *Le Traité du Narcisse*, is revealed in his letters to Paul Valéry. In a letter dated 15 November 1891, Gide exclaims 'I read a work by Hello on style. And I'm studying heraldry! It's wonderful. I'd never thought about it before.' Valéry's ironic response was: 'You must be curious seen in heraldic terms. How about "D'Azur au dextrochère d'or tenant une coupe vuyde du même, où souffre un monstre"?' This did not stop Gide returning to the subject in a letter written in December the same year: 'More treatises on heraldry' (A. Gide and P. Valéry, *Correspondance 1890–1942* (Paris, Gallimard, 1955), pp. 138ff. and 141).

6. *JI*, pp. 40ff., cf. *Journals 1889–1949*, translated by J. O'Brien, pp. 29–31; my italics. Considering the importance of this context, it is astonishing that it is so rarely quoted – and even more rarely exploited – by critics. It is discussed in exemplary fashion by M. Blanchot (*La Part du feu* (Paris, Gallimard, 1949), pp. 217ff. and *L'Espace littéraire* (Paris, Gallimard, 'Idées', 1968), pp. 104ff.), who, however, completely ignores the 'charter'!

7. J. Lacan, *Écrits* (Paris, Seuil, 1966), p. 298.

8. Cf. *Journals 1889–1949*, translated by J. O'Brien, p. 26 and *passim*, and also *The Counterfeiters*.

9. *Écrits*, pp. 93ff. Cf. also the famous 'schema L' (p. 53), and p. 181.

10. *JII*, p. 252; cf. *The Journals of André Gide*, translated by J. O'Brien, 4 vols (London, Secker and Warburg, 1947), I. 218 Cf. also p. 215 (I. 186) and *The Notebooks of André Walter*, translated by W. Baskin (London, Peter Owen, 1968), pp. 52 and 112ff. Gide's use of the mirror here can be compared with that of other Symbolists. One is, of course, reminded of *Monsieur Teste* (' "I am being, and seeing myself: seeing myself see myself, and so on" ') and of *La Jeune Parque* ('And in my tender bonds suspended from my blood / I saw myself seeing myself, sinuous … '). However, one of Valéry's aphorisms better expresses the basis of Gide's narcissism – not mere indulgence, but rather the attempt to overcome the eccentric movement from self to self of a subject that is (already) called into question: 'A mirror in which you see yourself, which makes you want to talk to yourself – this evokes and explains the strange text: *Dixit Dominus Domino meo* . . . it gives it a meaning' (P. Valéry, *Œuvres* (Paris, Gallimard, Pléiade, 1960), vol. II, p. 541).

11. This imperfect tense is an extended echo of the present tense that opens the text, which everything leads us to understand as 'I can see myself writing': it changes the scene into the reflection – or, as Gide says, into a 'double mirror' –

which enables the subject to find himself: 'I had never since written at this table. These last few evenings I have been recapturing my childhood sensations' (*The Journals of André Gide*, I. 218). Gide's bliss here is iterative in essence, because only (self-)repetition can give the obsessive person a feeling of his/her own identity, and it reaches asymptotically the end of a series of reflections that tend to drain away what was irreducible about the present, making it merely a benevolent double of the past, or, better still, of the earlier past of *childhood*. On the subject of this scene as temporal reappropriation and repercussion, see A. Py's fine analysis in 'Les Jeux du temps, du bonheur et de l'ennui dans le *Journal* d'André Gide', in *Sur 'Les Faux-Monnayeurs'* (Paris, Minard, 1974), pp. 140ff.

12. The illustrative value of the *Notebooks* (1890) – not to mention the even more limited value of *Le Traité du Narcisse* (1891) – seems to be restricted in that it only fully emerges once we know the external details Gide gives us about them elsewhere. These two *Notebooks* constitute the posthumous journal of a young novelist engaged in writing (in a barely veiled way) about the passion he has experienced. Apart from the difficult genesis of work (excerpts from which we can read), they also relate the way in which Walter is reflected by his double who precedes him into madness and death. Unfortunately, what the structure of the work does not reveal is the relationship between Walter and the author. If we are to suppose that he is Gide's double, and that Allain is the double of this double, where then would be the 'retroaction'? The fact is that it cannot be found in the *Notebooks*, but rather in *If It Die . . . .* The retroaction consisted in the exorcism the writing of the novel represented for the potential Walter-Werther that was the young Gide (Cf. *If It Die . . .* , translated by D. BUSSY (London, Secker and Warburg, 1950), p. 201). One of Gide's 'confessions' allows us to go even further: the work was conceived of as a scientific experiment (with a working hypothesis, which was to be tested against the character of Walter, etc.), intended to demonstrate that the renunciation of love was harmful and to convince Gide himself and also Madeleine Rondeaux of this. The marriage of a writer as a retroaction of the suicide of one of his characters would be a rather moving example – all the more so in Gide's case – of the complex relationship between the activity of writing and the desire for the other.

13. In the terminology of Genette, who coined the latter word, by analogy with 'destinateur'/'destinataire' (sender/addressee), to denote the internal agent of reception in a narrative.

14. *La Tentative Amoureuse*, in *Le Retour de l'enfant prodigue précédé de cinq autres traités* (Paris, Gallimard, 1967), p. 44.

15. This retroaction in Gide is not unlike the use of the 'work within the work' by another Symbolist writer, RÉMY DE GOURMONT. In *Sixtine, Roman de la vie cérébrale* (1890), the primary narrative is interspersed with travel notes, poems and, in particular, a novel written by the protagonist (d'Entragues), chapters of which appear at irregular intervals. Besides making the book alternate between the two stories, the function of this inserted novel (*L'Adorant*) is to transpose the quintessential elements of the hero's experience of love (the hero becoming the narrator), and thus to make the various ways in which art and life interrelate into one of the themes of the book. At first, the infrequently occurring chapters of *L'Adorant* reflect an experience after the event, and limit themselves to sublimating it. But, as the narrative progresses, these 'satellite' chapters occur more frequently, and end up having a dialectical relationship with 'life' – since they go as far as anticipating it – and even safeguarding it. However, the

meaning is rather ambiguous: d'Entragues kills off his substitute *alter ego* before he has even learnt of his own failure in love; and then, when he does learn of it, he seems less inclined to delight in the autonomy of literature (as a good Symbolist should) than to regret having devoted himself to it, and having been rejected. If he continues writing, it is not without a certain amount of bad faith, since, in line with a recurrent theme in *fin de siècle* literature (Huysmans, Thomas Mann), it is because of an inability to live that one resigns oneself (not without regret for what instinct would dictate) to opting for the dictates of the ideal: a sort of semi-sublimation.

16.   The pun seems permissible because of the context of Gide's 'charter', which itself contains a pun, as I have suggested, on the two meanings of the word 'subject': 'the active subject is oneself; the retroactive thing is a subject one imagines'; 'the subject of the work itself'; 'the retroaction of the subject on itself'. . . .

17.   e.g. M. BUTOR, *Répertoire III* (Paris, Éditions de minuit, 1968), pp. 17ff.

18.   Cf. MORRISSETTE, 'Un Héritage d'André Gide', *passim*.

7   Vinio Rossi on The Keyhole Metaphor and the Parable*

Vinio Rossi's aim in the book from which this extract is taken, is to trace the evolution of the young Gide's artistic techniques from the spontaneous adherence to symbolism that characterized his first writing, to those features associated with his mature work. In so doing Rossi assesses the extraordinary creative energies released in the years 1893–5, during the trips to Africa and the winter sojourns in the Alps at Neuchâtel. At the same time he pursues the impact on Gide's imagination of contact with physical reality, and the efforts of an intuitive intelligence to assimilate this experience. The period on which Rossi focuses saw Gide escape from a form of theologically-inspired essentialism, in which the work of art captured and restored religious truths obscured by the flux of time and the imperfection of human existence, as in *Le Traité du Narcisse*. Here the object used as a symbol is the poetic expression of an ineffable reality beyond words. However, in *Paludes*, as Rossi demonstrates, Gide reformulates his aesthetic so that the particular detail makes no claim to transcendental values, merely offering an invitation to generalize. This is the basis on which Gide's fiction can aspire to engage with the real world. Such an approach determines the nature of characterization in the novel; but it also has implications for narrative structure, and in this respect Rossi shows how Gide tested out the narrative patterns of ancient myth and biblical parable in his search for an appropriate instrument for his purposes. We have already seen O'Brien discuss the cross-fertilization of these two sources (Chapter 1 above); Rossi demonstrates that the two sets of narratives also offer images that embody forms of human conduct on which he can base his own fictional characters. Furthermore, these archetypal tales present patterns of meaning which can either be self-sufficient or refer outwards to a state of affairs in the real world. The particular ways in which the work of art can allude to concrete situations and moral issues while sacrificing none of its internal coherence and autonomy greatly exercised

---

* First published in his *André Gide, the Evolution of an Aesthetic* (New Brunswick, New Jersey, Rutgers University Press, 1967), pp. 128–42.

112

Gide. The realism of the novel he envisaged would not be that of a mirror, but would be achieved by the inner consistency of its composition. He was helped on his way to this conceptualization, according to Rossi, by considering the qualities of the parable.

The artist, we recall from *Paludes,* must depict a particular subject with such skill that the general truth upon which it depends can be clearly comprehended. Gide's narrator goes on to clarify this thought by resorting to a metaphor:

> . . . You will certainly understand me better if you think of all the enormous landscape that appears through a keyhole the moment your eye comes close enough to the door. He who sees no more than the lock, could see the whole world if he only knew enough to stoop down. It suffices that the possibility of generalization exists; it is then up to the reader or the critic to make the generalization.[1]

This paragraph admirably synthesizes the theory and the aesthetic achievement of *Paludes.* The image of the keyhole as a metaphorical description of Gidian fiction contains the heart of the Neuchâtel discoveries.[2]

In order to facilitate generalization, Gide further simplified his initial idea and scenario for *Angèle ou le pauvre petit voyage.* He transformed menacing sensuality and the voyage to a neighbourhood park into immobility and the joys of vegetation. Gide's final metaphors then came naturally: the swamp, *Paludes'* central image, 'Tityre *recubans*' its idea, and Tityre recumbent in the swamp and increasingly enjoying it, its scenario.

But Gide's *Paludes* is much more than the Tityre story, more than his narrator's *Paludes* and *Polders* taken together. Unlike many of Gide's later works, *Paludes* absorbs the scenario into its own fabric by the technique Gide identified as 'en abyme'. Previously used in *Les Cahiers d'André Walter, Le Traité du Narcisse,* and *La Tentative Amoureuse,* and not again until *Les Faux-Monnayeurs,* this technique was formulated in the summer of 1893. He borrowed the term from heraldry, where it signifies placing a figure or a reproduction of the coat of arms itself at the centre of the field. In the *Journal,* he stated his predilection for this device as he saw it transposed in painting and literature:

> In a work of art I rather like rediscovering the subject itself transposed on the scale of its characters. Nothing better clarifies and more surely establishes the proportions of the whole.

The Tityre story functions in *Paludes* in a similar manner: like the small convex mirror in the paintings of Memling, it reflects 'in its turn the interior of the room in which the depicted scene is taking place'.[3] But it goes further, for it tends to deform the reader's view of his own world as well. If the central or, metaphorically, the 'keyhole', figure of the *sotie* is Tityre in his lair, and the title *Paludes* seems to support this view, Gide is the first to make generalizations of his subject by underlining its traits in the world of the narrator; in so doing he invites us to do the same.

Gide then creates the possibility of generalization by obliging his protagonist to see paludal traits in the world about him and finally by forcing him to see himself as victim of these very same traits. We need only follow Gide's example and seek out Tityre in our own midst. The critics of the time were not misled by this device. '*Paludes* touches upon what makes us suffer,'[4] said Camille Mauclair, and, in an undated letter written to Gide probably at the same time, he went further in his appreciation of the book:

> Finally, I like *Paludes* because one has the feeling that you are really fed up, that you need some air, and these past few days I have seen all my friends startled by that, and I, too, am fed up and they all bore me and I would like to get away. The whole book is exquisite and instructive, like an indecency.[5]

Had Gide chosen to restrict his work to the Tityre story alone, the reader would have been obliged to make the first step in the direction of generalization on his own. This first step is not a great one to ask of a reader, for only by discovering a hidden meaning could he explain the author's insistence upon so special a subject. Less timid in his later works, Gide dispensed with this first step entirely and concentrated his efforts upon the elaboration of his special subject. In *Le Prométhée mal enchaîné*, *Philoctète*, *Le Roi Candaule*, and *Saül*, Gide concerns himself only with the 'keyhole' figures. Yet, again, in the preface to *Le Roi Candaule*, he felt it necessary to reiterate his hopes and intentions as well as suggest possible generalizations for his play.

> Let no one see 'symbols' here, but simply an invitation to generalize. And let the choice of such a subject, of the exceptional character of Candaule, find its explanation and its excuse in this invitation.[6]

But generalization is encouraged not only by the particular functioning in a general context but also by some of its own special qualities. The particular in *Paludes* is, of course, Tityre happily reconciled to his swamp. But as a human being totally dominated by one single trait, by his idiosyncrasy, he is unreal and implausible; he lives and functions in a world alien to our own. Still, he is a human being, whose force lies in the strength of his idiosyncracy. This is precisely the state of affairs that the fictional author of *Paludes* described in his rebuttal of Evariste's objections; for generalization is forthcoming if the particular is painted with sufficient intensity. The justification of this intensity lies only in Tityre's being a pretext for generalization, and the reader's awareness of this fact prompts him to suspend his disbelief in Tityre's plausibility as a real human being.

Because of this intensity and implausibility, Tityre belongs to another realm, the artificial one of art and poetry: he has a classical pedigree, he is the product of another age and culture. The narrator, on the other hand, is a somewhat diluted version of Tityre; as such, he is more easily recognized than his prototype and functions in a more plausible context, the modern world. By juxtaposing these two figures, separable not only by their varying degrees of intensity but by their cultural backgrounds, Gide reinforces his invitation to generalize. The juxtaposition of Virgil's Tityrus, the narrator's unlikely but more modern society, and the world of the reader produces the shock of anachronism which elevates Tityre's idiosyncrasy beyond an ethnic or historical to a more general human level.

The temporal distance a work of art places between the figures it depicts and their audience was discussed by Racine in his preface to *Bajazet*. Here, in order to excuse his choice of a contemporary subject, Racine stated that spatial distance can substitute for temporal distance in order to obtain the same end: respect for the tragic hero, which is not normally forthcoming if he is viewed by the spectators in the same way they see their own contemporaries. In his lecture of 1904, entitled 'L'Evolution du théâtre'. Gide further analyses the nature of this 'respect' and the mechanism of 'dépaysement' which yields it.

> An artist's choice of figures distant from us arises from the fact that time – or whatever distance is in question – gives us an image already shorn of the episodic, the bizarre, the ephemeral; it conserves only the core of profound truth upon which art can work.[7]

The truth in question is, of course, the idea perceived by the artist and is the standard about which the work is composed. Gide here echoes the narrator's discussion with Angèle concerning the opposition between psychological and realistic truth.[8] Anachronism and 'dépaysement' free the artist from concern with realistic truth so as to portray forcefully psychological truth; they free the spectators, too, from the distraction of a familiar world, enabling them to concentrate upon the artist's particularization of a truth which they can then extend more easily to themselves.

Anachronism for the sake of prompting generalizations is a technique Gide used in many of the works that followed *Paludes*. The 'en abyme' device, which aids the juxtaposition of different historical and cultural periods, is by no means limited to this function nor is it the only device available to fulfil it. Gide temporarily gave up the use of this device in favour of more subtle means to accomplish the same end. In *Le Prométhée mal enchaîné*, the classical and modern worlds are fused: Prometheus and his classical partners play out their roles in a contemporary Paris. In other mythological works, modern expressions and vocabulary, references to contemporary events and ideas are employed. In still others, such as *Philoctète* and *Le Roi Candaule*, anachronism is not stated but implied, thus leaving the reader the responsibility of generalizing.

Virgil's Tityrus was thus a happy find for Gide, not only because he served, by means of his idiosyncrasy, as a pretext for generalization applicable to Gide and his period, but also because he opened for exploitation the figures of another culture, who by their presence in a twentieth-century work of art could elevate it to a more general, human plane. Gide was thus drawn to the classical myths because they facilitated comprehension of what he had to say in a manner in keeping with it. Fully conscious of their efficacy while writing *Paludes*, he conceived of two new mythical works in addition to *Les Nourritures Terrestres* and mentioned them in letters to Marcel Drouin and Pierre Louÿs.[9] *Philoctète* was published in 1899; fragments of *Proserpine* not until 1912. Most of Gide's mythical and classical works, moreover, were written in the years immediately following *Paludes*; only three date from the latter part of his life: *Oedipe* (1931), *Perséphone* (1934), which is a reworking of the earlier *Proserpine*, and *Thésée* (1946). His interest in classical mythology nevertheless remained constant throughout his life. Frequent allusions and references to the myths in his journals, letters, and articles, a long projected treatise on the subject, which yielded the fragment 'Considérations sur la mythologie grecque,'[10] bear testimony to his continual interest in, if not utilization of, the myths.

Gide's attachment to the legends seems to go beyond the aesthetic advantages outlined above. What more did they offer him? One might acknowledge that for Gide the Greek myths contained the wisdom of the ages in poetic garb. But it would be more accurate to say that Gide considered and treated them as fertile points of departure. He did not feel that the Greeks had exhausted the image of man in the myths they left us or that the myths represent those eternal truths which may legitimately exert a despotic control over us. They contain wisdom simply because their authors and audiences took into account the totality of *their* age.

Their wisdom, so highly prized by Gide, consisted of a profound understanding 'of harmony of the individual, of the customs, of the city.'[11] Whether their instinctive need for harmony gave rise to their tolerance of diversity or arose from it, Gide was loath to conjecture. Diversity, in any case, was prevalent and existed authentically and harmoniously.

The individual did not become banal by compulsion, but pushed himself to his limits out of virtue; each required from himself only himself and, without becoming deformed, attached himself to a god. Hence the great number of gods, as numerous as men's instincts. . . . For them religion did not erect atop a cross or upon the earth this bundle of virtues or that moral specter which one had to resemble under threat of being held impious. The typical man was not unique but legion; or rather, there was no typical man.

In conclusion to these remarks in 'L'Évolution du théâtre' Gide affirmed that 'paganism was, at the same time, the triumph of individualism and the conviction that man cannot make himself other than he is.'[12] With the triumph of the individual and the divinization of all the instincts, the Greeks left to posterity an image of harmony and serenity. It becomes clear that Gide's attachment to the Greek heritage was based on the example and authorization it provided for him to follow his instincts and maintain a balance and harmony among them. But, more important for Gide's work, the Greeks also left in their myths an extremely rich source of ready-made distillations of various human experiences. The myths opened for exploration a mine of images into which he could infuse his own understanding by reworking them to make them relevant to his own purpose. Moreover, because these images were already distillates they suited Gide's own psychological needs for self-analysis. 'I lived on the Bible and the Greek myths,' he said in an interview with Léon Pierre-Quint. 'In both cases you know that I do not try to interpret them but to deepen their meaning, as I have done in *L'Enfant prodigue*.'[13] Louis Martin-Chauffier made a similar statement in a preface to a later volume of Gide's *Oeuvres complètes*. Gide used the myths to supply 'the admirably "prepared" material they afford for commentaries or entirely personal interpretations': they thus lose their own value and become 'admirable *pretexts*'.[14]

The Greek myths, then, did not present themselves to Gide as secrets in poetic form but as the distillations of a particular society to which he brought his own experience and reason. What he said about the work of art applies to his attitude towards the myths as well.

> The accomplished work of art is miraculous in that it always offers us more meaning than its author imagined; it constantly permits a richer interpretation.[15]

The applicability of this statement to the myths themselves is suggested by the context in which it is found, 'Considérations sur la mythologie grecque.' In this fragment, Gide insists that the Greek fables are essentially rational. They cease to teach us anything if we do not apply our reason to them, if we augment the role of Fate in the events they depict. But if we interpret them as we would interpret a consciously conceived work of art, they take on untold significance. The point is that this added meaning is bred in the eye and mind of the beholder, who brings his whole psychological and cultural orientation to bear upon the understanding of the work of art, or myth, in question. Gide affirmed this point in a letter to François Mauriac:

> I maintain that the Holy Scriptures, like Greek mythology, have infinite and inexhaustible resources, and are destined to enrich themselves with each interpretation that a new spiritual orientation offers. It is in order to question them further that I do not limit myself to their first answer.[16]

But Gide not only questioned the myths, he frequently relied upon them to provide the central images of his books. The human figure as an incarnation of an attitude can define himself in reaction to his physical environment, as does Tityre in *Paludes*; but he can do as well in reaction to other figures. The need of place can thus be superseded and with it the 'paysage – état d'âme' formula. With Tityre, Gide discovered the efficacy of the human figure alone as image, or more precisely, as an incarnation of a human posture. In this respect, the myths offered a multitude of such figures, which Gide later used freely in exactly this manner. As suggested by the success of Tityre, the myths and their use represent a convenient way out of his image-making dilemma and a logical outcome of his long grappling with the problem of the image.

In addition to being a vast storehouse of ready-made images, the myths offered Gide four other major advantages. First, each one was a pure and concentrated idea or attitude untainted by the bizarre, episodic, or ephemeral. Secondly, they answered his own needs for analysis by providing a means to identify and extend in fiction various aspects of his own personality. Thirdly, they represented the world of the imagination and poetry. Like André Walter, Gide profited from the poetry created by others before him. Lastly, because the mythical figures are common property, they preclude the need for elementary characterization and development, permitting Gide to begin *in medias res*. These advantages favoured a basic aesthetic tenet of Gide's, litotes, which is, in essence, the device the novelist of *Paludes* described by the metaphor of the keyhole. This metaphor is particularly apt as a characterization of Gide's aesthetic because it contains two levels of significance: the keyhole represents itself as object and also what it contains upon closer scrutiny, what lies beyond it. An examination of these two levels will further clarify Gide's use of the myths as metaphoric images.

In reading and studying the myths, the gospels, or any work of art, Gide was constantly searching for the idea of the work. He was less concerned with the work of art as self-image than as likeness, in the sense given these terms by Rudolf Arnheim. A self-image, he says, is 'an object that visibly expresses its own properties. Its functions derive from the properties it reveals.' On the other hand, 'a liknesss . . . is an object treated as a statement about other objects, kinds of objects, or general properties, which are recognized in the object.'[17] Gide himself has admitted this concern, suggesting it in his lecture on influence,[18] demonstrating it in much of his literary criticism, and stating it in *Propositions*:

> the work of an artist interests me fully only if I feel it exists in direct and sincere relationship with the external world and, at the same time, in intimate and secret relationship with its author.[19]

Now, in literature, what Arnheim calls the self-image is a work of art that finds its end in itself, that means only what it says, utilizing the virtues of language and of its genre for the sole purpose of communicating itself. In this class one should place the novels of Robert Louis Stevenson, *The Arabian Nights*, much of lyrical poetry, and many songs; that is to say, tales and emotions told only for the joy obtained and given in their telling. Gide applies to this class the term 'sensuality.'[20] In the case of pure likeness, on the other hand, the art object is but a means for contemplating or considering something beyond itself, yet with which it has important elements in common. The object itself tends to fade in the eyes of the viewer in favour of the ideal object. 'The pure likeness, unrelated in space and time to its environment, requires a beholder who is able to cut his own ties in space and time.' But, 'the true work of art,' Arnheim continues further on, 'is more than a statement floating adrift.' More than a pure likeness, it is also a self-image.

> It occupies, in the world of action, a place suitable to the exercise of its powers. It cannot be alone. Primitively it performs only as a thing among other things. At its most human, it rules as an embodied statement over a world in which every tool, every flower, and every rock also speaks as itself and through itself.[21]

The true work of art, then, blends to perfection both of these elements, self-image and likeness; it is a statement about the world, but inasmuch as this statement is embodied, what Gide would call 'composed' or 'organized' it is an object in a world of objects. The true work of art is an image of itself in time and space while at the same time it is an image alluding to something delivered of its spatial and temporal moorings, what Gide refers to as the idea. The art-object as self-image also clearly embodying an invitation to be considered as likeness, that is, as an invitation for generalization, was Gide's aesthetic ideal and his most frequently realized aesthetic tendency. It was during the composition of *Paludes* that he discovered it and during the years following that he formulated it, giving it full expression in *Littérature et morale*.

Thus, Albert Thibaudet refers to Gide as a 'myth-maker' and Germaine Brée notices that 'the essence of the Gidian novel . . . is its mythical character'.[22] We accept the understanding of the word 'myth' suggested by Thibaudet:

> Myth, introduced into art by Plato . . . is an idea carried by a narrative: an idea which is a soul, a narrative which is a body, and both of them are inseparable.[23]

But not all Gidian critics are of one mind in this matter. Jean-Michel Hennebert bluntly states,

> Gide never had the Greek sense of myth . . . but the Christian sense of parable. If his work on Greek mythology was never written, it is because the Greek fable is not essentially rational.[24]

The apparent contradiction between the two points of view as stated can be reduced to a problem of terminology. There is no doubt that Hennebert would use the term 'parable' to fit the definition of 'myth' offered by Thibaudet. It is interesting to note, in Hennebert's favour, that Plato's myths, which Thibaudet considers the first in literature, have been considered by others, including scholars of biblical exegesis, precisely as parable.

> The 'Myths of Plato' are not myths in the strict sense of the word but are rather the parables and allegories of an acute and extraordinarily developed intellect.[25]

The two terms are close enough in meaning to cause confusion and to merit closer examination. 'Myth' or 'mythos' meant originally, in the critical jargon of Aristotle, 'fable,' 'narrative', or 'plot'. It is easy to see how the legends received this appellation, since tragedy freely drew its plots from them. The legends originate in three basic needs of pre-scientific man, according to C. M. Bowra: 'to make sense of some ritual whose significance has been forgotten, if indeed it has ever been fully understood'; 'to explain natural phenomena through some dramatic, cosmological tale'; and, finally, 'not to explain, but to delight.'[26] Thus, the basic need that the myths satisfied was the establishment of a well-ordered universe, or, at best, well-ordered and comprehensible in terms of the real experience of the mytho-poets. Fantasy filled in where fact was lacking. Parable, on the other hand, is concerned to offer a more plausible explanation of things.[27] The parable is essentially rational. The work of one or several minds, it is a finished literary product; myth, a collective endeavour, is raw material.

'Parables employ fiction, but they do it knowingly, holding it apart, in order to teach fact.'[28]

Both myth and parable are particularizations of perceived or vaguely intuited abstractions. That is, both are stories, or narrative images, that function on two levels. But only for the parable was this double level a principle of composition. The parables illustrate spiritual truths in terms that were familiar to their intended listeners. As illustrations, they are plausible and realistic, thus supporting the 'conviction that there is no mere analogy, but an inward affinity, between the natural order and the spiritual order'. Since the parable brings its narrative into the home grounds of its audience, its realism serves to underline its problematic and argumentative nature. 'The parable has the character of an argument, in that it entices the hearer to a judgment upon the situation depicted, and then challenges him, directly or by implication.'[29]

This is precisely what the narrator, and Gide himself, try to do in *Paludes*; it is what characterizes so much of Gide's fiction. Many years later, in 1927, he articulated this very quality of his work:

> it is not so much by offering solutions to certain problems that I can render a real service to the reader, but rather by forcing him to reflect upon those problems to which I hardly admit that he can have any other than a personal and particular solution.[30]

To say, then, that his novels are mythical in tendency would be less accurate than to affirm their parabolical nature. For although he sins against a basic tenet of the parable by dispensing with realism, he does not try to approximate truth with fictions, as do the myths; rather, he tries to create the 'temptation' of a truth, that is, of an intuited idea concerning man and his condition. He becomes the articulate consciousness of this idea by creating the form by which it can be apprehended by his and future generations; moreover, he argues its plausibility by means of the parable.[31]

One might be further inclined to give credence to Hennebert's opinion for another essential reason: Gide's rigorous Protestant upbringing. Despite his own avowals,[32] his contact with the Greek world could not have been so profound as to undo the deep impression made upon him by the New Testament. His Protestant education coloured not only his way of seeing reality but his way of seeing literature as well. Extremely sensitive and intelligent, he inevitably applied the rigours of biblical exegesis to all he read.

[. . .] Just as Gide sought and found wisdom in the words and parables of Christ, because he believed they were the utterances of an inspired man, so, too, he sought and found wisdom in the Greek myths because he believed they were the products of a rational people. The myths were not, of course, the deliberate productions of a rational culture; they can be considered at best, if we follow Jung, as the significant workings of a collective subconscious rising up from the irrational depths of the human mind. Thus, when Gide considered the Greek myths in his essay of 1919 and postulated that they were 'raisonnables', he was treating them, however inadvertently, as parables. And in reconstructing them, choosing from their numerous and frequently contradictory details only those pertinent to his idea, he recast them in parabolical form.

Paludes, the first summit in Gide's literary career, expresses and implies with most consummate artistry the Gidian aesthetic and the form most of his fictional works take. This form is the parable, the natural and logical outcome of his long groping with the problem of that expressive aesthetic unit, the image.

Notes

1. *Paludes, OC, I*, 412.

2. [During his convalescence in Neuchâtel in the winter of 1894–5, Gide experienced a period of intense creativity that prepared the ground for much of his subsequent work.]

3. *JI*, 41.

4. CAMILLE MAUCLAIR, 'Paludes,' *Mercure de France*, XV (July, 1895), 102f.

5. From an unpublished letter in the Bibliothèque Littéraire JACQUES DOUCET, quoted in part in MICHEL DÉCAUDIN, *La Crise des valeurs symbolistes, vingt ans de poésie française, 1895–1914* (Toulouse: Privat, 1960), p. 52.

6. Preface to *Le Roi Candaule, OC, III*, 295.

7. 'L'Evolution du théâtre,' *OC, IV*, 205.

8. See *Paludes, OC*, I, 376.

9. 'Lettre à Marcel Drouin' (Fall, 1894), quoted in DAVET, *Autour des 'Nourritures terrestres,'* pp. 55f., and 'Lettre à Pierre Louÿs' (19 October, 1894), quoted in DELAY, II, 389.

10. 'Considérations sur la mythologie grecque,' *OC, IX*, 147ff. First published in March, 1919.

11. *JI*, 996. Entry dated July 8, 1930.

12. 'L'Evolution du théâtre,' *OC, IV*, 211, 214.

13. In LÉON PIERRE-QUINT, *André Gide* (Paris: Stock, 1952), p. 391. The interview is dated December, 1927.

14. LOUIS MARTIN-CHAUFFIER, "Notices," *OC, XIII*, xf.

15. 'Considérations sur la mythologie grecque,' *OC, IX*, 150.

16. 'Lettre d'André Gide à François Mauriac,' *La Table Ronde*, no. 61 (January, 1953), p. 93. The date of this letter is July 1, 1922.

17. RUDOLF ARNHEIM, 'The Robin and the Saint: on the twofold nature of the artistic image,' *The Journal of Aesthetics and Art Criticism, XVIII* (September, 1959), 74ff. In this article Arnheim analyses the semantic properties of the image, reducing them, in the ideal work, to these two mutually dependent elements: self-image and likeness.

18. 'De l'influence en littérature,' *OC, III*, 269: 'The true artist seeks the man behind the work, and it is from him that he learns.'

19. *Propositions, OC, VI*, 353f.

20. See 'Lettres à Angèle,' *OC, III*, 220.

21. Arnheim, 'The Robin and the Saint,' pp. 78f.

22. ALBERT THIBAUDET, *Histoire de la littérature française de 1789 à nos jours* (Paris: Stock, 1936), p. 445. BRÉE, *André Gide, l'insaisissable Protée*, p. 362.

23. Thibaudet, *Histoire*, p. 139.

24. JEAN-MICHEL HENNEBERT,''Du *Prométhée* à l'art d'André Gide,' *Prétexte*, no. 1 (February 15, 1952), p. 71.

25. GEORGE A. BUTTRICK, *The Parables of Jesus* (New York: Harper, 1928), p. xv. Consider also HARRY LEVIN's observation: 'Plato's myths are notable examples of argument reverting to parable,' in 'Some Meanings of Myth,' *Myth and Myth-Making*, ed. Henry A. Murray (New York: George Braziller, 1960), p. 105.

26. C. M. BOWRA, *The Greek Experience* (New York: World, 1959), pp. 115, 117f.

27. See ibid., p. 115.

28. Buttrick, *The Parables of Jesus*, p. xv.

29. CHARLES HAROLD DODD, *The Parables of the Kingdom*, revised edn. (New York: Scribner, 1961), pp. 10f.

30. *Journal des Faux-Monnayeurs, OC, XIII*, 15. In a letter to Marcel Drouin dated May 10, 1894, Gide says that the writer's conclusions must be questions addressed to the reader, that the writer must corner his reader and force him to answer. In Davet, *Autour des 'Nourritures terrestres,'* pp. 66f.

31. These remarks suggest another trait Gide's parables have in common with their biblical predecessors. The aim of both is to teach. Gide's 'côté didactique' can be discovered in all of his works, even in the *soties* where it is disguised by farce. For a long discussion of Gide's didacticism, see MAX MARCHAND, *Le Complexe pédagogique et didactique d'André Gide* (Oran: Fouque, 1954).

32. Cf. *Si le Grain ne meurt, I, II*, 497, and I, 859.

8   Albert Guérard on *L'Immoraliste**

Guérard was among the first to consider Gide's fiction from the point of view of its latent psychological content and the way in which it dealt with the author's homosexual inspiration. His reading of *Le Voyage d'Urien* (1893) is notable for the attention it draws to the psychoanalytical phantasms made manifest in the text's descriptive imagery; in *L'Immoraliste* he is concerned to highlight the combination of the autobiographical and the unconscious in a novel which aims to be overtly realistic. Guérard points out, however, that Michel, the narrator-protagonist, is only autobiographical insofar as, in accordance with Gide's theory of imaginative catharsis set out in a celebrated letter to Scheffer, the character is merely a virtual self Gide was not prepared to live out in reality and which he is at pains to dissociate himself from.

Critics who exclusively emphasized the book's moral point were misguided, according to Guérard. The story of a man who seeks to throw off the inhibiting shackles of civilization in an attempt to turn himself into a superman, rising beyond good and evil as Nietzsche had proclaimed, is little more than window-dressing behind which is played out a drama of repressed homosexuality. The hero is a man who cannot acknowledge the nature of his unconscious desires, and who is driven to various pseudo-ritual actions and patterns of behaviour which afford displaced forms of gratification. What prevents the novel from becoming the banal enactment of a sub-Freudian scenario, however, is the contribution made to the story by Michel's flawed intelligence and will. And when due allowance has been made for these factors, the problematic of culture versus anarchy remains unresolved, transcending its particular manifestation in this one individual.

The other source of the novel's richness is the part played in its narration by the protagonist's own deluded perception of events. The imperceptive

---

*First published in his *André Gide* (Cambridge, Mass., Harvard University Press, 1951) pp. 99–119.

narrator, though incapable of lucid self-analysis, nevertheless provides the reader with material that reveals what he himself cannot or will not see. Thus the casual detail in his account of the story can be seen to be charged with the unconscious obsession that drives him. In this way Gide finds a form of realism that extends to the depiction of the unconscious, and establishes the technique he will use in his subsequent first-person ironic narratives.

Gide wrote to Guérard that he was surprised by the critic's assessment of *L'Immoraliste* as his greatest achievement, but that there was some justification in his indicating that the novel was a latent precursor of Freudianism.

L'Immoraliste, finished in 1901, is the first, the most autobiographical, and the best of Gide's *récits*. Certainly it is the most frequently misunderstood of his novels, partly because its deceptive simplicity of surface invites casual and very literal reading. Like the unread *Voyage d'Urien*, the misread *Immoraliste* demands a fuller analysis than books as well or better known. Historically, it is an important moment in the development of the French psychological novel – which threatened to become, in the hands of Bourget, a lucid pondering of abstract problems and a vehicle for transparent instruction. *L'Immoraliste* brought to the French novel all the seriousness and much of the complexity of Dostoevsky's short novels – and did so first of all through its successful use of the 'imperceptive' or self-deluded narrator as subject of the story he tells. *L'Immoraliste* is not, to be sure, *The Possessed*, or even *Crime and Punishment*. But it exists as a touchstone for shorter and less ambitious fiction. It helps us to define a level of achievement which autobiographical and subjective fiction can rarely hope to surpass: fiction which concentrates on one man's destiny (a shadow of the author's own) and which offers no comprehensive understanding of society. Michel's revolt reflects his age (the age of Nietzschean hopes and destructions) but reflects even more the timeless conflict of the unconscious life and the conscious. Already the psychological realism of *L'Immoraliste* seems more important than its critique of individualism; its anticipation of Freud more valid than its oblique reflection of Nietzsche. Its more personal triumph lies in the successful avoidance of lyricism, of confused or angry self-justification, of special pleading – of all the evasions, in fact, to which autobiographical fiction is tempted. The precarious balance of the author's sympathy and detachment remains to the end under minute control.

Gide readily admitted the part which symbolic action played. He told Francis Jammes he had spent four years on the book, not writing but living it. He had struggled through the novel as through a disease, in order 'to go beyond.'[1] In a letter to Scheffer he reduces such symbolic action to an aesthetic principle:

That a germ of Michel exists in me goes without saying . . . How many germs we carry in us, which will burgeon only in our books! They are what the botanists call 'sleeping eyes.' But if, by an act of will, you suppress them, *all but one* – how it springs up at once and grows! How it seizes at once upon the sap! My recipe for creating a hero is simple enough. Take one of these germs, put it in the pot by itself – and you soon obtain an admirable individual. Advice: choose preferably (if it's true one can choose) the germ that most disturbs you. By doing so you rid yourself of it at once. Perhaps that is what Aristotle meant by the purgation of the passions. Purge ourselves, Scheffer, purge ourselves! There will always be passions enough.[2]

However, the process was not as simple as this letter implies. A fragment on Ménalque preceded *Les Nourritures Terrestres*, and in the completed book only Ménalque has a personal history of any significance. Was Gide long determined to fix the lesson and personality of Oscar Wilde for posterity, or did he imagine once again a fictional blend of Wilde and himself? *L'Immoraliste*, in any event, appears to have been planned as a 'life of Ménalque', to be told from the outside.[3] But Gide could not, in 1897 or later, tell a detailed story of subjective torment except in the first person and from the inside. For this or for some other reason a separation occurred. The Ménalque of *L'Immoraliste* is no longer a blend of Wilde and Gide, but a walking manual of hedonism who recalls only too obviously the recorded personality and recorded epigrams of Wilde. He is as sprightly and as unreal as the Protos of *Les Caves du Vatican*, and is therefore out of place in a sombre realistic novel. But Michel, transposed to a plane and life of tragic failure, is a potential or suppressed self, a refashioned image of the young André Gide.

There are differences, such differences as made the writing of *L'Immoraliste* possible. The fictional Michel is a latent and frustrated homosexual even after his marriage with Marceline, and is paralyzed by the freedom he has won. The freedom is of course incomplete, since to the very end he does not satisfy his pederast inclinations. Otherwise, the resemblances between the hero and his creator are striking and too obvious to insist on: the double oppression of childhood Huguenot teachings and an isolated bookish adolescence; an ill-advised marriage and the first fascinated observation of the children in Biskra; tuberculosis, convalescence, and the fierce egoism which accompanies it. Later, the dual impulses to concentration and dissolution of the self; the sense of estrangement on returning to the artificial Paris salons; the crucial meeting with a notorious hedonist. And at last the reckless unrest of the journeys to Switzerland and Italy, in roundabout obedience to the ineluctable pull of North Africa, where the last discoveries must be made. Gide thus 'used' extensively his first two trips to North Africa and their surrounding moral complication, though the poachers of the second part derive from much older memories.[4]

Not everything was so retrospective, however. Gide also used certain more recent events: memories of ice-skating in St Moritz on his honeymoon, of his wife's illnesses in Switzerland and North Africa in 1897 and 1898, of her carriage accident in 1900.[5] A brief 1897 letter to Jammes from Switzerland – mentioning both his wife's illness and Athman – reminds us of the very dilemma which Michel could not define.[6] Weighed against such living forces and memories, the influence of Nietzsche on the novel scarcely seems worth mentioning. This other 'source' was in any event negative. The translation of Nietzsche's books into French freed Gide from the obligation to theorize on individualism at length. We can only regret that he did not feel free to dispense with Ménalque as well. But this is perhaps the hardest thing for any novelist to do: to cut away all traces of what he had once (and wrongly) supposed to be his real subject.

In personal terms, *L'Immoraliste* was a symbolic act of dissociation from Michel. Had Gide not discovered himself so fully, he too might have been driven to such a harsh and aimless individualism. This is the book's 'personal' subject. *L'Immoraliste* is also, of course, a critique (not rejection) of Nietzschean individualism. But most of all it is a study of latent homosexuality, of repression and compensation, of the effect preconscious energies may have on a man's acts, feelings, and ideas. It is no wonder, since the book was all these things, that it was little read and little understood at first. A very few early readers – and readers as different as Madame Rachilde and Francis Jammes – saw that the conflict was a sexual one. Yet a large majority of the book's critics (including some very recent ones) have considered *L'Immoraliste* to be a novel 'about individualism' and have not seen Michel's homosexuality at all. Some, to be sure, may have simply refused to acknowledge what they saw. Thus Charles du Bos candidly admits that he could not take up 'le problème Wilde' with the particular audience of his early lecture on the book.[7] Unlike French biography, French criticism has long resisted the influence of psychology and has also remained curiously discreet.

There is the further fact that Michel's revolt against repression and conformity may be transferred to any plane of experience, and so may invite the sympathy of a critic differently repressed. But the strongest obstacle to understanding has probably been the inveterate tendency of critics to take a narrative told in the first person at its face value and to confuse the narrator's consciousness with the author's. It is nevertheless hard to understand why so few critics (including those who return constantly to 'intention') have referred to Gide's statement that Michel was an unconscious homosexual.[8][. . .]

L'Immoraliste is one of the first modern novels to deal at all seriously with homosexuality. But it is most important to keep in mind that Michel never participates in a homosexual act. The reader who assumes that such acts occur but are not mentioned, for reasons of discretion, is likely to misinterpret everything else. One can imagine Gide's exasperation when Paul Bourget asked him, as late as 1915 (and as soon as Edith Wharton had left the room) whether Michel was a 'practicing pederast'.[9] Through many pages of a first reading we have every right to share Michel's bewilderment. We explore him with the same curiosity that he explored himself. And how much would be lost if the last revealing lines of the novel were its first ones! But on second and subsequent readings the ambiguities should dissolve. Not till then, perhaps, does the reader notice that Michel possessed Marceline only after fighting with the drunken coachman; that he felt 'obliged' (in an hour of frustration) to caress a strangely textured shrub; that his period of tranquillity at La Morinière ends abruptly with the coming of the boy Charles; that he longs to sleep in the barn because the boy Alcide sleeps there; that, in fact, he never proceeds beyond the stage of longing for these boys. The important fact about Michel is not that he is a homosexual, but that he is a latent homosexual, a homosexual without knowing it.

Thus *l'Immoraliste* is not a case study of a particular and manifest neurosis, but a story of unconscious repression. In the light of this, but only in this light, various unexplained ritual acts take on meaning: the shaving of the beard, or the ceremonial undressing, sun-bathing, and immersion in the pool near Ravello. The vengeance of what has been suppressed touches every fibre of Michel's intellectual and moral life; determines his self-destructiveness and his anti-intellectualism alike. Restrained from sexual satisfaction and even from self-discovery by an unconscious force, Michel rebels in other ways. The outburst may be sudden and specific, as when he leaps into the draining lake and takes a savage excitement in catching eels with Charles. More generally, Michel rebels against his early intellectual training in his philosophical defence of barbarism; against his inherited Norman prudence in trying to destroy the harmony and order of his farm. *L'Immoraliste* dramatizes as clearly as Dostoevsky's *Gambler* the compulsion to risk – and lose. Payment must eventually be made to the internalized parental authority. But the first impulse is to destroy not appease this superego. The harshness of Michel's individualism – and this, in general terms, is no less than the 'subject' of the novel – is determined by the harshness of the repression.

The hidden victim of this hidden restraint reveals itself in a curious hostility toward the convention-bound and in an abnormal sympathy for the free. Michel's acts seemed to many early readers (and even at times to himself) unmotivated and 'Satanic'. [. . .] *L'Immoraliste* dramatizes unconscious or half-conscious identification. The lawless buried self is attracted to all whom the superego and the waking conscience deem guilty, and repelled by all the well-behaved. Even when he is most determined to lead a regulated life, Michel's affections go out to the immoral, the corrupt, the unrestrained. He has a 'horror of honest folk', but is paralyzed by 'joy' when he sees Moktir steal the scissors, when he learns that Alcide is a poacher – or when he uncovers, in the lifeless pages of his research, the youthful savagery of Athalaric. He envies Pierre's drunken brutality as he envies Ménalque's refined selfishness. The movement toward discovery is not, to be sure, uninterrupted. The alternating and sometimes simultaneous impulses to concentrate and to destroy the ego – to use Baudelaire's terminology rather than Freud's – increase or weaken according to the self at the moment dominant and the self at the moment suppressed. The frustrated Huguenot as well as the frustrated homosexual may demand satisfaction. In the final chapters, however, the inward aggressions become frenzied as the 'authentic self' nears the surface.

Not all of Michel's feelings may be so simply explained. Does he resent the dying Marceline because he fears a return of his own tuberculosis, or because he has equated weakness and virtue, or simply because he longs to be rid of her? One strength of *L'Immoraliste* lies in its awareness of the close interdependence of Michel's health, his degree of sexual adjustment, his moral heritage, and his intellectual interests. The novel's over-all 'meaning' is reducible to the barest Freudian terms, but Michel as a character is not. His intelligence and will, however weak, do play some part. His tenderness toward Marceline develops into love at the same time as his cruelty toward her – and at the same time as his homosexual impulses. And if his ideas are determined by unconscious needs, his arguments still demand attention. The problem of individualism, though provoked in this instance by a specific sexual situation, nevertheless transcends neurosis.

For Gide knew that the problem of the emancipated individualist goes on, even after sexual adjustments have been made. Must one choose between a refusal to live and an individualism which makes others suffer? Marceline justly observes that Michel's doctrine may be a 'fine one,' but that it threatens to suppress the weak. And can the individualist cut himself off to be free, yet live in that rarefied air? 'To know how to free oneself is nothing; the arduous thing is to know what to do with one's freedom.' It is here, in its critique of Nietzschean individualism, that *L'Immoraliste* is necessarily imperfect – and first of all because Michel is an imperfect Nietzschean. Gide agreed with Michel and Nietzsche that the world is divided into the strong and the weak, and many of Michel's arguments are transcribed from *Les Nourritures Terrestres*. But Michel was incapable of the solution Gide elsewhere proposed: to become fully conscious of the inner dialogue between order and anarchy, and to suppress by an act of will whichever voice threatens to become too strong. The very fact that makes Michel so interesting dramatically and psychologically – his imperfect understanding of himself – makes him a poor vehicle for Gidean and Nietzschean ideas. His story could not answer the question raised in the Prologue: how is society to use the energies of the free man? 'I fear the failures of individualism,' Gide wrote in 1898.* Michel is such a failure; he is not a free man.

Thus the aspect of *L'Immoraliste* most emphasized by critics is in fact unsatisfactory. The novel's strength lies rather in its art and psychological understanding, and in its controlled transposition of personal experience. For it is a 'fruit filled with bitter ashes'[10], a novel written severely from memory, but also out of mind and nerve. The triumph of intelligence reveals itself in the close pressure of form. Not a single irrelevant memory has survived this pressure, other than the memory of Wilde's epigrams. This required a conscious separation of the author's consciousness from Michel's, and a careful use of the 'imperceptive' narrator as a technical device [. . .] It remains one of the few ways of saving psychological fiction from pedagogical abstractness, and perhaps the best way to convey (rather than 'explain') a conflict between conscious and unconscious energies. The problem for the novelist is to keep his narrator self-deluded, imperceptive, blind; incapable of accurate self-analysis – yet have that narrator supply all the evidence necessary to the reader's understanding. He must say enough to convey his daily suffering and betray his true difficulties, but not say too much more.

Critics have more and more come to realize that a novelist's 'technique' has some intimate relationship with his understanding of his characters, as well as a more obvious bearing on the mobility, energy, and persuasiveness of his books. But it is nearly impossible to demonstrate these relationships specifically, and even discussions of 'point of view' are often disappointingly vague. The device of the obtuse narrator or observer is, however, a particular and definable one, and Gide's major success in using it deserves close analysis. [. . .]

L'Immoraliste [. . .] offers the structural firmness and inward connections of a fully dramatized psychic situation. Most obvious are the falling then rising line of Michel's health, as Marceline's line rises and declines; the balance of the two visits to La Morinière as Michel preserves then destroys his estate, and the vast circular movement from Biskra back to Biskra. Even these unities (if we accept the common view that

---

*For Gide's intellectual conclusions at this time, we must look to the 'Lettres à Angèle' (*OC*, III, 222–41). In 1898 Gide failed to distinguish clearly between the final affirmation of Nietzsche and the final renunciation of Dostoevsky, and brought them too close together by verbal legerdemain. If the individualist's energies are stifled, they may break out in some violent antisocial way. A universally accepted individualism, on the other hand, would ruin both the strong and the weak. The true 'exceptional' man would be lost in the crowd of 'meaningless eccentrics'. There is no rule of thumb, Gide observes, by which we may distinguish the successes from the failures, the Nietzsches from the Stirners. We would therefore repudiate 'individualism', out of respect for the individualist. Gide argued in much the same terms during his communist period.

tuberculosis is often a neurotic illness) seem psychologically necessary.
More specifically, each step in Michel's journey looks forward to some
future step: the fight with the drunken coachman near Positano to the
kissing of the coachmen in Taormina; the gardens of Biskra to the gardens
of Ravello; the daylight rides with Charles to the nighttime poaching with
Alcide. Yet these anticipations are never fortuitous, as the gondolier's
anticipation of the entertainer is fortuitous. The changed Michel is
compelled to return to the same places and experiences, if only to discover
how he has changed.

Still more challenging, to the student of realism, is the fact that nearly
everything Michel says and nearly everything he sees has a direct bearing
on his sexual problem. He keeps Moktir's theft secret not merely because
he sees in it an acting-out of his own longing to rebel against accepted
decencies, but because he here enters into a first clandestine relationship
with a child. A large psychological situation is thus perfectly dramatized in
the action or inaction of a moment; the 'gratuitous act' of sympathetic
identification is in no sense gratuitous. Yet Michel's prolonged compulsive
need to spend all his money is, to the reader of Menninger and Freud, fully
as convincing.[11] The novel offers very little 'neutral' or innocent imagery.
Lassif's canals and Lachmi's gourd for collecting the sap from palm trees
are images as primary, for this latent homosexual, as the eels he caught
with Charles; clay and shrub alike have a fleshy texture. How could Gide,
using so much significant imagery, yet contrive to give an impression of
real life, of unselected experience? [. . .] One answer is that Gide's
significant images also serve as casual images – *and so serve because never
explained*. No single image or experience, but the cumulative effect of them
all, drives us very slowly to an awareness of Michel's trouble. Everything
in Michel's story leads to his revelation in the last line, yet no particular
page seems to lead there in an obvious way. The minutiae of style and
technique thus disguise an economy as extreme as any in modern fiction.
Could Gide achieve a latent homosexual's vision of experience so exactly
and so economically only because he had been, himself, a latent
homosexual? To ask this is to take a very naïve view of the art of fiction –
and to forget the imperfections of certain earlier books. In *L'Immoraliste* he
reduced a most confused personal experience to an order which even the
best-adjusted writers rarely achieve.

It is hardly the intention of this book to defend realism as such, and the
anti-realism of *Les Faux-Monnayeurs* may have done more for the modern
novel. But *L'Immoraliste* is a great realistic novel, and perhaps the best novel
Gide would write. It [. . .] shows us, at the outset, the characteristic tactics
and strategy of Gide's other *récits*. Beyond this it proves that even the
realistic and subjective psychological novel may be economical. The
neurotic experience of a Michel can be more than neurotic experience; it can
reflect a universal conflict.

Notes

1. Undated letter to F.J., *OC, III*, 562.

2. Undated letter to Scheffer, *OC, IV*, 616–17.

3. Letter to Jammes of July 1897, Francis Jammes et André Gide, *Correspondance 1893–1938* (Paris, 1948), pp. 117, 330.

4. 'Jeunesse', *OC, XV*, 83.

5. See JEAN SCHLUMBERGER, *Eveils*, p. 144; Jammes et Gide, *Correspondance*, pp. 109–10, 144, 158.

6. Jammes et Gide, *Correspondance*, pp. 109–10.

7. DU BOS, *Le Dialogue avec André Gide* (Paris, 1947), p. 218.

8. *Journal*, 26 November, 1915.

9. Ibid.

10. Gide's Preface to *L'Immoraliste*.

11. [See DAVID STEEL's essay on prodigality in the present volume.]

9   Emily Apter, on *L'Immoraliste*: Slips of the Text*

Apter's approach is inspired by a comment of **Roland Barthes** to the effect that Gide's work had been unduly neglected. The implication is not that Gide had been overlooked by critics in general, but that a certain kind of criticism had not engaged with his writing.

This criticism, of which Barthes' writing is a leading example, is inspired by the theories of structural linguistics and the renewal of psychoanalysis which came in their wake, specifically in the writings of Jacques Lacan. Lacan argued that the unconscious is structured like language and that the signifier, or concrete manifestation of language (the sound, or signs of the word on the page) provides a vehicle through which unconscious desire pursues an ever-deferred fulfilment, just as language gestures towards a meaning which remains forever unattainable.

The 'postmodernist Gide' whom Apter aims to present is also coloured by the concerns of feminist criticism. In a patriarchal world, language is subject to masculine sensibilities and tends to suppress the female voice. This gendering of language means that misogyny is inscribed within literary texts, and Apter is concerned to show this 'homotextuality' working through Gide's writing. His case is particularly interesting because of his homosexuality, which, marginalizing him and thus placing him alongside women in our society, might make him a better spokesman for feminism, for a 'gynotextual' sensibility, than a heterosexual male author. Such is the prospect seemingly held out by his ceding territory to a female narrator in *La Porte Étroite* and *L'Ecole des femmes*. Apter's reading of *L'Immoraliste*, highlighting the 'Freudian slips' that betray a misogynistic drive in Michel's narration, effectively challenges this hypothesis.

*Originally published in her *André Gide and the codes of Homotextuality* (Saratoga, Anma Libri, Stanford French and Italian Studies, 1987), pp. 110–24.

An incompletely formulated yet nonetheless coherent definition of the slip or lapsus can be discovered *in nuce* within Gide's oeuvre, not in relation to his *récits* (where we intend to resituate it), but in the context of his critical remarks on the nature of myth and his efforts to transpose classical myths into the idiom of modern theatre. As Walter Benjamin noted in his review of Gide's *Oedipe* (staged in 1930), this was a theatre of language – of excessive 'bavardage' in which arche typal heroes (Oedipus, Saul, Theseus) were allowed to define themselves as *myths* in an outburst of anger, a flash of tenderness, or a slip of the tongue. Benjamin emphasized in his essay entitled 'Oedipe ou le mythe raisonnable,' that unlike the Sophoclean Oedipus who remains a mute pawn of Fate, Gide's Oedipe dares to speak out, to interpret his destiny subjectively. During the second act of the play, he angrily refuses Tiresias' orthodox recourse to the God's will as a means of explaining the origin of his personal and political tribulations: 'What should I go looking to God for? Answers. I felt I was myself an answer to I knew not what question'.[1] The fact that Gide's Oedipe is allowed to 'answer back' to the supercilious prophet is, according to Benjamin, a long overdue settling of accounts:

> Sophocle's drama has five acts; it is at the end of the second that the seer Tiresias leaves the stage. Oedipus will have had to wait two millennia to engage him, in Gide's play, in the great debate during which he expresses what, in Sophocles' play, he would not even have dared to think.[2]

As wilful author of both question and answer, this Oedipus reserves the right to define his own fate even when this necessitates the recognition of his own inner 'monstrosity': 'I have been asleep for twenty years, lulled by my reward. But now at last I listen to the new monster that is stirring within me. A great destiny awaits me, lurking in the shadows of evening. Oedipus, the time for calm is past. Rouse yourself from your happiness.'[3] Oedipe's premonition of his future monstrosity (as a myth) gives him the right to both define the crime and determine the nature of his punishment. No longer is his guilt the result of parricide and incest; it resides instead in the realization that his twenty years of 'bonheur' were purchased through ignorance of the power-hungry motives of his family. He chooses to blind himself not because he aims to do penance for crimes that were accidents of fate, but because he can no longer endure contemplating the ignominious scheming of Etéocle, Polynice, Créon, Ismène and Antigone.

In his reading of Oedipus, Gide seems intent on travelling beyond Freud. Where Freud stops at a psychological allegory of mother-loving and father-killing (the inherent drama of which is heightened by theatrical representation), Gide gravitates towards the more prosaic moment of the subject's verbal cure – often brought on by a slip of the tongue. In *Thésée*,

Gide's final *récit* (1946), it is the 'bêtise' lodged in pure 'bavardage' that dismantles the protective facade of repression. Here, in the course of his uncontrollable chatter to himself, Theseus stumbles unwittingly on the explanation for his 'forgetting' of the black sails (thereby provoking his father's suicide):

> I regret that I caused his death by a fatal oversight: I omitted to hoist white sails in place of the black sails on the boat that brought me back from Crete, as I had agreed to do if I returned victorious from my risky enterprise. One can't think of everything. But to tell the truth, and if I question my motives, something I never do willingly, I can't swear that it was really an oversight. Aegeas stood in my way, you see, and especially so when, thanks to the potions of the enchantress Medea, who considered, as he himself did, that for a husband he was getting on a bit, he took it into his head, on an unfortunate impulse, to help himself to another dose of youth, thereby obstructing my career, whereas each should take his turn. Anyway, on catching sight of the black sails . . . I discovered when I got back to Athens that he had thrown himself into the sea.[4]

In the colloquial expressions and commonplaces littered throughout Theseus' monologue, phrases such as 'One can't think of everything,' 'considered [. . .] that for a husband he was getting on a bit', 'help himself to another dose of youth' or 'each should take his turn' one can locate instances of verbal lapsus. To carefully attuned post-Freudian ears, it is painfully obvious that 'each should take his turn' is a euphemism for patriarchal displacement – an act the violence of which is elided yet conveyed by the gap in the last sentence. In addition to euphemisms that have the effect of blocking out unpleasant truths, Theseus exhibits (and even admits to) the same tendency towards resisting self-questioning as do typical patients in analysis ('if I question my motives, something I never do willingly . . .'). But as resistance erodes and the unconscious ploy of the 'oubli' is abandoned, Theseus approaches the verge of speaking the unspeakable – acknowledging his parricide outright. By catching him at this pivotal moment in his 'talking cure' Gide rewrites the legend of Theseus as Freud might have rewritten it – as a symbolic rendering of 'dénégation', or the function of resistance in the affirmation of repression. Indeed, it is this rationality of repression (explicated so brilliantly by Freud in psychoanalytical terms) that constitutes what Benjamin identified as the 'reasonableness' of the Gidean myth, noting how his characters 'speak' the logic of their unconscious desires and fears. Gide himself, long before writing *Thésée*, had given theoretical expression to this notion in a brief essay on Greek mythology (1919):

One has understood nothing of the character of Theseus, for example, ıe simply accepts that the bold hero 'Who shall dishonour the bed ıe god of the dead' inadvertently left the black sail on the ship that ᴜ.ᵢᵢgs him back to Greece, that 'fatal' black sail which, misleading his sorrowful father, induces him to throw himself into the sea, by virtue of which Theseus takes over his kingdom. An oversight? Come now! He forgets to change the sail like he forgets Ariadne on Naxos. And I can understand that fathers might not teach their children that; but to end the process whereby the story of Theseus is reduced to the insignificance of a fairy-tale, one need only restore to the hero his self-awareness and his resolve.[5]

Insisting on the implausibility of Theseus' plea of 'not guilty' on the grounds of faulty recollection, Gide insinuates that the metonymy of the fatal black sails is itself the equivalent of a textual lapsus in the Greek version of the myth, thinly concealing yet exposing Theseus's underlying wish-fulfilment. In his modern adaptation of the myth, Gide, following the implied prescription of his argument, devised linguistic corollaries for the black veil – the insipid blunders, horrendous clichés and maladroit euphemisms that festoon Theseus' speech.

One of the major differences between the use of the lapsus in *Thésée* (Gide's final *récit*) and its uses in the early *L'Immoraliste,* lies in the fact that Theseus is a far less intelligent, hence less manipulative, narrator than Michel. The latter reveals himself as constantly on guard against the reader's powers of supposition, which means that Michel's slips of the tongue, like the author's slips of the text, are more difficult to localize. Frequently, evidence of Michel's narratorial circumspection is registered through anacoluthon, technically defined as 'the failure, accidental or deliberate, to complete a sentence according to the structural plan on which it was started' and used more loosely by Barthes to signify 'a break in sense or construction.'[6] The first instance of this rupture occurs when Michel, having summoned his friends to North Africa to listen to his story, finds himself unable to articulate precisely why he needs them or what he wishes to say: 'For I have reached a point in my life beyond which I cannot go. Not from weariness though. But I can no longer understand things. I want . . . I want to talk, I tell you.' (p. 1)[7] Here, the verb 'parler' is ironically substituted for the 'faille' or temporary failure of speech on Michel's part. As in the discourse of Theseus, it is the impromptu utterance or uncontrolled pause that signals the speaker's fear of disclosure.

What is it that Michel fears to disclose? Initially it appears to be the ambivalence of his sentiments towards his new bride Marceline: 'I was accustomed to her grace . . . For the first time now I was struck with astonishment, it seemed to me so great' (I, 33;5). Here, the gap records the shock as he recognizes his former indifference to Marceline. Suddenly, he senses her presence and though he claims at this moment to welcome it, assuring the reader of his pleasure, the ellipsis foreshadows the awkward moments of silence that will occur when communication between them deteriorates, and Marceline's presence is resented as an imposition. This begins to happen soon enough during what turns out to be a grotesque travesty of a conventional wedding night. The blood which is shed comes not from Marceline's deflowering, but from Michel's diseased lungs, and, as if to add to the horror, it is staunched by a scarf that Marceline wears around her waist (a symbolic chastity belt), stealthily procured by Michel while she sleeps. Throughout this scene, Michel engages in a debate with himself marked by hesitations and ellipses, which themselves signal the textual spaces of transgression:

> I was feeling very weak, however, and ordered some tea to be brought. And as she was pouring it out, a little pale herself, but very calm and smiling, a kind of irritation seized me to think she had not had the sense to see anything. I felt indeed that I was being unjust, and said to myself that she saw nothing only because I had hidden it from her so cleverly; but I couldn't help it – the feeling grew in me like an instinct, filled me . . . and at last became too strong; I could contain myself no longer; the words slipped out, as though absent-mindedly:
> 'I spat blood last night'. (I, 37;10)

Michel's 'irritation' at Marceline escalates rapidly into rage as he struggles inwardly against uttering the unspeakable revelation of his illness. Here the rupture in his narration, directly following the allusion to an 'invading instinct', provides a clue, perhaps, to what he fears to divulge for it is this very instinct, so strong as to defy constraint, that will ultimately impel him away from his wife and towards members of his own sex.

If Michel's latent homosexuality is *pre*-figured in the 'creux' or hollows of a spoken sentence, it also emerges after his return to health, as a *sub*-text in the analogy drawn between himself and a palimpsest:

> And I compared myself to a palimpsest; I tasted the scholar's joy when he discovers under more recent writing, and on the same paper, a very ancient and infinitely more precious text. What was this occult text? In order to read it, was it not first of all necessary to efface the more recent texts? (I, 60;39)

The palimpsest is used as a metaphor of the quest for lost origins, both in the historical sense (Adamic man, the Greek pagans) and in the personal sense (childhood, freedom from social inhibitions, the novelty of sensual experience). All this seems laudable in the context of Michel's renewed resolve to live and fortify himself until one recalls that the 'textes récents' of the life that he would so eagerly 'efface' include his marriage to Marceline. Moreover, as we gradually learn, references to 'origins' are encoded as the original nature of the 'vieil homme', which, like the palimpsest, has been submerged in artificial layers of civilization. It is for this reason that the new Michel no longer devotes his intellectual energies to abstract, philological research, but rather to studying the periods in history where political authority is undermined (as when Athalaric, a young Italian king, rebels against his mother and aligns himself with the wicked Goths) or when high culture begins to degenerate. In the course that he offers at the Collège de France, he delights in focusing on the most decadent phase of the late Roman empire for it permits him to fashion a thesis with Nietzschean and Spenglerian overtones in its prophecy of decline and fall in the West.

In Michel's description of the public's reaction to his lectures, Gide may be seen not only to be alluding to the unstated subtext of homoeroticism, but also to be committing a slip of the text in relation to his own narrative control over the reader. Implying that only the inferior scholar is capable of enthusiasm ('The historians criticized a tendency, as they phrased it, to too rapid generalization. Other people blamed my method; *and those who complimented me most were those who understood me least'* (I, 93;77; my emphasis). Michel places the scholar-reader in a double-bind. If, like the historians in relation to Michel's interpretation of history, we discern in *L'Immoraliste* a certain 'tendency', then we reveal ourselves as morally prudish and narrow-minded. If, on the other hand, we admit to being moved by the text, then we betray our ignorance of its subversive content. The work apparently falls at this point into its own trap: Michel's scorn of the sympathetic reader parallels Gide's, who, by implication, exhorts the reader to relinquish his naïveté and adopt an attitude of suspicion towards the ruses of writing. But, by rendering the reader less susceptible, *L'Immoraliste* undoes a measure of its reader-manipulation. Is this accident or plan? Certainly it can be interpreted as a version of the Freudian 'unobserved error'.

A comparable example of textual lapsus occurs in the treatment of a hallowed (even hackneyed) Gidean theme: the relationship between truth and sincerity. After an extenuating soirée during which he has been compelled to 'feign his feint', that is, disguise the fact that he is pretending to share the views of his colleagues, Michel concludes: 'One cannot both be sincere and seem so' (I, 90;74). Whether this is interpreted as a statement of fact or a moral admonition, the axiom unwittingly drives a wedge between the reader and the text, for *L'Immoraliste* is replete with instruments of literary artifice specifically chosen for their effectiveness in making the text *appear* sincere. From the frame conceit of multiple prefaces (with each narrator echoing the sincerity claims of the other), to the use of the gaze as a mirror of the lie (a kind of 'regard regardé', as when Moktir watches Michel watch him steal Marceline's scissors), to an inverted rhetoric of self-exposure that grotesquely ranks dissimulation as the highest expression of truth, these techniques are in evidence. The last is particularly well exemplified in one of Michel's reports on the evolving patterns of his married life:

> For the time being, therefore, my relationship with Marceline
> remained the same, though it was every day getting more intense by
> reason of my growing love. My dissimulation (if that expression can be
> applied to the need I felt of protecting my thoughts from her
> judgment), my very dissimulation increased that love. I mean that it
> kept me incessantly occupied with Marceline. At first, perhaps, this
> necessity for falsehood cost me a little effort; but I soon came to
> understand that the things that are reputed worst (lying, to mention
> only one) are only difficult to do as long as one has never done them;
> but that they become – and very quickly too – easy, pleasant and
> agreeable to do over again, and soon even natural. So then, as is
> always the case when one overcomes an initial disgust, I ended by
> taking pleasure in my dissimulation itself, by protracting it, as if it
> afforded opportunity for the play of my undiscovered faculties. (I,
> 66;46–7)

According to this convoluted logic, dissimulation 'protects' from the truth, and the artifice of dissimulation – the tricks that forge the appearance of sincerity – are perversely valorized as a labour of love. Even the lie is naturalized ('even natural'), presented as a vice which, like tobacco or alcohol, becomes through force of habit, a sophisticated, acquired taste. If one re-juxtaposes this passage to the previously cited axiom – 'one cannot be sincere and appear to be so at the same time' – it would seem that the narrator is deceiving us with the appearance of appearances, craftily substituting an ethic of falsehood for what seems to be a version of the noble lie. The axiom, however, belies the lie – like a slip or mistake, it signals the aesthetics of mimetic truth that undermine Michel's courageous avowals of duplicity and render his entire discourse of sincerity a kind of preamble or founding text for the post-modernist practice of dissemblance. As Alice Jardine, expanding on Deleuze's post-Nietzschean reflections on the modern status of falsehood has surmised:

> In effect, for many contemporary theorists and writers, to be radical in
> our culture may require new kinds of mental acrobatics: for example,
> to be radical may no longer be to work for the side that is 'right',
> speaks the 'truth', is most 'just.' It may in fact be to work rather for the
> *Pseudos*, for 'the highest power of falsehood'; it may be to opt for
> overwhelming falsehood, thereby confusing and finally destroying the
> oppressive system of representation which would have us believe not
> only in its sub-systems of models (the real, the first) versus simulacra
> (the unreal, inauthentic), good versus bad, true versus false; but would

also have us believe in a world ultimately obsessed with self-destruction.[8]

Examined thus from the hindsight of our own critical climate, Michel emerges as the prototypically Nietzschean king of the 'Pseudos', even more than Ménalque, Michel's sinister mentor, whose characterization parodies and oversimplifies the stereotypical essentials of Nietzsche's thought. Privileging the simulacrum or semblance of truth over truth itself by means of such techniques as the partial avowal, the withheld inference, or the deceptive sign, Michel makes of the error a textual precondition.

In the cat and mouse encounters between Michel and Ménalque, the latter stalks the former and eventually traps him through the rhetorical manipulation of silence. As if to emphasize this point, Ménalque's persona is introduced under the sign of the unspoken; in his first words to Michel, he indicates his fundamental antipathy to idle chatter: 'I don't much care about talking, but I should like to talk to you' (I, 94;78). By breaking his habitual 'code of silence', Ménalque begins his initiation of Michel into a secret society whose members recognize each other by their reserve in conversation. For this reason, Ménalque's discourse, with its pregnant pauses and pointed omissions, serves a didactic function as a model of the coded language that Michel has yet to master. The first lesson posits the necessity of indiscretion (foreshadowing the voyeurism in which Michel will later indulge after learning of the bestial sexual practices of some of his labourers). In the ellipsis into which Ménalque's speech trails, Michel receives his first prodding to respond in code:

> It's my habit to be discreet only about things that are confided to me; for things that I find out myself, I'll admit that I have an unbounded curiosity. So I searched, poked about, questioned wherever I could. My indiscretion was rewarded, since it has made me wish to meet you again; since instead of the learned man of habit you seemed to be in the old days, I know now that you are . . . it's for you to tell me what.
> I felt myself blushing. (I, 95;80)

Michel's blush – the biblical sign of shame – shows that he is beginning to divine the missing texts of his interlocutor. When he reddens for a second time, it is because the unspoken comes dangerously close to enunciation; but ironically, what is revealed is yet another silence – Michel's silence as, on that fatal day, he watched Moktir furtively pocket Marceline's scissors:

> 'You saw the theft and said nothing! Moktir was very much astonished at this silence – and so was I.'
> 'And I am too at what you have just said. What! Do you mean to say he knew I had caught him at it?'

'It isn't that that matters; you were trying to be more cunning than
he; it's a game at which children like that will always get the better of
us. You thought you had him, and in reality it was he who had you . . .
But that's not what matters. I should like an explanation of your
silence.'

'I should like one myself.'

Some time passed without a word from either of us. (I, 96;81)

Here it becomes evident that in remaining silent in the face of Moktir's
theft, Michel was giving the sign of his assent to the tacit contract that will,
in future, hold between them. The contract is grounded in a masochistic
paradigm described by Fredric Jameson as 'stealing from oneself'.[9] Jameson
identifies the pattern in relation to a later episode in which Michel is
portrayed poaching on his own land, an accomplice to his most brutish
farmhands. For Jameson, the travesty of the trope lies in its perversion of
capitalism, and indeed, this is the explicit reproof communicated by the
young manager of Michel's estate, Charles Bocage: 'One ought to take one's
duties seriously and not play with them . . . or else one doesn't deserve to
have possessions' (I, 125;114). Taken as a figure, however, this 'stealing
from oneself' may be interpreted in its wider ramifications as a synonym of
the self-undermining text; the text that robs itself, depleting its stock of
moral integrity just as Michel depletes his own territories of valuable game,
because he simply is unable to resist the temptation to 'play with them . . .'.

What is it about these games that excites Michel so profoundly? More
than just the risk of being caught, his reputation tarnished by scandal, his
name (and that of his wife) the object of public ridicule, it is the delight in
being duped that spurs Michel towards danger. Having learned that
Alcide, the wildest of the poachers, has tricked old Bocage into paying him
to destroy illegal traps which he himself has laid, Michel confesses:

And what specially vexed me in the business was not so much Alcide's
threefold traffic as his deceitfulness. And then what did he and Bute
do with the money? I don't know. I should never know anything about
creatures like them. They would always lie; they would go on
deceiving me for the sake of deceiving. (I, 122;111)

Like both Swann and Marcel in *A la Recherche du temps perdu*, Michel
reveals his vulnerability to the seductive powers of what Deleuze has
called the 'deceptive sign', a sign which, by 'concealing what it expresses'
alludes to those mysterious 'possible worlds' of concupiscence and
coquetry from which the jealous lover is excluded by the beloved.

Alcide, through his transparent lies, draws Michel deeper into the
underworld of deception, a world governed, as Deleuze has advanced, by
its own inverted 'system', of rules and 'laws':

If the lie obeys laws, this is because it implies a certain tension in the liar himself, as it were a system of physical relations between the truth and the denials or inventions behind which one aspires to hide it: thus there are laws of contact, of attraction and repulsion, which form a veritable 'physics' of the lie. Indeed, the truth is there, present in the loved one who lies; he is permanently cognizant of it, he does not forget it, whereas he rapidly forgets an improvised lie. The thing hidden acts within him in such a way that he extracts from its context a small true fact designed to authenticate the lie as a whole. But it is precisely this small fact which betrays him, because its corners don't fit properly with the rest, revealing a different origin, a source in another system. Or else the thing hidden acts from a distance, attracts the liar who ceaselessly draws nearer to it.[10]

When Michel covers for Alcide, fabricating excuses that will in turn signal his complicity to the young criminal even at the expense of putting his own credibility into question, he discovers the magic point of contact that connects him to that 'other system', that society of marginals tainted by poverty, incest and rape ('la famille Heurtevent'). But as Alcide is to Michel, so Michel is to Marceline: her point of intersection with the shady, mediated world of middle-class deception: her prevaricating beloved. Often, as Deleuze points out in relation to Proust's Marcel, Michel's 'improvised lie' is forgotten, as when he pretends to Marceline during the period of his malady that she should continue to engage young Arab companions, only in order to keep the enviable example of their health (rather than their animal sensuality) before him. Alternatively, in some of the subtle, almost imperceptible shifts in his interior monologues, one can discern the 'small true fact' which according to Deleuze gives away the lie. At one point, after exclaiming selfishly over the cost of a proper apartment for his ailing wife, he cunningly reverses his position: 'Besides, what need have I of money? What need have I of all this? . . . I am strong now . . . [. . .] Marceline, of course, requires luxury; she is weak' (I, 131;120). The sudden change in attitude from respect to scorn for private property acts as a disguise for Michel's shift in allegiance from the weak to the strong, the strong being the unbridled clan instructed by Ménalque, deserting responsibility, sleeping in barns, and heaping contempt on bourgeois moral protocol.

In his gradual withdrawal from Marceline, Michel saturates his own discourse with deceptive signs, as he progressively bankrupts the discourse of Marceline, and it is in this rhetorical negation of the female signifier, that one can begin to observe the broader relationship between negation and gender. Although he would never be so brutal as to voice openly the complaint that Marceline's conversation amounts to little more than a tissue of moral platitudes, the complaint is nonetheless communicated through textual juxtaposition, the requotation of her phrases in a hostile context. Shortly after one of their habitual evening 'causeries', Michel remarks angrily on the conformity of opinion that appears to prevail among their friends, to which his wife replies: 'But, my dear [. . .] you can't expect each of them to be different from all the others'. He retorts, 'The greater their likeness to each other, the more unlike they are to me' (I, 91;75). The manifest vehemence of this rebuke renders what happens later in the course of his discussion with Ménalque all the more astonishing:

> I let Ménalque speak on; he was saying exactly what I myself had said the month before to Marceline; I ought to have approved him. For what reason, through what moral cowardice did I interrupt him and say, in imitation of Marceline, the very sentence word for word with which she had interrupted me then?
> – But, my dear Ménalque, you can't expect each one of them to be different from all the others. (I, 101;87)

Repetition of the trivial phrase brings on swift and exigent punishment. Ménalque turns his back abruptly on Michel and only subsequently relents on the condition that Michel disowns his words. Michel capitulates, condemning the phrase as a worthless commonplace, then further condemning its speakers ('I hate people of principle') (I, 102;87), thereby implicitly repudiating his wife. This seems to be what is understood by Ménalque who concurs, with satisfaction, that 'there is nothing more detestable in the world' than 'people of principle' (I, 102;87). Marceline's words, read metonymically for her entire person, are thus radically negated, but with impunity, for Michel has not actually uttered a single word against her directly. Indeed, he even allows himself the luxury of 'forgetting' the slip, as he masquerades as the most devoted of husbands after she has lost her child. The only overt signs of his betrayal can be found in the silent recrimination of the dead infant (a ghoulish metaphor of absence) and in the prohibition of all speech pertaining to the miscarriage: 'Not a word was exchanged about the melancholy accident that had shattered our hopes' (I, 108;95). Here, Barthes's concept of the 'Inter-dite', as that which is linguistically forbidden or taboo, as well as 'read between the lines', appropriately describes the new mode of censorship to which all future exchange between them will be subjected.

If on one level, Marceline's discourse is rhetorically negated (judged to be conformist, 'detestable', and finally unspeakable by Michel), on another and even more sinister level, the representation of her diseased and decomposing body merges horrifically with the textual figuration of the 'abîme' or abyss. The association between the feminine body and the 'abîme' as a hole or gap acquires further semiotic dimensions with the help of its secondary meaning, the verb 'abîmer' denoting the process of rotting, spoiling or deterioration. It is in this sense that Michel initially uses the word in conjunction with Marceline's metonymical scissors after their theft by Moktir: 'Why did the little wretch steal them', he wonders, 'if it was only to spoil [*abîmer*] and destroy them at once?' (I, 100;85 my emphasis). Michel's perplexity in regard to the motives of a thief who defaces the booty which he has run such risks to procure is left unresolved, but perhaps, as is intimated, Moktir's perversely destructive gesture was guided by the unconscious wish-fulfilments of Michel. Is it simply a slip of the text that as Marceline's condition worsens, her body becoming the mirror of her husband's growing immoralism, it is as 'a thing that had been spoiled [*abîmée*]' that she appears to Michel? 'Disease had taken hold of Marceline, never again to leave her; it had marked her, stained her. Henceforth she was a thing that had been spoiled,' he observes with chilling detachment (I, 109;96). The semantic links implicit in the verb 'abîmer' between organic decay (the body as transitively decomposed, reduced to the holes of the death's head), are luridly personified in the description of Marceline's face as it reflects the advanced stages of the disease: 'How weak and changed she looks! In the shadow there, I should hardly recognize her. How drawn her features are! Used those two *black holes* of her nostrils always to be so visible?' (I, 131;119 my emphasis).

Michel's projected vision of the 'black holes' in Marceline's head is prefigured several times in *Les Cahiers d'André Walter*, conforming with the alarming exactitude of a classic case history, to the Freudian description of fetishism. The curious gaze that travels from below to above, pruriently investigating beneath a woman's skirt, is duly recorded by the tormented narrator of *André Walter*: 'Oh! I would like to snuggle close to you, sit at your feet, be enveloped by your warmth, my head on your knees, in the deep folds of your dress,' And if here the 'deep folds' evokes the dark space of the absent female phallus, so terrifying to the fetishist, it later develops into the even more redoubtable apparition of a 'nothingness,' featured as 'black as a hole':

> Nightmare:
> She appeared to me, very beautiful, clothed in an unpleated rochet which fell to her feet like a stole; [. . .]
>   Under her dress there was nothing; it was black, black as a hole; I wept in despair. Then with both hands she grasped the hem of her dress and threw it over her face. She turned herself inside out like a sack. And I saw nothing more; darkness enveloped her . . . [11]

André Walter's nightmare of the womb shockingly emptied like a bag (another figure of female castration) foreshadows the placement in later works of the female signifier 'en abyme'. The text of Marceline's body becomes the site of gaps, disfigurations, and defamiliarizing anatomical displacements. Most sinister is the grotesque displacement of the eyes, and by implication the spiritual value of her gaze, to the nostrils, which encircle the black hollow of physical dematerialization:

> O taste of ashes! O deadly lassitude! O the sadness of superhuman effort! I hardly dare look at her; I am too certain that my eyes, instead of seeking hers, will fasten *horribly* on the *black holes* of her nostrils; the suffering expression of her face is agonizing. Nor does she look at me either. (I, 146;136: my emphases)

In addition to the 'trous noirs', the adverbial qualifier 'affreusement' (denoting 'horror' from the root *affre*, but also, significantly enough, that which is 'détestable') serves to underscore the fine line between Michel's sympathy and contempt for his wife. The repressed signification of 'détestable' (the very word used by Ménalque in reference to people like Marceline) resurfaces in the ambivalent word 'affreux'. The adverb is even carried over as an adjective in the description of Marceline's death-throes, in which the awful silence between husband and wife is transferred back from the gaze to the lips, just as the abyssal signs of lifelessness are redisplaced back to the eyes from the nose:

> She is half sitting on the bed, one of her thin arms clutching the bars and supporting her in an upright position; her sheets, her hands, her nightdress are flooded with a stream of blood; her face is soiled with it; *her eyes have grown hideously big*; and no cry of agony could be more appalling than *her silence*. Her face is bathed in sweat; I try to find a little place on it where I can put a *horrible kiss*; I feel the taste of her sweat on my lips. (I, 147;137: my emphases)

The transfixed expression of Marceline's cavernous eyes is harrowingly transcribed yet again a moment before her death ('but her eyes are still wide open' (I, 148;138), as if to punctuate the end-point in the abyssal chain stretching from the dark patches of discoloration on her body, to the blank spaces in dialogue, to the black orifices of nose and eyes.

Without imputing a vulgar misogyny to Michel, or for that matter to Gide, we are nonetheless left with the dilemma of how to interpret this censorship of the feminine – of the woman's body and the woman's 'parole'. Has Marceline simply been sublated, interred and inscribed in the homotextual 'inquiétude' that reverberates in each of the *récit*'s elisions? Or can her negation, her disappearance into the 'abîme', be read as a protofeminist fable in which masculine and feminine 'jouissance' are presented as mutually exclusive? Perhaps it is only in the slips of the text, in those flashes of simultaneous concealment and disclosure that the full complexity of these unspoken issues can be glimpsed.

Notes

1. André Gide, *Oedipe* in *Théâtre* (Paris: Gallimard, 1942), p. 288.

2. WALTER BENJAMIN, 'Oedipe et le mythe raisonnable,' *Walter Benjamin: Oeuvres, II,* tr. Maurice de Gandillac (Paris: Denoël, 1971), p. 47.

3. Gide, *Oedipe*, p. 289.

4. Gide, *Thésée* in *Romans, récits et sôties*, pp. 1416–17.

5. André Gide, 'Considérations sur la mythologie grecque,' *Incidences* (Paris: Gallimard, 1924), p. 129.

6. Barthes, 'Pierre Loti,' *Nouveaux Essais*, p. 173 (my paraphrase).

7. André Gide, *L'Immoraliste*, ed. ELAINE MARKS and RICHARD TEDESCHI (Toronto: Macmillan, 1963), p. 29; All further references to this work will appear in the text abbreviated *I*. I have used this edition because of its useful notes.

8. ALICE JARDINE, *Gynesis* (Ithaca: Cornell University Press, 1985), p. 146.

9. FREDRIC JAMESON, *The Prison-House of Language* (Princeton: Princeton University Press, 1972), p. 178. Jameson writes: 'Vice, said Sartre once, is a taste for failure; and it is in Gide (think of the situation in which Michel ends up helping the poachers steal from himself) the penalty for an allegiance to the myth of some absolute and original presence.'

10. GILLES DELEUZE, *Proust et les signes* (Paris: PUF, 1964), pp. 93–4.

11. André Gide, *Les Cahiers d'André Walter*, in *Oeuvres complètes*, ed. L. MARTIN CHAUFFIER, I (Paris: Editions de la Nouvelle Revue Français, 1932–1938), 144, 169–70. *Notebooks of André Walter*, trs. WADE BASKIN, (London, Peter Owen, 1968), pp. 115, 133.

10 Albert Sonnenfeld on Readers and Reading in *'La Porte Étroite'**

The technique perfected by Gide in his first-person narratives lent itself at the outset to a certain psychological analysis. This concentrated on the tell-tale traces in the story in which the deluded narrator, unaware of the full implications of what he or she is saying, provides clues for the alert reader to see a fuller picture. Such is the source of the **irony** in the Gidian *récit*: Gide as implied author enters into a tacit pact with the reader over the head of his character, enabling the reader to understand more than the protagonist who is recounting the story.

Developments in critical theory beginning in the 1960s highlighted the formal devices involved in telling stories. Gérard Genette, in *Narrative Discourse* (1980; translated from *Figures III*, 1972), brought an unprecedented degree of systematic critical scrutiny to the process and inaugurated what became known as **narratology**. Such attention to the detailed circumstances whereby narrative comes into being was particularly appropriate in the case of Gide's *récits*, and the climate created by the theoretical work of Genette and others fostered increasingly sophisticated readings.

A by-product of this perspective was to highlight the extent to which literature and literary practices form an integral part of the characters' lives. Their sense of identity and their relationships are bound up with reading the texts of others – singly or together – and writing to each other (sometimes about what they have read). Albert Sonnenfeld's seminal article provides crucial insights into the way in which the love between Alissa and Jérôme, while intensely and tragically moving as a spectacle, is inseparable from elaborate literary ploys involving reading, writing, rereading, editing and rewriting which give the lie to the notion that such passion is essentially natural or spontaneous.

---

*From a text originally published in *Romantic Review*, LXVII (1976), pp. 172–80.

Some people might have made a book out of it; but the story I am going to tell is one which took all my strength to live and over which I spent all my virtue. So I shall set down my recollections quite simply, and if in places they are ragged I shall have *recourse to no invention, and neither patch nor connect them*; any effort I might make to dress them up would take away the last pleasure I hope to get in telling them. (495;5)

Set off in a solitude of white space almost as though it were an epigraph or invocation to the Muses before the real story begins ('I lost my father before I was twelve years old' (495;5); 'It really begins, I may say, in the year of my father's death' (497;8); 'Yes, it was certainly the year of my father's death' (497;8), this complex and rich 'Au lecteur' might be relegated to the obscurity of a rhetorical flourish, an authorial protestation of inadequacy before ineffable emotions.[1] 'My strength' went into living the story; 'my virtue' (in the etymological sense) was eroded by the experience, and my narration is but the poor reflection of *l'histoire*. Its very fragmentation is the mirror of personal disintegration and there is delight in that the painful pleasure of the form of the narrative faithfully reflects the formlessness of contradictory emotions that cannot be expressed.[2] The weakness of the structure reiterates the erosion of strength and virtue, the continuous melody of *L'Immoraliste*, where Michel retains his self-delusion of strength even in the epilogue, has yielded here to the ragged. The traditional poet usually invokes the transport of inspiration, whereas Jérôme is *dispossessed* by the Muses. One might, moreover, find here a conventionalized appeal to truth or truthfulness. A well-wrought story (*book, invention, patch, connect, effort, dress up*), it is implied, is less 'true' than a dislocated one; the natural ('So I shall set down my recollections quite simply') will make *La Porte Étroite* superior to the fearful symmetry of *L'Immoraliste*. But beyond the rhetorical, something far more secret and significant, both for *La Porte Étroite* and for Gide's work as a whole, is happening. The narrator is removing his work from the realm of literature (*un livre*) back to the autobiographical and even toward the *Journal* (*in places they are ragged*). He is reversing the traditional hierarchy of modern literature (*vide* Joyce's *lyric, epic* and *dramatic*, Flaubert's *époque barbare* to *époque d'analyse* in the *Carnets*, Gide's own evolution from *André Walter* through the *récits*), implying that the autobiographical fragment or the journal are more faithful than the book which others might have written.[3] The obvious subterfuge here is that *La Porte Étroite* is not a journal or autobiography but a well-wrought *récit* (more artful even than *L'Immoraliste*), that where Jérôme aspires to the naturally *unformed*, Gide is in fact *informing* with satanic precision. What may seem more recondite but somehow more shocking is the pretence that *mémoires*, autobiographies and journals bring us closer to the actually lived story. In the Gidian perspective, the first-person narrator of a journal or autobiography is a *created character* (in many ways like Proust's Marcel)[4] who exists only in the *word* and not in historical *fact*: the Self is a narrated Self, not a living one – Gide becomes the *Je* of the *Journal*, he invents himself through the act of writing, he can correct his real defects and frailties in recomposing his Self through the Word; and he makes of the reader his unwilling accomplice in this recreation since even the semblance of spontaneity ('So I shall set down my recollections quite simply') is a literary and psychological stratagem. What is astonishing in *La Porte Étroite* is that the book itself seems to be formed around, or based on, this problematic. It is not something that the critic adduces from a remote theoretical domain but rather the very matrix of the *récit* itself.

The rejection of *un livre*, in favour of the apparently more improvisational (*set down my recollections quite simply, ragged, no invention, telling them*), leads us straight to that part of the novel which is overtly aleatory, Alissa's *Journal*, where the *Je* is purportedly elaborating itself in fragmentary entries, with *recourse to no invention, and neither patch nor connect them*. Now this most famous section of *La Porte Étroite* has too often been misconstrued as the sincere record of a misguided but nonetheless admirable mystical quest, particularly by pious would-be admirers, from Claudel on.[5] I have tried to show elsewhere the degree to which the *récit* is far more obtrusively critical of both Alissa and Jérôme as 'theatrical' instead of 'religious' than most critics or Gide himself ('the critique of a certain mystical tendency,' etc.[6]) have been willing to concede.[7] What concerns me here is that Alissa's *Journal* poses the problematic of the fictitious self as the inevitable creative mask, even in writing that is not 'book' but supposedly unformed confession, spontaneous and unpremeditated. Any word, whether written or spoken, signals the creation of a self-in-words which exists in the eyes or ears of a reader or listener. This creation is, moreover, structured by a need to form a particular self (or mask) for another self (the recipient-reader-listener).

How does the *Journal* enter the book as a counterweight to the implicit Journal-Autobiography of Jérôme's narrative? In her last will, she asked that the notary transmit a sealed packet of papers to be opened only by Jérôme.[8] 'The sealed packet which the lawyer sent me contained Alissa's *journal* ' (580; 119). In a theatrically ritualistic request, she also specifies that she is to be buried wearing the amethyst cross which she had wanted Jérôme to give to the daughter he might father one day. We can deduce therefore that the *Journal* itself was composed with a continuous, though possibly unconscious, calculation of the effect each line would produce on the intended reader, Jérôme; that Alissa in the *Journal* is a self, created in words, activated in projected response to an anticipated reader; that reader, Jérôme, then appropriates the *Journal* when he becomes its editor and transcriber; that he incorporates it into his own narrative, into *his* creation of a fictive self, projecting towards yet another readership, the public of 1909, or perhaps Madeleine-André-Gide. 'I here transcribe a considerable number of its pages. I transcribe them without commentary. You will imagine well enough the reflections I made as I read, and the commotion of my heart, of which I could but give a too imperfect idea' (580; 119). Some questions the mysterious 'you' might ask would be: What proportion of the pages in the diary does Jérôme transcribe? What did the suppressed pages contain? What were the reflections those pages inspired in Jérôme as reader? Is not the choice of pages to transcribe itself the *commentaires* Jérôme denies making? And finally *we* might ask: who is the *you* to whom his remarks are addressed.

The *Journal d'Alissa* might be considered a peculiar form of posthumous revenge designed to keep a particular image of the diarist alive in Jérôme-the-Reader's sensibility; but even if Alissa had no intimations of mortality in the early pages of its inception, she composed the diary with Jérôme reading 'over her shoulder,' as it were, as she was writing:

> Sometimes as I listen to him talking I seem to be watching myself think. He explains me and discovers me to myself. Should I exist without him? I *am* only when I am with him. (584; 124)

> Just as I was going to throw this journal into the fire, I felt a kind of warning which held me back. It seemed to me that it no longer belonged to me, that I had no right to deprive Jérôme of it, that I had never written it except for him. (594; 139)

When she writes: 'Re-read my journal before destroying it' (594; 138), she is more than the poet-critic of the post-Baudelairian modernist æsthetic; she has become Poet-as-Reader, Alissa as Jérôme, calculating the effect of what she writes in the gestation of a new self-in-words to be read by the reader. In romantic first-person narratives, (*vide* Gœthe's *Werther*[9] or Bernanos' *Journal d'un Curé de Campagne*),[10] obliterated or missing passages express the ineffable by activating silence through wilful fragmentation.[11] Jérôme aspires to the same expressivity when he recounts his memories though *in places they are ragged.* And Alissa appears to be in the tradition when she tears out many pages (584; 124); even destroying an entire notebook 'for in the papers which Alissa left behind the Journal did not begin again till three years later' (590; 133). But Gide forces her to reveal herself as anything but a hapless victim of the ineffable passion when she *herself* notes her erasures and deletions:

> I have torn up all the pages which seemed to me to be *well written*. (I know what I mean by this.) I ought to have torn up all those in which there was any question of him. I ought to have torn them all up. I could not. (588; 129)

Tore up my letter, then wrote again . . . Here is the dawn [. . .] My letter shall not go. (593; 137)

Re-read my journal before destroying it. (594; 138)

Clearly, her gestures form part of her created personality and are performed (and duly noted) in full awareness that a reader (Jérôme) is necessary as a witness to confirm her created personality. A truly spontaneous mystical victim of the incommunicable would have simply torn out the pages without self-conscious explanation. Unwittingly, Alissa comes to resemble Rodolphe Boulanger,[12] dropping water on his signature to simulate tears, more than Bernanos' Curé d'Ambricourt.

Alissa's preoccupation with style offers further confirmation of the process of self-creation through the word. Just as Jérôme presents himself as a hapless and sincere victim of his own higher aspirations in denying his story the status of *un livre*, so Alissa becomes aware of a foolish, wicked anxiety to write well (588; 129) and notes that she tears out pages which seem well-written. 'Sometimes I force myself to write badly in order to escape from the rhythm of his phrases' (588; 130). This too is a public, rather than a private gesture, the creation of a fictive self which manifests itself, both in the *Journal* and in Jérôme's narrative, in her banishing literature from her library in favour of 'insignificant little works of vulgar piety' (569; 104).

> These are humble souls who talk to me simply, and express themselves as best they can. I take pleasure in their society. I know beforehand that they will not fall into any snare of fine language, and that I, as I read, shall not be tempted by any profane admiration. (569; 104)

Again, what should have been private and unnoticed has become part of a public symbolic ceremonial staged for the benefit of Jérôme as worshipper or as reader of the *Journal*. One could, of course, comment on every aspect of the *Journal* to show that every admission and every intention is addressed to Jérôme as reader, as the name on the sealed packet of papers transmitted by the executor of Alissa's last will. Every entry marks another stage of self-creation (as a *Je* in a *Journal*) of a new and fictive self. That the *Journal* succeeds in imposing its image of Alissa can be seen in the narrative itself, since one must assume that Jérôme recreated Alissa in his *souvenirs* AFTER her death and AFTER reading her Journal. Alissa has thus become the creator of herself in what purports to be Jérôme's tale, but she needs his presence as a *reader* to avoid 'the sudden and disenchanting *illumination* of my life' (595; 140). Early in the novel, Jérôme visits Alissa unannounced in her room:

> She was putting on a coral necklace, and, her arms raised to fasten it,
> she was bending forward, with her back turned to the door, looking at
> herself over her shoulder, in a mirror between two lighted candles. It
> was in the mirror that she first caught sight of me, and she continued
> to look at me in it for some moments without turning round. (520; 38)

One cannot worship on the altar of the Self alone; the mirror must reflect
the witness-reader hovering over Alissa and framed between the
sacramental tapers.

Daniel Moutote has written extensively and well about 'the literary self
of André Gide, he who says *I* in the Journal'.[13] Alissa's 'moi littéraire' is in
her Journal, to be sure, but perhaps even more manifest in her letters to
Jérôme, which she intended to be read immediately, not posthumously.
When Madeleine burned Gide's letters to her, he was to lament: 'Without
that virtually day-to-day testimony of my entire inner life, I am nothing
more than posturing. It seems to me that there never were more beautiful
letters.'[14] It is not that French literature, as Trahard maintains, was
deprived of a masterpiece; the act of destruction, the ultimate expression of
the fragmentation Jérôme ascribes to his ragged non-book, must itself be a
literary gesture by the author, a part of the creation of a self in the eyes of a
reader. From the very first, Jérôme can only evince perplexity that the very
act of reading has been appropriated by his correspondent: 'What could be
the meaning of this letter? What were those words that she was grieved not
to have uttered . . .' (512; 27). He does not realize that Alissa must flee his
presence because only the *written* word will allow her the ceremonial
creation of self:

> Listen Jérôme, I can't speak to you this evening – don't let's spoil our
> last minutes. No, no, I'm as fond of you as ever; don't be afraid. I'll write
> to you; I'll explain, I promise I'll write to you – tomorrow – as soon as
> you have gone. Leave me now! See, I am crying. You must go. (521; 39)

Unwittingly, Jérôme realizes: 'Now that I am here, I feel as if it would
have been easier to write, and I blame myself for coming' (524; 43).

That the only form of knowledge is the act of reading (despite Gide's
'Throw away this book, and go out!'*) has already been amply
demonstrated in the *récit*. Lucile, that embodiment of life's energies and
sensual indulgence, always holds a *closed* book, whereas for Jérôme and
Alissa (even for Juliette and Abel) the book has so long been open that it
has become a part of them: they quote freely from Dante, from Baudelaire,
from Pascal, they read aloud from Swinburne, casually adapt Shakespeare
into the very fabric of their dialogue. Indeed, they have made a book out of
their lives, and it is no accident that at the very centre of the definition of

---

* [An exhortation Gide addresses to the reader of *Les Nourritures Terrestres*.]

their reciprocal ritual of self-abnegation, there is the Book, the text. 'Enter ye in at the strait gate,' around which there are grouped two readerships: Pastor Vautier's straightforward rendering; Alissa's and above all Jérôme's secretly erotic misinterpretation:

> I fancied it, in the dream in which I was plunged, as a sort of press into which I passed with effort and with an extremity of pain, that yet had in it as well, a foretaste of heavenly felicity. And again this gate became the door of Alissa's room; in order to enter in at it, I squeezed myself – I emptied myself of all that I contained of selfishness. (505;18)

The pastor had chosen his text 'doubtless unintentionally', and Jérôme hears the sermon while staring at Alissa 'with such self-oblivion that it seemed as though it were through her that I heard the words I listened to with such passionate eagerness' (505; 18). We have here the very paradigm of the complexities of the created self in the created reader. It is not only Jérôme's Puritanical upbringing which makes of him a 'soul ready prepared' (506; 20) for the austere teaching, but his devotion to the self created by the text and recreated in the perceiving self of the reader. Small wonder then that after the ceremony of worship 'without attempting to see my cousin [. . .] I fled' (506; 19). The relationship of Alissa and Jérôme is ultimately symbolized by 'the shelf on which she kept her bedside reading': 'This little collection had been gradually formed, partly by the books I had given her, partly by others which we had read together' (569; 104). The book even usurps the bed, when the bookcase presides over the scene of abstinence. Though literature will be replaced by works of vulgar piety, Alissa remains faithful to the ceremonial of reading, and at her final moment becomes (or remains) the reader of the created self in the word: 'Even now I am writing to reassure myself, to calm myself' (595; 140).

Alissa's letters to Jérôme create her self in written form and in the eyes of a reader, and Gide plays with optic complexities in a way prophetic of *Les Faux-Monnayeurs*. There are letters from Alissa read by Jérôme; a letter first read by Jérôme, then analysed by Jérôme and Abel and passed on for further interpretation by Juliette; a letter from Alissa to Aunt Plantier with implied instructions to let Jérôme see it; letters from Alissa written while rereading Jérôme's missives; a letter from Alissa with the injunction not to communicate its contents to Abel and Juliette, and so on. This is not the place to analyse the increasingly rhetorical and epigrammatic flourishes of Alissa's style and its calculated effects. But let us recall that the texts of Alissa's letters are themselves edited by Jérôme's own narrative needs, so that they form part both of Alissa's creation of a self in letters and of Jérôme's creation of a fragmented self in narrative. Thus, Jérôme receives a letter transmitted by the aunt 'from which I copy out the part that throws light on my story' (542; 67); another group in which 'I copy . . . all that bears upon my tale' (548; 75); he then comments that 'I do not give all her letters' (551; 79); in one of his own lengthy replies, 'I remember the only passage of my letter that was at all clear-sighted' (565; 99). In other words, as 'editor', Jérôme practices a rhetorical strategy toward his own reader analogous to the projected self of Alissa in her *Journal*. 'No doubt you can easily imagine with what transports of joy I read this letter' (547; 74). Who is the *you* to whose instinctive understanding Jérôme appeals here except a reader standing in relationship to his narrative as Jérôme stands to Alissa's *Journal*? The very phrase 'transports de joie' anticipates (or rather recalls, since Jérôme has read Alissa's *Journal* before composing his narrative) Alissa's quotation from Pascal's *Memorial* in the penultimate entry in her diary (p. 595; 139). Also reminiscent of her strategies in the *Journal* are the admissions of deletions and revisions:

> The next three days were wholly occupied by my pleading; I wished to reply to Alissa; I was afraid of incurably inflaming the wound by too deliberate a discussion; by too vehement protestations, by the slightest clumsy word; twenty times over I began the letter in which my love struggled for its life. I cannot to this day re-read, without weeping, the tear-stained paper, which is the copy of the one I at last decided to send. (560; 91)

To which one might respond with Alissa's announced tactic: 'I tore up that letter, it is true; but now I am writing it over again, almost the same' (559; 90). While other rhetorical effects are almost operatic: 'since [. . .] I have not strength to bear another letter like the last – please, for a time, let us stop all communication' (Jérôme to Alissa, 560; 92). Or this reply to Jérôme's lengthy, tender letters:

> The summer is not far off. I propose that we give up our correspondence for a time, and that you come and spend the last fortnight of September with me at Fongueusemare. I shall take your silence for consent, and hope, therefore, that you will not answer (566; 100).

But this invitation to forsake letters for 'life' is only to allow Alissa to demonstrate her conversion from 'literature' to 'those humble souls': 'I know beforehand that they will not fall into any snare of fine language, and that I, as I read, shall not be tempted by any profane admiration' (569; 104). Which is itself a veritable writhing in the trap of language as mask!

At various points in his retrospective narrative, Jérôme shows awareness of Alissa's preemption of his freedom as a reader, of her rhetorical dominance, of 'the subtlety of her feint' (565; 99). Early in their correspondence, he comments on the sacramental aspect of their dominical correspondence and the uneasiness her letters caused him through what he discerns as her keenness to keep up with his work:

> and it even seemed to me that, while on my part reflections, discussions, criticisms were only means towards expressing my thoughts, she, on the contrary, took advantage of all these things to conceal hers. Sometimes I wondered whether she were not actually taking pleasure in this as in a kind of game. No matter! I was firmly resolved to complain of nothing, and I let no trace of anxiety transpire in my letters. (530; 51)

Jérôme's activity of *costruirsi*, to use the Pirandellian[15] phrase, is nowhere more apparent: he maintains that words for him were only 'means towards expressing my thoughts,' whereas we have seen that his wilfully fragmented narrative, his editing of Alissa's letters and diary, his rhetoric, were in fact elements in the construction of a fictive self through words; that omission is a form of subjective statement. That Alissa herself works with words 'to conceal her [thoughts]' is doubtless true (though we are too dependent on Jérôme as reader of her words), since he transcribes *in toto* (at least with no statement that he is fragmenting) her letter written a fortnight after Juliette's marriage (pp. 545–547; 71–74). Here she is acknowledging that what she thought was a paraphrase of Corneille's is in fact the fourth *Cantique spirituel* by Racine.[16] We see Alissa in the act of writing (or of copying) while reading, and characteristically she suppresses two revealing stanzas, the first beginning 'O wisdom, thy word / brought the universe into being' the second begins 'The Word, image of the Father / Came down from his eternal throne.'[17] It is revealing indeed that Alissa incorporates those stanzas dealing with her self-created being as would-be Saint (the angelic instead of earthly bread, the captive soul, content to be entrapped in God's yoke) and omits those extolling the flesh and God as Word. For it is to the word that Alissa and Jérôme have recourse to control and manipulate the Reader – Jérôme as reader of Alissa, Alissa as reader of herself pretending to be Jérôme, Jérôme the narrator as 'reader' of his narration. Alissa is mistaken (whether wilfully or unconsciously) when she felt 'our correspondence was nothing but a vast mirage that we were each writing, alas! only to ourselves' (559; 90); in fact she was always writing for 'the other,' the reader, Jérôme! Every impulse in *La Porte Étroite* stems from the act of readership, from the Pastor's sermon to Alissa's rejection of Pascal. And if in the beginning was the Word, that 'brought the universe into being,' so Jérôme's last vision of Alissa (before Juliette's letter announcing her death) is of her as reader:

> 'Look what I brought here to read for the last three evenings,' she interrupted, and held out to me a packet of letters; I recognized those I had written her from Italy. (576; 113)

Jérôme exists for Alissa-the-reader in his letters; Alissa's being, her created self, exists within the most sacred of Mallarmé's words: 'the sealed packet [*le pli*] [. . .] contained Alissa's journal' (580; 119). [. . .]

Notes

1. See PHILIPPE LEJEUNE, *Exercices d'ambiguïté*, (Paris: 1974), p. 40.

2. 'I admire now all the things I succeeded *in not saying*, in KEEPING BACK. (I think for some time of the virtue that "reserve" can become in a writer)' (*JI*, 170; *J1*, 144: 31 July 1905).

3. See my article 'Answering Voices: The Novelist and the Supernatural,' *French Studies* (October 1968), 307–320, for discussion of the expressive value of the 'fragment.'

4. [Marcel is the name of the first-person narrator in the multi-volume novel *À la recherche du temps perdu* (1913–1927) by MARCEL PROUST (1871–1922).]

5. See D MOUTOTE, *Le Journal de Gide et les problèmes du moi* (Paris, 1968): 'The ascension by means of which Alissa progresses from a somewhat profane and almost Stendhalian renunciation to pure saintliness . . . '

6. [A well-known comment by Gide on *La Porte Étroite*, grouping the book among his 'ironic books [. . .] books of criticism'. See 'Feuillets', *OC, XIII*, p. 439–40].]

7. See my essay '*Strait is the Gate*: Byroads in Gide's Labyrinth,' *Novel* (Winter 1968), 118–132, for comments on the stage-games of Alissa and Jérôme.

8. 'I was shortly to receive some papers which she had put in a sealed packet addressed to me' (580; 119).

9. [*The Sufferings of Young Werther* (1774), an early novel by JOHANN WOLFGANG VON GOETHE (1749–1832), which used the letter form to convey the hopeless passion of its young hero and contributed significantly to the definition of romantic love.]

10. [*Le Journal d'un curé de compagne* (1936), a novel in the form of the diary of a parish priest, by the Catholic writer GEORGES BERNANOS (1888–1948).]

11. See my 'Answering Voices,' esp. p. 308.

12. [RODOLPHE BOULANGER, the mock-romantic lover satirized by GUSTAVE FLAUBERT in his novel *Madame Bovary* (1857).]

13. *Le Journal de Gide*, etc., p. 336.

14. Quoted by M VAN RYSSELBERGHE, *Les Cahiers de la Petite Dame*, vol. 1 (Paris, Gallimard, 1973), p. 11.

15. [Pirandellian: associated with the Italian dramatist and writer LUIGI PIRANDELLO (1867–1936), whose characters struggle to construct an identity for themselves in the face of the internal contradictions and opposing views of others which bedevil the human personality.]

16. See my analysis of this mistake in 'Byroads in Gide's Labyrinth,' pp. 127–29.

17. RACINE, *Oeuvres complètes*, I (Paris: Pléïade, 1950), 1000–1001.

11   W. M. L. Bell on Religion and its avatar in *La Porte Étroite**

This article traces the history of readings of the text and indicates the problematics it has given rise to. Gide himself indicated a preference for the sections attributed to Alissa, declaring that the 'flaccid character' of Jérôme dictated a dull presentation and uninteresting style when he express himself (*JI*, 276; *J1*, 240: November 1909). This in turn encouraged critics to concentrate on the analysis of Alissa and on her religious leanings as the core of the novel; such approaches were only gradually modified by attention paid to the parallels with Gide's own life (though he asserted that Madeleine was *not* Alissa, he suggested that she *became* Alissa . . .). Consideration of the sexual elements in the drama and hence of the text's pioneering exploration of Freudian matters, though initially focusing on Alissa, have made for different approaches to both the principal characters. More recent analyses have varied between 'Alissa' readings and 'Jérôme' readings, whether the method adopted be psychological or narratological (as in Sonnenfeld's essay included in the present volume). Bell's essay surveys some of this critical history, but seeks in particular to draw attention back to the original context from which the novel emerged. Above all, this critic stresses the literary context and generic affinities, showing that *La Porte Étroite* draws on a particular mix of cultural traditions relating to the depiction of courtly love and engages with specific expectations the cultural antecedents condition in the alert reader. Ultimately, the critic argues, these antecedents undermine Gide's own claim to be criticizing a particular point of protestant theology, since rather than being in conflict in the novel, the sentimental and the religious in fact work in subtle complicity within the courtly tradition on which it builds.

*Originally published in *Romance Studies*, no. 10, Summer 1987, pp. 7–20.

A simple view of the relationship between literature and religion in *La Porte Étroite* might be that the form is literary and the subject religious. *La Porte Étroite* belongs to the novel genre, whether we call it *récit* or *roman*, and we are invited by Gide to construe the work in terms of Alissa, 'the portrait of a protestant soul, in whom the essential drama of protestantism is (played out)'. It has been suggested[1] that Gide, when finally he embarked in 1905 on a not entirely congenial subject, was reacting to the preoccupations of close friends and correspondents, conspicuously Claudel and Jammes. What is certain is that their reaction to the work largely focused on subject-matter, and subject-matter perceived as having particular interest for the believer. Claudel spots the heretical, quietest element in Alissa's faith. More generally, he wonders whether the work is 'Christian'. Jammes, in contrast, has no misgivings; where Jérôme sees only a wasted life, 'I consider, as a Roman Catholic, that Alissa sacrificed in this way radiates a beauty which is incomparably finer.'[2] With varying degrees of enthusiasm then, Claudel and Jammes salute the novel as one which is likely to promote the good cause.

Claudel was of course right to query the author's commitment. By comparison with the message of his own plays, the ending of *La Porte Étroite* would strike him as highly ambiguous. Alissa's diary reveals her as achieving neither peace of mind nor any sense of a saving presence. Even the admiring reader will pause, one imagines, before adopting Alissa as a model of conduct.[3]

What the reader infers, in this case the author confirms. In Gide's reply to Claudel (10 May 1909), he speaks of 'a school of heroism whose error I believe my book brings out quite well'. In the letter to André Beaunier concerning *Les Caves du Vatican*: 'I have up to now written nothing but *ironic* – or, if you prefer, critical – books' (*Journal*, 12 July 1914). And in the 1912 *Projet de préface pour 'La Porte Étroite'*, he insists that *L'Immoraliste* and *La Porte Étroite* are complementary: 'each is the counterpart of the other; they sustain each other; it is in the excess of the one that I find a sort of permission for the excess of the other'. On the strength of this last remark, Gide can be made to seem extraordinarily trite.[4]

Gide's glossing of the text stands to confirm our sense of the heroine's error. The same effect is produced if we bring to bear on the *récit* a knowledge of the whole corpus. We know that Gide moved from a Christian to a classical viewpoint, from heroism to harmony, cult of the eagle to cult of Prometheus. By the 1940s, the possibility that Alissa represents unorthodox Christianity – unorthodox even by Protestant standards – has been forgotten. The paradigm of the religious man is Oedipe, and Oedipe learns what Tiresias had always known: 'We must cease to see the world, in order to see God' (1452). There is an instructive parallel between the argument of *Thésée* and the criticism of Pascal voiced by Alissa: 'If he had not first emptied this life of its joy [. . .] it would weigh heavier in the balance . . . ' (570; 105). Viewed as part of a development, rather than in isolation or in simple juxtaposition to *L'Immoraliste*, it is not difficult to see that the transcendental preoccupations of Alissa, however sympathetically presented, are not endorsed.

'A critical work' then, despite the terms of the preface to *L'Immoraliste*: 'For the rest, I have not tried to prove anything. . ., etc.', and Gide's insistence that they hold good equally for *La Porte Étroite*. Gide disapproves of the *roman à thèse* (Barrès), condemns the attitude which would put literature at the service of low-level moralising (M. le sénateur Béranger[5]), wishes to secure for the writer the maximum artistic licence, but there is never the least disposition on his part to marginalize literature, empty it of meaning and moral seriousness. Thus, the stance of the Cornelian heroine[6] is not merely depicted, it is qualified; not just *héroisme* but *héroisme gratuit*. As we witness the conflict within and between the protagonists, *bonheur* (happiness) versus *sainteté* (saintliness), we are made to feel that, while the former is elusive and precarious, the latter is chimerical. In her diary, Alissa expresses the hope that Jérôme, as eventual reader, may detect therein 'the unskilled accent of a heart, desirous *to the point of madness* of urging him to those heights of virtue which I myself despaired of reaching' (595: 139). The term *madness* is the last in a rising scale: *enthusiasm, exaltation, madness*. It is Alissa herself who, having chosen against happiness, paradoxically proposes happiness (in the way that Gide himself was to do) as the criterion by which her enterprise might be judged: 'I understand that my whole life has been vain, except in so far as it culminates in happiness' (595; 139). By such a test, her failure is absolute. By juxtaposing the first and last sentences of the final entry, Gide underscores the irony: 'Jerome, I wish I could teach you perfect joy'; 'I should like to die now, quickly, before again realising that I am alone' (595; 140).

The claim that *La Porte Étroite* has a religious subject is, I suggest, uncontroversial. It corresponds to the experience of many readers and to Gide's own sense of what he was about. Gide scholars will know very well however that a powerful challenge to the notion that the work is fundamentally concerned with religion, was mounted some thirty years ago by Germaine Brée,[7] and they will know that her argument has carried weight with later critics. Professor Brée redirects our attention, on the one hand giving prominence to Jérôme (omitted from Gide's description of his subject as 'the portrait of a protestant soul'), and on the other identifying obstacles to the fulfilment of the relationship which are psychologically prior to the obstacle afforded by religion. We are encouraged by Jérôme as narrator to believe that Alissa acts and he merely reacts. Brée inverts matters: at the source of the drama, in her account, is the stance of Jérôme: 'hatred of Lucile Bucolin . . . refusal of "possession" . . . impotence'. As the story of a couple, it is a novel about *repression*; therein lies its novelty. Alissa's religion is a mask, a compensation, a search for an alternative form of happiness to the one which subconsciously she knows to be unobtainable inasmuch as it depends upon Jérôme. Professor Brée is led to conclude (stating her point of view more forcefully, perhaps, as a corrective to a conventional view):

> With *La Porte Étroite*, Gide has not written a mystical book; he has not even written a religious book. The forces which lead Alissa and Jerome are psychological, imaginative, sentimental, but not religious. (p. 203)

The Brée line on *La Porte Étroite* is taken up by L. D. Knecht in an article which has become part of the new orthodoxy on the novel. Knecht, like Brée, turns the spotlight on Jérôme, develops the implications of Gide's description of Jérôme as 'flaccid hero', i.e. sexually inhibited or sexually impotent, gives prominence to those parts of the text in which Alissa's spontaneity, appetite, responsiveness are touched upon, and, again like Brée, sees her as forced into religion; hers is a tragedy not of renunciation but of resignation. Support for this reading is found, not surprisingly, in Gide's private problematic: the *mariage blanc* to Madeleine André Gide. The case of Jérôme is then akin to that of Octave in *Armance*, except that Gide unconsciously suppresses and conceals that part of the subject at which Stendhal was concerned to hint.[8]

Knecht makes greater play than Brée with an alleged contrast between Jérôme and Alissa and ties the explanation for Jérôme's behaviour more firmly to Gide's own dilemmas, but the total effect on one's view of the book is similar: the religious element, which seemed so important to readers such as Claudel and Jammes, tends to be eclipsed by a secular reading which places the emphasis on sexuality, repression and sublimation. Gide criticism, post Brée and Knecht, has on the whole tended to reflect this shift of emphasis.

There is, of course, an inherent plausibility about a line of interpretation which explores the links between the presentation of heterosexual relationships in the fiction and the author's deviant sexuality. One might argue too that the shift of emphasis has produced a more modern reading of the novel, one which is more in tune with sensibilities shaped by Freud and Erich Fromm. But still, Knecht's argument – and in this respect it is different from that of Brée – strikes me as in some ways extremely crude. Crude in its continual appeals to the idea of the normal in matters of love and sexual behaviour. Crude in invoking Gide's deviance as the only factor which might sufficiently explain Jérôme's pussy-footing in areas where red-blooded males such as Abel know what is expected of them. Crude above all (and despite a reference to *La Princesse de Clèves*[9]) in paying virtually no attention to the literary traditions in which the novel is situated.

Knecht suggests that Jérôme, in his conduct toward Alissa, is lacking in 'normal male aggressiveness'. But why does Nemours finally disqualify himself in the eyes of Mme de Clèves, if not precisely because of his 'male aggressiveness'? What may we infer about their respective worths from the contrast between the behaviour of Bernard during the fateful hunt with Edmée in *Mauprat*[10] and that of Rodolphe during the *promenade à cheval* with Emma Bovary?[11] What does Fromentin encourage us to believe about the relationship between love and aggression on the strength of the last encounter between Dominique and Madeleine?[12] Knecht would have it that Alissa loses faith in her charms because of an absence of 'concrete manifestations' on the part of her lover (p. 105). Perhaps she is like Tartuffe:

> Sweet words are not enough to win my trust,
> Unless some of your favors, which I burn for,
> Should give the reassurance that I yearn for . . . . (IV, 5)
> (Trans. Donald Frame)

The comparison is of course absurd and I make it only with a view to showing how incongruous it is to impute to Alissa the desire that their love should be confirmed 'par des réalités'.

I have discussed the contributions of Brée and Knecht because they have been largely responsible for the displacement of religion from the centre of *La Porte Étroite*. I would agree that there are elements in the novel which compete with religion for our interest. But to my mind, a far more important factor than sexuality is literature. What makes Knecht's account unsatisfactory and, in the long run, unsophisticated is the fact that he loses sight first of the generic affinities of the novel, second of the value system which obtains within the courtly tradition to which the novel belongs, and third of the extent to which the intellectual, highly literate protagonists in the sentimental drama are conscious of that tradition and of its main exemplars. An account of the novel which did justice to its complexity would not, I think, be one which saw literature as a vehicle for religion. Neither would it be one which discovered in Jérôme the unstated sexual problematic of the author. Rather it would be an account which recognized the importance of literature as an explicit theme within the book (a theme which sometimes accords and sometimes conflicts with the religious theme), and as a factor which, scarcely less than Alissa's mysticism, determines the fate of the lovers.

The extent to which literature dominates the converse of the young people in *La Porte Étroite* is, of course, striking. The letters and diary of Alissa are filled with quotation, as to a lesser extent is Jérôme's narrative. Characters identify their feelings and attitudes in terms of their reading. They borrow the eloquence of great writers, appeal to them, argue with them. This aspect of the novel has been judged sufficiently important for J. Mallion and II. Daudin to devote to it an article, 'Quotations in *La Porte Étroite*'.[13] Their concern is part pedantic: to make a list and furnish references. At the same time, they show how Gide, given that Jérôme, Alissa and Abel are 'intellectuals, with a very keen taste for literature', uses quotation as a means of drawing character and marking states of emotion. 'You are what you quote': there is a propriety to Jérôme's quoting Ronsard, 'whose vein of idealistic and platonic Petrarchism captures his attention',[14] as there is to Alissa's quoting Clotilde de Vaux.[15] Mallion and Baudin note the predominance of the seventeenth century as a source of quotations other than Biblical – testimony perhaps to an attempt by Gide to write a less convoluted prose.

The literary dimension of the text, where it takes the form of quotation, is explicit and easy to recognize. In contrast, intertextual study has revealed a range of hidden possibilities – features of rhetoric or style, more often shades of meaning, which will register only with readers of adequate erudition. The opening sentences are derived from Montaigne;[16] the description of landscape from Balzac,[17] the vision of happiness from Virgil.[18] The whole novel is a disguised tribute to Baudelaire.[19] Gide's moral and metaphysical concerns are shaped by Charles de Rémusat and the letters of Abélard and Eloïse.[20] A similar claim is entered on behalf of the letters of St. Jérôme.[21] In retrospect, one of the strangest remarks ever to have been made about *La Porte Étroite* must surely be that of Georges Pelissier: 'No literary artifice, nothing bookish . . .'.[22]

Let us assume that two things have been established by those critics who have dwelt upon what might be called the erudite or literary dimension of the text: that Gide's characters derive from literature the models for their conduct and the means of interpreting their situation, and that Gide's readers must similarly derive from literature the means of interpreting his texts. What follows?

In describing the relationship between Jérôme and Alissa, Gide describes a mode of conduct (characterized by *obstacle, refusal*) which he goes out of his way to qualify as strange (cf. Abel: 'there's something I can't understand in your tale' (523; 41)). The reader is put on his mettle to understand, with the benefit of hindsight and in the light of the diary, what is opaque to the narrator as actor and to the narrator as narrator. What does the reader understand? That the association of sexuality and guilt is made at the level of both experience and precept (Lucile's betrayal and Vautier's sermon) and that the 'natural' expression of love between Jérôme and Alissa is thereby permanently inhibited. Jérôme is locked into negative patterns of behaviour ('the snare of virtue' (565; 99)) and Alissa, in an effort to deny the maternal legacy, embarks upon her quest for transcendental worth: 'by force of love, beyond love' (586; 128). The novel is then about fear: 'to shelter this child from fear, from evil, from life' (504; 17). As she pursues the distinction between *life* and *life everlasting, daily bread* and *bread of heaven, muddy springs* and *living water*, Alissa commits a kind of moral suicide: askesis carried to the point of self-destruction.

What room is there in this account for literary models? The values are derived from Scripture, either direct (St Luke: the metaphor of the door) or via an intermediary (Racine: the metaphors of food and drink). On the other hand, when we consider *La Porte Étroite* as a sentimental novel, the literary models come into play. The first hint of a possible model comes in the opening chapter with the mention of the 'Florentine statuette of the time of Dante' (501; 14)[23] and the consequent mention of Beatrice. We are not however told that Jérôme takes Dante as a model, in the way that Julien Sorel takes Napoleon.[24] His model is unspecific: it is that of the *donnoi*, that most ancient and common romantic paradigm.[25] Jérôme relates to Alissa as knight to lady, the latter the inspiration and the prize, the former entirely submissive, making no claim, seeking only by patience, endurance, valour to establish such credentials as might warrant the lady's freely giving of herself. Jérôme strives, in effect, to be the 'parfit gentil knight'. Confirmation is to be found at the level of narrative detail, e.g. in the notion of the trial or test:

> without attempting to see my cousin, as soon as the service was over, I fled – out of pride, already desiring to put my resolutions (. . .) to the test, and thinking that I should best *be worthy of* her *by immediately avoiding her*. (506; 19)

> I did not answer. No doubt this silence was only the last trial to which she was subjecting me. (566; 100)

These acts of a quasi-penitential kind are performed early and late in the relationship. In between, Jérôme subjects himself to the mental disciplines of the rue d'Ulm and to the military disciplines of Nancy; he travels in foreign lands, in Italy and later in Palestine: as the details accumulate, we recognize in him an analogue of the crusader, a modern Rinaldo.[26]

The episode of the cross as sign belongs unambiguously to the world of the romance:

> Let us settle on a sign, which shall mean, 'Tomorrow you must leave Fongueusemare'. The next day I will go, without recrimination, without complaint. (562; 95)

Understanding the conventions, Alissa proposes that he remain only for as long as she wears her amethyst cross: 'But will you be able to go without a tear or a sigh? . . .'. He submits, and the bargain is sealed with a gesture which implies, on both parts, an understanding of ancient ceremony:

> She held out her hand; as I raised it to my lips, I added: 'But from now till the *fateful* evening, not an allusion to make me feel that it is coming'. (562; 95)

The episode of the cross has tragic overtones: 'till the *fateful* evening' – the parting *must* come. But in the days which follow, all sense of foreboding disappears:

> Hope sprang up again, confidently, in my breast. Hope, do I say? No! it was already certainty (. . .) 'Alissa,' I said to her one morning when all the air breathed laughter and delight and our hearts were opening like the flowers . . .. (563; 96–7)

How to explain this? Inconsequence? An ironic failure to appreciate the force of his own language, of the adjective: '*fateful* evening', and the tense: 'parting that *will* follow'? We have to keep in mind that submission is the means of success: in Sand's *Mauprat*, the interminably suffering Bernard wins Edmée. Jérôme is no different in that he hopes, by virtue of a series of trials successfully overcome, to justify Alissa's good opinion ('Do you think that he will become a remarkable man?' (508; 23)) and earn her hand.

In developing the theme of chivalry, am I making too much of what are no more than traces, linguistic relics – *vertu* (virtue), *courage, téméraire* (bold), *épreuve* (test), *éperonner* (spur on) – of values and modes of relationship which have no relevance to the world of the Le Havre merchant classes at the turn of the century? The objection is met in part by the sense the lovers have of themselves *beings set apart*, and by their frequent feeling that they are engaged in some sort of game, that their behaviour is unreal. The first games mentioned are the games that children play: '(I) cared only for the games which need reflection or effort' (506; 20); then the games that lovers play: 'Alissa seemed to lend herself to this child's play' (516; 32); 'And as, on the contrary, at sight of this gesture I came to a standstill in a spirit of playfulness . . .' (525; 44); then the games become serious: at the beginning of Chapter IV, games are associated with the idea of deception and unhappiness: 'Sometimes I wondered whether she were not actually taking pleasure in this as in a kind of game. No matter! I was firmly resolved to complain of nothing, and I let no trace of anxiety transpire in my letters' (530; 51). Before the end, the game is being used to qualify both the spiritual aspirations of Alissa and the chivalric pose of Jérôme: the same episode of the amethyst cross prompts, in Alissa's diary, the reflection: 'The reasons which make me fly from him? I no longer believe in them . . .' (587; 129), and in the letter – 'the strange letter which I give below' – which she writes immediately on his departure:

> I looked for you the whole morning, my brother. I could not believe that you had gone. I felt resentful against you for having kept to our engagement. I thought it must be a jest [*un jeu*]. (564; 97–8)

With the notion of game, Gide inhibits, at the same time as he promotes, our sense of the extravagance of the romantic dream. We believe because they disbelieve. Sometimes however we share their disbelief.[27] By comparison with the treatment of chivalric themes in *Les Caves du Vatican*, however, their treatment here is serious and respectful; the tone of voice represented by Abel is quickly suppressed.[28]

Besides furnishing the courtly model, literature is constantly present as · an intensifier, a noumenal extra. Jérôme is an adept in literature; to share in the secrets, Alissa is prepared to learn Latin and Juliette Italian. Life, to Jérôme, appears as 'a long journey – with her, through books and people and countries' (519; 36); as the glossing of that idea with Juliette involves appeals to Mallarmé's 'Brise marine' and to Baudelaire's 'Le Voyage', we might think that the first term, *books*, is the most important. Poetry is the means chosen by Juliette of communing with Jérôme, as it is the means of communing with Juliette chosen by Abel. In the garden, before the amorous confusions are revealed, the lovers read Swinburne, taking turns. It is against such a background that the marriage to Tessières, '(who) doesn't like music and hasn't much taste for books' (553; 83), and the transformation of Alissa, 'her hair in a new way, which flattened it and dragged it back . . . an unbecoming dress, dull in colour' (567; 101), must be judged.

In withdrawing his love, or seeming to withdraw his love, when confronted with the *dépoétisation* of Alissa, Jérôme responds in the only way he can. Love cannot sustain itself except on a diet of poetry. The formula in which he expresses his bafflement is full of irony: 'Alissa! . . . why do you tear off your wings?' (570; 106). Alissa's purpose is the acquiring of wings; she is 'the woman who wants to play the angel' [Pascal], a second Icarus. From the point of view of the lover and the poet however, Alissa refuses fancy and the flights of fancy.

Music, love, fancy: the three are linked in the passage of *Twelfth Night* from which Alissa culls the epigraph to her penultimate letter. Heine and Mendelssohn[29] conspire to keep alive that most seductive of romantic tropes, 'Auf Flügeln des Gesanges' ['The Wings of Song']. It is the office of poetry so to order the external world as to bring it into harmony with the heart's desire. Hence the notion of the *pays d'élection* [chosen country]: 'My mind has turned traveller; it is only my body that makes believe to stay behind here; in truth I am with you on the white roads of Umbria' (548; 75). Hence the importance of poetic décor in a novel such as this: 'The summer that year was splendid. The whole world seemed steeped in azure' (515; 31); 'She was at the bottom of the orchard, picking the first chrysanthemums at the foot of a low wall' (525; 44); the finest example occurs at the moment of the last interview between the lovers (576; 114). The description of Alissa's room, with its Baudelairian echoes (frequently remarked), stands as a tribute to the notion of a physical world which has been wholly assimilated into the world of the spirit. As Fromentin's Madeleine says, when at last she visits Les Trembles: 'Your countryside resembles you'.

Much has been made, in Gide criticism, of the contrast between Fongueusemare and Aigues-Vives, the latter revealing to Alissa an aspect of her being which she is reluctant to acknowledge. Scarcely less important is the difference between the contingent world and the world of poetry, the world outside the garden and the world within:

> already I wished for nothing beyond her smile, and to walk with her thus, hand in hand, along a sun-warmed, flower- bordered path (526; 45);
>
> 'Did you ever think what our life would be without each other?' 'No! Never': 'Now you see! For the last three years, without you, I have been drifting miserably about . . .'. (578; 116)

The extent of the hero's dereliction in the world outside the garden is suggested by an earlier detail in the text. Among the works of art which Alissa banishes from her room, there are, Jérôme tells us, 'two large photographs of Masaccios, which I had brought back from Italy' (568–9; 103–4). What were their subjects? The frescoes in the Church of Santa Maria del Carmine in Florence spring to mind, and of these, two scenes especially: *Adam and Eve in Paradise*, and the still more famous *Expulsion from Paradise*.[30]

The poetry of the relationship is a self-conscious poetry, and the courtly model is consciously adopted, yet the tragic implications of the model seem to escape the protagonists. Jérôme never consciously aims at anything other than happiness. It is his question: 'What can the soul prefer to happiness?' (563; 97) which creates the pretext for the opposition, *bonheur/sainteté*. His hope of happiness centres on Alissa. 'I seemed to have no other reason for living than my love' (540; 65). But the most powerful myth thrown up by courtly literature is the myth of Tristan and the pattern of the myth, in Rougemont's striking formulation, is that of *reciprocal unhappy love*.[31]

The central feature of Rougemont's reading of the myth is his demonstration of the way in which, when the obstacle to love is removed, there is the need artificially to invent an obstacle. Ultimately, the obstacle is internalized; love becomes a pretext for suffering and the intensification of emotion; the relationship between the lovers is sadomasochistic in character. Love is not love of the other but rather love of self, love of love, and in the last analysis love of death.

We know from Delay how interested Gide was in Rougemont's thesis,[32] and we know how brilliantly that thesis was exploited by Delay in the course of showing how Gide's *angélisme*, Beatrice complex, *mariage blanc*, arise from the coincidence of the myth and a certain disposition:

(the myth of angelism) would trouble only a courtly spirit, one that is prepared for the potion by temperament, as well as by an early and decisive fixation on the image of a venerated woman. (p. 220)

In the course of a discussion of a central feature of Gide's psychology, Delay offers an extended reading of *Les Cahiers d'André Walter* and shows how its patterns are repeated in *La Porte Étroite*:

> What André Walter and Alissa want is not the happiness of the couple but the obstacles that will prevent it, and of such obstacles death is obviously the most conclusive. These words of Chrétien de Troyes apply equally to both: 'Of all ills, mine is different; it pleases me; I enjoy it'. [p. 219: abridged version expanded]

Consistent with these statements is the claim: '*La Porte Étroite*, with its feminine replica of André Walter, is itself an anachronistic book, a novel of chivalry, and its heroine a thirteenth-century virgin, a figure from a stained-glass window.' (id.)

Delay couches his argument mainly in terms of Alissa, seeing in her (and the reading is conventional in this respect) the dominant partner. In fact, Jérôme's role as narrator and the sequence of the narrative ensure that courtly motifs, when they first appear, appear in relation to the hero. I have earlier cited the concluding sentence of Chapter I: 'without attempting to see my cousin, [. . .] I fled – out of pride . . . , etc.' (506; 19), but as he responds to the distress of Alissa, already Jérôme identifies himself as paladin – to be compared, for example, with the hero of Keats's fragment, 'Calidore', who burns:

> To hear of knightly deeds, and gallant spurning
> Of all unworthiness; and how the strong of arm
> Kept off dismay, and terror, and alarm
> From lovely woman . . .[33]

Courtly motif merges with *jeu de l'amour*, then gives way to something more serious, though whether by virtue of its own momentum or because it is annexed to other, more strictly religious purposes, we are not required to decide.[34] What matters is that we recognize the tradition:

> In French romantic literature a whole courtly tradition, from *Le Roman de la Rose* to innumerable modern novels, corresponds to the Tristan myth. (Delay, p. 220)

La Porte Étroite is one such novel; in recognizing the type and allowing our imagination to be guided by it, we acknowledge a preference for the tragic outcome.

By what signs do we recognize the type? The retrospective quality of the narrative, the elegiac mood, the preference for autumn among the seasons, a sense of time and the ravages of time, the suggestion that the figure and manners belong to another age: all of these are recurrent features. 'Lucile Bucolin, I wish I no longer bore you malice . . .' (499; 11); 'But, Aunt, I didn't choose to love her . . .' (513; 29); 'The summer sped by . . .' (516–7; 32–3); 'Ah! blind wretch that I was . . .' (520; 37); with a minimum of emphasis, the tragic tone insinuates itself. If we miss these indications, some explicit reference to earlier examples of the tradition will be made – as here, to Beatrice or to Swinburne.

How considered is the reference to Swinburne?[35] In 'The Triumph of Time', an unrequited lover reflects on what might have been and vows to take his love and pain unspoken to the grave. The persona is that of the 'flaccid hero', in whom self-immolation combines with resentment and a sense of failure. Two passages especially are of interest. The firsts reads as commentary upon the novel:

> But will it not one day in heaven repent you?
> Will it solace you wholly, the days that were?
> Will you lift up your eyes between sadness and bliss
> Meet mine and see where the great love is,
> And tremble and turn and be changed? Content you;
> The gate is strait; I shall not be there.
>
> But you, had you chosen, had you stretched hand,
> Had you seen good such a thing were done,
> I too might have stood with the souls that stand
> In the sun's sight, clothed with the light of the sun . . .

The second pays tribute to the source of all such material:

> There lived a singer in France of old
> By the tideless dolorous midland sea.
> In a land of sand and ruin and gold
> There shone one woman and none but she.
> And finding life for her love's sake fail,
> Being fain to see her, he bade set sail,
> Touched land, and saw her as life grew cold,
> And praised God, seeing; and so died he.[36]

The speaker's purpose, in retelling the story, is to compare his fate unfavourably with that of the quasi-Tristan. More generally, the stanza acts as a marker, linking Swinburne's theme to the themes of the legend. The mention of Swinburne's title in the Gide text performs the same function.

For most readers of *La Porte Étroite*, nearer to home than Swinburne is Fromentin and the novel which Gide would appear not only to have admired, but discreetly to have imitated.[37] Juliette, rival in love to her sister, is a more developed Julie; Abel shares a mocking, man-of-the-world tone with Olivier; marriage to Tessières ('A tradesman!') teaches (perhaps) the positive lessons which Augustin tried to impart. In Dominique, whose cast of mind is elegiac and whose self-esteem is low, Gide's hero is partially anticipated. The similarity is of kind as well as detail. *Dominique* is squarely in the Tristan tradition: it is when the obstacle appears (Nièvres) that the passion declares itself: 'What I saw, dawned on me in a few seconds: "Madeleine is lost to me and I love her" '.[38] In the lengthy ordeal which follows, Madeleine's brief sojourn at Les Trembles is a perfect analogue of those fleeting moments of happiness in the garden at Fongueusemare:

> Madeleine came upon me once in the winding alleys of the park, lost in memories. Julie followed behind, carrying an enormous sheaf of chrysanthemums which she had picked for the vases in the drawing-room. Between us, a clump of laurels formed a light screen. 'Are you composing a sonnet?' she called to me through the trees. (p. 170)

The cast and the settings correspond; the coincidence of tone is unmistakable. And again we find those references which link the story to earlier examples of the tradition – references to *Werther*:

> The sound of bells, accompanied these walks, gothic chimes for German walks where I was no Werther but where Madeleine, I do believe, was worthy of Charlotte (p. 101);

and to *Mauprat*:

> For at least a minute, like Bernard de Mauprat in the footsteps of Edmée, I watched her flee beneath the tall colonnade of oak trees . . . . (p. 263)

Even where the reference is negatively formulated, as in the former case, the suggestion is that we are dealing with variants upon a single story.

Roman religieux? Professor Brée thought not. *Roman de chevalerie*, then? The description is Delay's and if we accept it, we have to accept the implications. First among them is the fact that there can be no limit to the spiritualization of the relationship and no drawing back from the tragic ending: 'But to have kept her, to have forced the door [. . .] no, it was not possible to me' (579; 117). If that is so, what becomes of the suggestion that the novel is ironic? On what grounds can we disavow the heroine's idealist preference? Alissa is anti-life, certainly, but so is Tristan, and it is as a genetic derivative from the Tristan legend that the work presents itself to us.

What of the ménage Tessières, Juliette's multiple pregnancies and the notion of happiness 'tailor-made' for the individual? Even without the epilogue in the 'small rather dark room', shrine to Alissa, it is difficult to see how these elements could be prestigious enough to overthrow the values implicit in the lovers' stance in favour of the viewpoint of those '[who] [don't] like music and [haven't] much taste for books' (553; 83). The arguments in favour of a passionate Alissa whose religion is factitious are similarly hard to swallow. We infer her nature from the scene in which she first appears as actor in the drama: 'she was on her knees by the bedside; through the window behind her came the last glimmer of expiring daylight' (503; 16). The scene resembles an Annunciation,[39] hence the presence later in her story of those symbolic attributes of the Virgin: *hortus conclusus, porta clausa, speculum sine macula,* the flawless mirror to which the remark concerning Frau von Stein,[40] certainly, and the mirror incident in Chapter II, possibly, allude.

If Alissa's spirituality is innate and not a characteristic acquired by way of compensation, it makes no difference whether she is sacrificed on the altar of religion or the altar of love. Superficially conflicting, the religious and the sentimental preoccupations reinforce one another. The presence of the courtly material makes it difficult if not impossible for Gide to press home his criticism of Protestant excess. In any case, Rougemont, and after him Delay, have shown that between heretical religion and courtly love, Cathar and troubadour, there is no contradiction. *Roman religieux* and *de chevalerie*? Perhaps the best approach to *La Porte Étroite* might set out from those lines in which Nerval imagines the poet

> Modulant, tour à tour, sur la lyre d'Orphée
> Les soupirs de la sainte et les cris de la fée.[41]

NOTES

1. See, for example, FRIEDA S. BROWN. 'Montaigne and Gide's *La Porte Étroite*', *PMLA*, 82 (1967), 136–41 (p. 139).

2. *Correspondance Jammes – Gide* (Paris, 1948), pp. 310–11; Jammes makes the remark in the final sentence of the review of the novel which he wrote for *L'Occident* (July 1909).

3. Compare JAMMES: 'The very haughtiness of the Christian suffering defies an all too human proselytising' (*Corr. Jammes – Gide*, p. 310).

4. Compare J. C. DAVIES, *Gide: 'L'Immoraliste' and 'La Porte Étroite'* (London, 1968), pp. 8–9: 'Alissa breaks her cousin's heart, and brings about her own death. This

occurs because of the *excess* to which both protagonists carry their ideal, so that it becomes a dangerous obsession, almost a temporary insanity. It should, after all, be possible for reasonable people to reconcile a desire for self-realisation or a longing for God with the claims of a normal married life'.

5. [See 'Licentiousness, depravity and the declarations of Senator Béreanger' in *Pretexts*.]

6. [*Cornelian*: associated with the tragedies of Pierre Corneille (1606–1684), whose plays such as *Le Cid* (1636–7) notably hinge on conflicts between human love and moral or religious duty.]

7. In *André Gide. L'Insaisissable Protée* (Paris, 1953), esp. ch. VII, pp. 183–208.

8. Knecht's article first appeared in *PMLA*, 82 (1967), 640–48. Knecht entitles his contribution 'A New Reading'; as I see it, it is rather a sequel to Brée. The last point, comparing Jérôme and Octave, is a development out of Knecht by DENNIS DRUMMOND, 'Une influence stendhalienne sur *La Porte Étroite* d'André Gide', *Stendhal Club*, 18 (1975), 148–57. [Octave, hero of the novel *Armance* (1827) by STENDHAL (1783–1842), appears to suffer from sexual impotence – though the condition is not made explicit in the text.]

9. [Novel (1678) by MADAME DE LAFAYETTE, commonly held to be the starting point of the modern novel of psychological analysis, whose plot concerns the heroine's resistance to the charms of Nemours and the temptation of extramarital love.]

10. [Novel (1837) of romantic passion by GEORGE SAND (1804–1876) in which the hero Bernard de Mauprat pursues the love of Edmée.]

11. [*Madame Bovary* (1857) by FLAUBERT, tells how the heroine is led into adultery by her attachment to romantic dreams.]

12. [*Dominique*, novel of 1863 by EUGÈNE FROMENTIN (1820–1876) presenting a psychological study of an impossible love.]

13. *Recherches et travaux*, Université de Grenoble, U.E.R. Lettres, 5 (March 1972), 3–11.

14. [The poet Ronsard (1524–1585) wrote in part in imitation of the Italian Petrarch whose poems celebrate his chaste, platonic love for his muse Laura.]

15. [CLOTILDE DE VAUX (1815–1846), a tormented and sickly woman, inspired a passionate love in the philosopher Auguste Comte from the moment he met her in 1844. Under her influence he turned from positivism to religion and mysticism and after her early death declared her a patron saint of humanity.]

16. BROWN, 'Montaigne and Gide's *La Porte Étroite*', p. 137.

17. DOROTHY Y. KADISH, ' ''Alissa dans la vallée'': Intertextual Echoes of Balzac in Two Novels by Gide', *French Forum*, 10 (1985), 67–83.

18. GÉRARD DEFAUX, 'Sur des vers de Virgile; Alissa et le mythe gidien du bonheur', *Revue des lettres modernes, André Gide* 3 (1972) 97–121. Some of the same ground is covered in EIKO NAKAMURA, 'Les deux jardins de *La Porte Étroite*', *Bulletin des Amis d'André Gide*, 10, no. 53 (jan. 1982), 29–37.

19. ALBERT SONNENFELD, 'Baudelaire et Gide: *La Porte Étroite*', 232 (May 1967), 79–90; this article overlaps with Sonnenfeld, '*Strait is the Gate*: Byroads in Gide's Labyrinth', *Novel*, 1 (Winter 1968), 118–32.

20. TONY HUNT, 'Alissa-Eloissa', *Orbis Litterarum*, 33 (1978), 183–90. [Charles de Rémusat (1797–1875), in his monograph *Abélard* (1845) and his 1877 drama of the same title, celebrated the love of Abélard and Héloïse, which transcended their respective careers as monk and nun. Their bodies shared the same tomb in 1163 and their remains were placed together in Père Lachaise cemetery in Paris in 1817.

21. KEITH CAMERON, 'Gide, Jérôme et Saint Jérôme', *Bulletin des Amis d'André Gide*, 6, no. 39 (1978), 58–65.

22. Pelissier's review of the novel, from *La Revue* (15 August 1909), is reproduced in PIERRE TRAHARD, *'La Porte Étroite' d'André Gide* (Paris, 1968), 138–9.

23. [The Italian poet DANTE ALIGHIERI (1265–1321), who in the poems of the *Vita Nuova* and *The Divine Comedy*, celebrates Beatrice as his chaste muse.]

24. [In Stendhal's novel *Le Rouge et le Noir* (1830).]

25. *'Donnoi*, or *domnei* in Provençal, depicts the relation of vassalage instituted between the lover- chevalier and his lady, or *domina*', Denis de Rougemont, *L'Amour et l'Occident* (Paris, 1939), Union générale d'éditions, 1962, p. 27.

26. [One of the crusaders who features in the epics of Charlemagne such as the medieval *Chanson de Roland*. Rinaldo or Renaud was a suitor for the hand of Angelica and conqueror of the Saracen enchantress Armida, who having converted to Christianity adopted him as her knight.]

27. There are the letters ('My heart melts with joy as I read you' (548; 75)) and the 'melancholy meeting' (558; 89); there is the *amour de tête* and 'the contact of our damp hands which made us unclasp them' (557: 87); there is the *correspondance-mirage* and the 'fall into reality' (560; 92). The old house has flawed windows: between the mind and reality, imagination – *le 'bouillon'* or 'bubble' (496; 6) – interposes itself.

28. 'It's all over! I am no longer worthy': thus Amédée [in *Les Caves du Vatican*], after his seduction by Carola. Abel has already failed the test; as Jérôme tells him: 'You aren't worthy to love her' (544; 71).

29. [HEINRICH HEINE (1797–1856), German lyric poet, author notably of the *Buch der Lieder*, many of which were set to music by composers such as Felix Mendelssohn (1809–1847).]

30. In the *Feuillets* which appear at the end of the diary entries for 1893, Gide mentions Masaccio as one of the painters whose work might be compatible with study: 'In the workroom no works of art or very few and very serious ones: (no Botticelli) Masaccio, Michelangelo, Raphael's *School of Athens* . . . , etc. (*JI*, 49; *J1*, 36). Alissa's sense of the profane element in art has reached the point where she is no longer willing to discriminate.

31. Rougemont, op.cit., p. 43.

32. JEAN DELAY, *The Youth of André Gide*, abridged and trs. by JUNE GUICHARNAUD, Chicago and London, Chicago University Press, 1963, p. 218.

33. *The Poetical Works of John Keats*, edited by H. Buxton Forman (Oxford, 1908), pp. 14–15.

34. Compare Alissa's remark (to Jérôme), recorded in her diary: 'And you, my dear, you yourself, and in spite of yourself, can no longer act otherwise than as if you

were inspired by the liveliest faith. And I should not love you if you were different' (585; 125).

35. Faint traces of an interest in Swinburne are to be found in *Le 'Subjectif'* (*Cahiers André Gide, 1*) and in the *Correspondance Gide-Valéry*. The most interesting piece of evidence is however supplied by Claude Martin, *LaMaturité d'André Gide* (Paris, 1977): Martin relates how, in Florence in 1895, Gide presented a copy of *Les Cahiers d'André Walter* to an American lady, Mrs Andrews, 'inscribing in it three lines of Swinburne in gallant illustration of the dedication: "Nothing is better, I well think, than love . . ." ' (p. 100, n. 66). [CHRISTOPHER BETTINSON, in 'Gide, Swinburne et *La Porte Étroite*', in *André Gide et l'Angleterre*, ed. Patrick Pollard, London, Birkbeck College, 1986, pp. 18–23, concludes that Gide was well-acquainted with the poet's work and perhaps also with those elements in Swinburne's marriage that were analogous to Gide's drama with Madeleine.]

36. *The Poems of Algernon Charles Swinburne*, 6 vols (London, 1904), I, 34–47.

37. DELAY (op.cit) reports Gide as acknowledging the kinship of *La Porte Étroite* and *Dominique*: 'he had greatly admired Fromentin's discreet masterpiece during his youth' [*I*, p. 511, n. 1: the reference does not appear in the English translation].

38. FROMENTIN, *Dominique*, ed. Emile Henriot (Paris, Garnier, 1961), p. 110. Further references to this edition are given after translated quotations in the text.

39. Or perhaps a false Annunciation: in place of light, Gabriel and a miraculous fecundity, darkness, Jérôme and the promise ('shelter this child . . . from life') of sterility.

40. 'For we remembered Goethe's saying about Madame de Stein: "It would be beautiful to see the world reflected in that soul" ' (515; 31). According to Mallion and Baudin (see above), the remark is recorded by Zimmermann in a letter to Frau von Stein (25 May 1775); it reflects, I would suggest, a popular belief concerning the Virgin, of which a mirror is the iconographic representation.

41. [Gérard de Nerval, 'El Desdichado':
    Rendering in turn on Orpheus' lyre
    The sighs of the saint and the cries of the fairy.]

12 Alain Goulet on The Figurative Representation of the Literary Process in *La Symphonie Pastorale**

The critical revolution of the 1960s transformed the way in which writing was viewed. Under the influence of Saussure's structuralist theories of language, Jacques Derrida and Roland Barthes formulated a notion of *écriture* as a system of signs which explores the multiple possibilities of producing meaning through the plurality of structural, semantic and other relations which it generates within itself (see *L'écriture et la différence*, Paris, Seuil 1967; *S/Z*, Paris, Seuil, 1970). Hence writing does not transcribe preexisting messages emanating from the writer's intentions or the world about which he or she writes: rather, the language of the written text explores its own signifying process – and in this respect, a text is **scriptible**, as Barthes puts it: reading such a text is itself a form of rewriting in pursuit of a meaning which is perpetually deferred. A radical version of this perspective was formulated by Jean Ricardou, who declared memorably that the business of literature was not *l'écriture d'une aventure* (the writing of an adventure) but *l'aventure d'une écriture* (the adventure of a writing). Moreover, he asserted, such was the self-consciousness of literature that, in a development from the internal mirroring associated with the *mise en abyme*, 'great narratives are distinguishable by the fact that the fiction they present is nothing other than the dramatisation of their own functioning' (*Problèmes du nouveau roman*, Paris, Seuil, 1967, pp. 111, 178). The literal narrative as such, therefore, is a pretext for a reflection on the text's own internal workings.

Gide's writing can be seen to anticipate some of these notions. Alain Goulet, a prominent Gide scholar who has written numerous substantial studies, brings this *avant-garde* perspective to bear on one of the *récits*. His reading centres on images deriving from water which can be read as metaphors for various stages of the writing process. In the evolution and interrelation of such motifs, Goulet discerns a network of signification which highlights the

---

* Originally published in *André Gide 3, Gide et la fonction de la littérature*, ed. Claude Martin, *Revue des Lettres modernes*, nos. 331–35, 1972, pp. 27–55. Translated and abridged by David Walker.

relation of the pastor-narrator to his own writing and the uses to which he puts it as a means of determining his relationships with the other characters in his tale: Gertrude, the orphan he takes in and falls in love with; Amélie, the wife he forsakes; and Jacques, the son who challenges him. While seeking to control them as the subjects of his narration, the pastor is defeated by the very flux and indeterminancy of writing: it becomes available for reading by others – first of all by Gertrude herself – who constructs ironic counterreadings that defeat his deluded dream of fixing its meaning, stopping the flow of signification. Such readings show the literary text moving beyond realism – the transcribing of ready-made meaning, for consumption by a passive reader – towards an adventure in the production of meaning, in which reading and writing are two aspects of the same process.

> I think of something Gide once said: 'It is above all necessary to study my work on the level of aesthetics', which does not prevent one, having started from aesthetics, from ending up with morality, theology, etc.

> André Berne-Joffroy, *Entretiens sur André Gide*, Paris, Mouton, 1967, p. 298.

> 'Read me better; re-read me.' Gide, *Divers*, p. 62.

[. . .] We propose to sound out, in *La Symphonie Pastorale*, the manner in which the literary process – that is to say the couple formed of the scriptural/reading function – is implicated within Gide's texts, is designated in and by the fiction.[1]

We shall not concern ourselves with Gide as author, except incidentally in so far as the Pastor-narrator represents one of his possible selves. Gide spoke too frequently of the 'moral purging' which led him to 'deliver up [his] various possibilities in [his] books and expel from [him]self the contradictory characters who inhabited [him]'[2] for us not to discern the author behind the narrator. And yet we must distinguish the links between the man and his work, which have been studied exhaustively in the case of *La Symphonie Pastorale* by Claude Martin after Francis Pruner, from the manner in which the narration implicates the narrator, that is to say how the writing process is inscribed within the narrative discourse.

1. Snow

Three paragraphs, clearly set apart in the first editions, inaugurate the discourse of the narrator and form an exordium which is to justify the story that follows. We note first of all that it is the snow which motivates and triggers the narration, on the specific date of 10 February: 'The snow has been falling continuously [. . .] and all the roads are blocked. [. . .] I will take advantage of the leisure this enforced confinement affords me to think over the past and set down how I came to take charge of Gertrude. [. . .] I proposed to write here [. . .]' (4; 9). This correlation of snow and writing is far from fortuitous. It is repeated as soon as the narrator takes up his pen again ('The snow fell heavily again last night. [. . .] I take advantage of it to go on with the tale [. . .]' (20–2; 18)), and is invoked *a contrario* to account for the interruption of the writing between the two Notebooks:

> I have been obliged to put this book aside for some time. The snow melted at last [. . .] (86; 50)

An extended metaphor, developed in connection with Gertrude's rapid progress, renders explicit what the snow can represent:

> How often have I wondered at the melting of the snow; its white cloak seems to wear thin from underneath, while to all appearance it remains unchanged. Every winter Amélie falls into the trap: ' The snow is as thick as ever,' she declares. And indeed it still seems so, when all at once there comes a break and suddenly, in patches here and there, life once more shows through. (36; 25)

The snow is a cover which provisionally conceals life, superimposes itself upon life – which erodes it meanwhile and which it will presently reveal. Let us hazard a preliminary interpretation: on the one hand the snow – and writing, which it prompts – is a seamless 'cloak' (the tissue of the text) which encloses a secret life; on the other hand it stands in the way of a direct involvement in life. Writing, in this view, would thus be a mediating element which becomes necessary when one is not directly involved in life, when life has lost its transparency.[3] It is the site of a search, and when the narrator claims to 'set down how [he] came to take charge of Gertrude' and then 'her formation and development' (4; 9) we are to understand that this is only the alleged object of his account. This account is not preconstituted, but, taking the circumstances of the past as a pretext, he will set out to discover, in the present, what he has to say. The narrator is thus driven by a need for elucidation which can conceal a 'need for justification'.[4] This indeed is the dual purpose of the diary kept by Gide, and this is what will induce the tale to take the form of a diary after the snows have melted, that is to say at the moment when writing will superimpose itself directly upon the 'reality' it is to illuminate.[5] On the other hand when the narrator finally sees things clearly, writing ceases to have a purpose and the tale abruptly stops: the narrator and his characters are restored to life[6] . . . or to oblivion.

Before leaving this exordium, let us note further what has been cut from it. The text of the manuscript given in Note 8 does much more than evoke Christmas as does that of Notes 1, 2 and 6. Alongside writing it also situates the word, underlining thereby the double status of the Pastor, a veritable Janus: as narrator, he holds the redoubtable privilege of binding the characters in his discourse and illuminating them as he likes; as a pastor he has the advantage, over the other characters in the tale, of the scriptural authority of the Word. 'J'ai *parlé*, ce jour de Noël, sur cette *parole* du Luc' ('My text, this Christmas day, was taken from Luke'):[7] the repetition in the French is eloquent and signifies that the Pastor tends to identify his words with those of the Gospels – or at least to make them coincide. It is evident at the outset, therefore, that this prerogative constitutes a pitfall from which derives a good part of the equivocations and ambiguities in the tale, since the Pastor is able to use his double authority, both divine and regal, to trap the reader while deluding himself. But this process is complicated in so far as the author, hidden behind the narrator, rapidly establishes a connivance with the reader to the detriment of his character whose privileges then rebound against him: this is the founding principle of the ironic or critical *récit*.

But that is not the only source of ambiguities. The play of scripture (Word/text) also covers a more complex play of thoughts, of tacit meanings, of more or less conscious tactical ploys which constitute a sub-text, highlighted here at the level of the word, that is of the fiction:

> [. . .] *meditating on* this *text* these last few days, I *had cause to think* sometimes of [Marceline] Gertrude, for whom my wife *declared* [. . .] *It goes without saying* that I *avoided any allusion* to that in *my sermon*; but it *is possible* nonetheless that my wife *thought about* it.

This habit the characters have of prevaricating with words – which ramify in a dense skein of what we might call 'infra-words' – , is analogous to the manner the narrator adopts at the scriptural level. The text is not closed off within the surface of its signs; its purpose is to suggest, to leave hints without being explicit, via the network of its component parts, and in one and the same movement, to dissemble that which it nevertheless denounces. What is written – and this is all the more true of an account which presents itself as autobiographical – is always a surface to be scrutinized, probed, reinterpreted.

2. Lake and stream

After the opening, the tale gets under way by means of a break, the Pastor's leap into the unknown, in accordance with the tradition of the *roman d'aventure* which remains for Gide the archetype of the novel.[8] The hero embarks on 'a road which [he] had never ventured down before and concludes: 'I had certainly never been there before' (6; 9–10). Framed by this double reference to a literary genre, is a fairly lengthy addition to the text which could appear solely descriptive:

> . . . however, I *recognized* on the left-hand side a *mysterious little lake*, where I had sometimes been to *skate* as a young man. I had not seen it for fifteen years, for none of my pastoral duties take me that way; *I could not have said* where it lay and it had so entirely *dropped out of my mind* that when I suddenly *recognized* it *in the gold enchantment* of the rose-flecked evening sky, I felt as though I had only seen it before *in a dream.*
>
> The road ran alongside the stream that falls out of the lake, cut across the extreme end of the forest and then skirted a peat-moss.

What we read into this is a metaphorical representation of the writing of the tale which is venturing to recognize a partially forgotten past. The fifteen-year gap noted in the fiction seems to correspond to the time-lag of 'two years and six months' which separates the lived adventure from this account of it – or if one prefers, the character from the narrator. Action ('skate') is replaced by contemplation in an 'enchantment' which is so misleading that the original era appears to have been only a 'dream', that is to say that the memory has subsided into the unconscious, offering resistance to the pastor's attempts at retrieval. The absence of utterance ('I could not have said') and of awareness ('out of my mind') represents the span of time preceding the start of the tale whose function indeed will consist of bringing into the open this past in which people only skated, that is to say only skimmed the surface of life. If recognition is not yet understanding, it will at least break the initial torpor of the enchantment and permit the scriptural process to go forward.

This is why the frozen lake of yore has become 'a mysterious little lake' akin to that unconscious past which the narrator carries within him. This lake flows into 'the stream that falls out of the lake [*s'en échappait*]', which in turn determines the course of the path followed by our Pastor, a route which he creates for the reader as he takes it. Thus does writing flow in a linear fashion from its origin in the narrator who fabricates his story progressively as he follows up that which he carries within him. To his double status noted above, we can now add that of being his own first reader.

If it has not previously occurred to anyone to consider that the paired evocation of the lake and the stream could well represent, in the text, an image of the text,[9] many readers of *La Symphonie Pastorale* had nevertheless resorted spontaneously to these images to define the impression given by the apparent limpidity of its surface ('stream') and its mysterious background depths, composed of ambiguities and secret motivations to which the narrator is blind ('mysterious little lake' and 'peat-moss' which are situated at the source and on the fringe of the writing). One of the most perspicacious among them, Charles du Bos, praised 'the turbidness of the content showing through the limpidity of the form',[10] whilst Anna de Noailles spoke of the debate which 'develops with a regular beauty, patient, mysterious, but swollen with its torrent', and of the 'perpetual transparencies,' the 'veiled light' of the story: 'Nothing is evaded, all is layered'.[11] This is the crux of the matter, in fact: the text indicates everything whilst making nothing explicit.[12] The stream of its words constantly leads us back to the mystery of the lake, and the Pastor perpetually maps a surface without looking into all that his writing conceals and reveals, indeed so far as possible avoiding understanding himself by means of his writing. It is therefore the role of the reader to illuminate the multiplicity of meanings which are layered one upon the other, to trace out a path through the polysemy of the work by considering the techniques of enunciation and articulation of the facts, instead of letting him/herself be smothered by the complex latticing as happened to the unfortunate Fontainas.[13]

3. Tears

There is therefore a circulation of water which might be taken to represent the work of the writing and which, like water, assumes various forms, linked with the narration, with the telling, with the wish to say something or the absence of things said. This is so literally the case that the tale stops when its source dries up, in other words when the narrator states: 'I would have wept, but I felt my heart *more arid than the desert*' (132; 71). The entire extent of the writing is contained between the two extremes of 'the snow' and 'the desert'.

A different level of textual investigation corresponds to each form that the water assumes: the snow, an opaque cloak, enabled us to envisage writing as a means of elucidation; the mysterious lake and the stream involved both the link between writing and the subject of the discourse and the linear unfolding of the action. Tears, on the other hand, permit us to engage with the problems of psychology and morality.[14]

Tears are in the first instance a means of establishing the limits of writing, signifying feelings without saying them, soundings taken inside the characters in such a way that they reveal themselves without the need to spell things out. Tears, then, are the limit terms of discourse for enunciating limited feelings. For one should not forget that the characters are never viewed 'objectively', but by the narrator who introduces them. This latter, deploying his writing like a set of masks by means of which he seeks to vindicate himself, is highly likely to divert the sense in the tears of others – as in their words – if he takes it upon himself to explain them. This is especially so in the case of Amélie, who provokes references to her 'fit of sobbing' (18; 16) and her 'voice trembling with tears' (76; 45).

It is clear that tears too are explicitly connected in the text with language. Ultimately they are in fact the equivalent of the supreme language, prayer – albeit negatively, since in the final sentence of the story the term 'pray' is the effect of a last-minute substitution for 'weep'.[15] In this respect, they will function as the privileged vehicle for the moral problem of lying and deception.

> Do you remember the day you answered me that you weren't *crying*, when my aunt (that is what she called my wife) had reproached you with being no help to her? And I cried out, 'Pastor, that's *not true [vous mentez]*!' Oh, I felt at once from your voice that you *weren't telling me the truth*; there was no need for me to feel your cheeks to know that *you had been crying*. (96; 31)

Because these tears revealed to Gertrude that the word could be false, she will take the opportunity to put the Pastor's sincerity to the test by establishing an equivalence between 'wanting to cry' and 'not telling the truth':

> 'And yet you *cry* sometimes?'
> 'I have *cried* sometimes.'
> 'Not since that time?'
> 'No, I *have not cried* since that time.'
> 'And you have not *felt inclined to cry*?'
> 'No, Gertrude.'
> 'And . . . tell me, have you *felt inclined since then not to speak the truth*?'
> 'No, dear child.'
> 'Can you promise *never to try to deceive me*?' (48; 31)

The parallels in the dialogue are unequivocal. And when, a few moments later, Gertrude perceives the deception of the Pastor in his attachment to her before denouncing it at the end of the Second Notebook, she in turn cries. Her sudden realization, brought about by Amélie's words, leads her to take upon herself the tears that the Pastor, in his obtuseness, is unable to shed:

'You see,' I said, 'this time I am not crying.'

'No,' answered she, trying to smile, 'this time it is my turn.' And as she looked up at me, I suddenly saw her face was flooded with tears. (52; 33)

Of course, as these tears are ambiguous in the way that language is, the reader will only grasp their meaning through their recurrence, when the *dénouement* of the story sheds light on the various paradigmatic indications scattered throughout the text.

4. Undine

Thus Gertrude, who is linked in a privileged fashion to the problem of writing, deciphering the implied meanings of the text and unmasking its falsehoods, has a particular affinity with water.

When she first appears, she is merely an object, a raw material, ill-defined, covered in filth and vermin. Then in Amélie's hands she is cleaned up, washed, purified. This is the occasion of her first metamorphosis: she accedes to the status of a character and is given a name. Washing and naming are undeniably connected in the text, the one seeming to be a preliminary to the other (22; 19). In a Christian perspective this signifies baptism, and in a Rousseauistic perspective, the revelation of the original being who has recovered her natural simplicity, in other words her identity.[16] Gertrude becomes a symbol of purity and naïvety, a touchstone for the truth and sincerity of others. The Pastor describes her as 'a limpid soul' (106; 59), and her limpidity is contagious:

> the smile that dawned for me one morning on that marble face of hers, when she seemed suddenly touched to understanding and interest by what I had been trying for so many days to teach her, *flooded my heart* with a more seraphic joy than was ever given me by any child of my own. (32; 24)

This smile, the first form of communication and language in her, is noted as a 'transfiguration' that confers on Gertrude a supernatural dimension – she is 'angelic', 'mysterious':

> Her features flashed into life – a *sudden illumination*, like the crimson glow that precedes dawn in the high Alps, thrilling the *snowy peak on which it lights* and calling it up out of darkness – such a flood, it seemed, of *mystic colour*; and I thought too of the *pool of Bethesda* at the moment the *angel* descends to *stir the slumbering water*. A kind of *ecstasy* rapt me at sight of the *angelic expression* that came over Gertrude's face so suddenly [. . .] (34; 24)

To understand this passage fully, we must connect it with the one analysed in Section 2 above. Gertrude is not merely visited by the angel, she becomes the angel, endowed with an 'angelic expression'; and the 'slumbering water' leads us back to the 'mysterious lake' at the start of the novel. The 'ecstasy' which seizes the Pastor here is akin to the 'enchantment' he experienced initially, a sort of illumination that precedes his plunge into adventure. The essential difference arises from the fact that the status of the character has changed. At the outset of the narrative, he stood as the narrator, the source of the writing; now he is a character in his tale. And if that 'slumbering water' is stirred up, it is because, after all the preceding preparatory detail, we have reached the point at which the action of the story will be initiated, bringing ineluctably in its wake all the future incidents from the moment when, in his rapturous delight, the hero kisses Gertrude for the first time. Let us resume our quotation from the point at which we had left it:

> [. . .] for it was clear to me that this heavenly visitor was not so much intelligence as love. And in a very transport of gratitude I kissed her forehead and felt that I was offering thanks to God. (34; 24)

The drama begins in this confusion between *eros* and *agape*. As for the 'snowy peak' picked out in the 'night' of the action by the heroine transformed into light, it announces the 'dawn' of the writing, that is to say the moment when the snow heaped up on life will constrain the Pastor to begin his narrative. This is why the tragic action begins with a reference back to the beginning of the narration which must recall this same action before conducting it to its conclusion.

This system of cross reference is more explicit in the episode of the concert at Neuchâtel which justifies the title of the story. If the title functions ambiguously in relation to the text which it announces and subsumes,[17] it is primarily nonetheless the symbol of it, and gathers within itself – especially in this particular instance – all the book's equivocal features. And yet the fact that it is the primary representation of the text can open the way to a privileged meaning for us, provided that we let ourselves be guided by the narrative thread. The manner in which the *Pastoral Symphony* is introduced into the story incites us forcefully to do so: 'It was actually (*précisément*) the *Pastoral Symphony* that was being played! I say *actually* because, as will be easily understood, there is no work I could have more wished her to hear' (44; 30). The truth is, not only does the second sentence not explain the first at all, but it actually deepens the mystery: at the level of straightforward denotation, both 'actually' and 'as will be easily understood' can have equally little meaning and constitute an insoluble enigma, unless they 'actually' refer to the title. Which is to say that, beyond the fiction written by the Pastor-narrator, it is the author who by this means is drawing the reader's attention to the wording he has introduced.

Thereupon we notice that in fact for us the symphony comprises only the 'scene on the bank of a stream', the allusion which will lead to the first explicit formulation of the major theme of 'evil' and 'sin' in opposition to the beauty of 'those ineffable harmonies' (46; 30). And the upshot of the episode is to suggest that hearing the music brought about a third metamorphosis in Gertrude. She remains 'silent, as though **drowned** in ecstasy'; [18] she becomes a nix, an undine, water-sprite.[19] She has passed through to the other side of the mirror of appearances which the Pastor merely skates over with his writing, and this is why she remains 'silent', like 'those ineffable harmonies': she is at one with nature, with creation, and thus has no further need of speech, of the words which convey falsehood and manifest in any case a distance from the things which they designate.

We know that for Beethoven, the *Pastoral Symphony* was 'the moving call to contact with the eternal things in nature. From nature emanates a deeper element: the comforting sensation of an immanent divinity, which unites the soul of man and the palpitation of the universe in a current of life'.[20] This is expressed in particular in the second movement, the 'scene on the bank of a stream'. Beethoven was to say of it, in 1823, speaking to Schindler as the two of them sat together beneath an elm tree beside a stream situated between Heiligenstadt and Grinzig: 'This is where I wrote the "scene on the bank of a stream", and the buntings up there, the quails, the nightingales and the cuckoos composed it with me.'[21]

Just as Beethoven, though deaf, composed to the sound of the birdsong, so Gertrude, though blind, will be able to read – that is to say spell out, write – the book of natural harmony with the 'flowers' for 'words', helped along in her decipherment by 'the cows'. In a scene with the Pastor which seems a pendant to that which followed the concert, the heroine is now able to *see* nature, at one with it. She alone can discern 'the lilies of the fields' whose presence her companion cannot even guess at. And after this overture, she composes her own 'scene on the bank of a stream', a replica of Beethoven's:

> At our feet, *like an open book* on the sloping *desk* of the mountain, lies the broad green meadow, shot with shifting colours – blue in the shade, golden in the sun, and *speaking in clear words of flowers* – gentians, pulsatillas, ranunculus and Solomon's beautiful lilies; *the cows come and spell them out* with their bells; and the *angels come and read them* – for you say that the eyes of men are closed. **At the bottom of the page** I see a great smoky, misty *river of milk*, hiding *abysses of mystery* – an immense river, whose only shore is the beautiful, dazzling Alps far, far away in the distance. (80; 48)

In this passage, all the elements of the literary process are gathered together, which makes of it a miniature reproduction of the work, placed at its centre. We can thus draw three types of consequences from it. At the level of the fiction, the meaning of the work is enunciated by the Pastor, making the Gospel text his own: 'I thank Thee, O Lord, that Thou revealest to the humble what Thou hidest from the wise' (80; 47); or alternatively 'the blind shall see', if being blind is being like Gertrude in union with nature so that each is transparent to the other and each is revealed through the other. We can sense here a formulation of the Gidean conception of poetic writing, close to the great models of Mallarmé and Valéry: to write is to collaborate with words – flower-words, cowbell-words;[22] – at the same time writing is a form of reading, a decipherment of the world which is articulated as if of its own accord. Finally we find 'en abyme' in this micro-text – itself *en abyme* in the narrative – the reference to the 'river' of writing, opaque, concealing 'abysses of mystery'. This 'great smoky, misty river of milk' is an end-result at one and the same time of the 'mysterious little lake' and of the 'stream' at the beginning of the novel. It is the announcement, at the conclusion of the First Notebook, of the change of form which will affect the writing in the Second Notebook. That part of the *récit* which is reaching its conclusion has, like the stream, followed a linear course, in a homogeneous time, apparently dominated by the writing, presenting a false appearance of transparency due to the stability of the vision which the narrator retained of himself and of events.[23] The lake-narrator and stream-narrative were therefore dissociated here. The 'misty river of milk' announces by contrast the *Diary* which will take over the story when in the entry dated 3 May the writing will be joined by events in the present. The stream has then merged with the lake to form the 'immense river', smoky with the unconscious of the narrator and his bad faith. For as Claude Martin most pertinently puts it, 'the diary is the mode of expression of a man who lacks distance and detachment, of a man whom critical intelligence abandons' (ciii). This privileged instrument for achieving self-awareness, for elucidating one's omissions and falsehoods, becomes, for the Pastor, the site of a wilful blindness into which he plunges. The gap between what is apparently said in it (denotation) and what the reader actually reads in it (connotation) thus represents the measure of the narrator's bad faith.

The 'great smoky, misty river of milk, hiding abysses of mystery' is also a premonitory vision, indistinct as yet, hinting at the catastrophe of which we have an intimation on the scriptural horizon: 'at the bottom of the page' flows an immense river waiting to engulf this sinful world. For the fundamental harmony of the world, the Paradise regained by the innocent blind girl, proves short-lived. No sooner are they flawed by slight dissonances caused by certain of the Pastor's words, than they are brusquely broken apart when sight is restored to the heroine; then follows her suicide in the river. After being carried along by the flow of the text ('walking by the river', 120; 66),[24] she seeks to end it by cutting it short, by positioning herself like an obstacle to the current ('crossed the [. . .] bridge'), and like Narcissus, she 'stoop[s] and disappear[s]'. The Pastor, seeing her 'sunk [*plongée*]' in 'stupor' and 'lassitude', is drawn in after her, and with him all the people in his story: 'in what abominable darkness I am plunged [*plongé*]' (120; 65).

For Gertrude, who up to now, has been a blind plaything of the writing, has become a reader of the text as she stoops over the flowing river: now she sees, she reads in it her impossible love, the evil and disruption which she has occasioned. In positioning herself as an obstacle to the text, she is seeking to put a final tragic stop[25] to its dramatic progression. Being a figure of the reader as well as an actress in the drama, she illuminates with her gesture all that the reader has as yet been unable to discern or has only perceived confusedly up to now. Her suicide, followed by the justification she gives for it, restores limpidity to the cloudy water of the text. One can, therefore, understand the aesthetic necessity for the notorious 'contraction' of the ending. Instead of condemning it or justifying it with reference to external biographical considerations, one should see that the pages which follow the leap into the river are pages of explanation, which decant everything that has been fermenting in the shadow of the text. So these pages could not be very rapid, restricted to a few brief notations, for fear of dragging the narrative down into thesis literature, with all the defects of didacticism.

If it has seemed appropriate to speak of Gertrude's 'suicide', this is because her plunge into the river has returned her henceforth to her status of undine. From this point on she is bound to die, being held back only by 'the little sluice, where she had been carried by the stream'. The writing specifies very clearly that she has become a water-sprite, that she has definitely passed through to the other side of the mirror, the other side of words and life: she maintains 'a smile which seemed to *stream* from her eyes like *tears*' whilst her hair is 'still *wet and like seaweed*' (122–4; 66–7).[26] Like a fish out of water – her element in which all was transparency, truth, where words and things coincided, where she could be one with nature[27] – she aspires only to return to it: 'I saw the *sweat* on her **moist** forehead. Then she closed her eyes and kept them shut for a time, as though to concentrate her thoughts or *to recover her former state of blindness*' (126; 69), that is to say the state of beatitude which made nature transparent and edenic to her. This is why her last words to the Pastor will be: 'I am thirsty [. . .] I can't breathe [. . .] We must say goodbye' (130; 70).

J'ai soif/I thirst. Such are also the penultimate words of Christ on the Cross,[28] and this suggests one final metamorphosis, or rather, renders perceptible the ghost of another set of meanings which have been present throughout the narrative. It will be remembered that at the moment of

Gertrude's 'transfiguration', she became an 'angel'; that the water of the 'pool of Bethesda' was likened to the 'crimson glow' that arises from the darkness like a 'mystic colour' (34; 24); and that her suicide attempt was disguised as an outing to pick forget-me-nots in which 'sky' and 'river' combine: 'What do you call those little blue flowers that I wanted to pick by the *river*? Flowers the colour of the *sky*?' (124; 67). To be in water is therefore, for her, to go to heaven,[29] just as the celestial Christ was symbolized by the fish in the primitive church. To see through writing and blend with it is to make contact with the archetypes which remain, beneath surface appearances, in the heaven of Ideas. And the sky-coloured forget-me-nots will be woven into a crown and funeral wreath for Gertrude: 'Her hair was now fastened up, with the forget-me-nots I had brought her twisted into the plaits above her forehead' (124; 68).

This messianic hypostasis may further illuminate three basic elements in the text. First the original opening, evoking Christmas and the child of Bethlehem with the explicit allusion to Gertrude for whom 'there was "no room at the house"'. Secondly the tears shed by the girl instead of the Pastor are analogous to the only tears of Christ, shed on the death of Lazarus (John, XI: 35: 'Jesus wept'), for Amélie's reproaches have in effect announced her death in expiation for the Pastor's sin. Finally her very function in the narrative is clarified by this means: she has come to sow trouble and discord within a peaceful family. 'Suppose ye that I am come to give peace on earth? I tell you, Nay; but rather division. For from henceforth there shall be five in one house divided, three against two and two against three. The father shall be divided against the son, and the son against the father; the mother against the daughter, and the daughter against the mother; the mother-in-law against her daughter-in-law, and the daughter-in-law against her mother-in-law' (Luke, XII: 51–53). This is what remains for us to see at present.

5. Ice

In order to teach Gertrude, I had had to learn the Braille alphabet myself; but she was soon able to read much quicker than I could; I had some difficulty in deciphering the writing, and besides found it easier to follow with my eyes than with my fingers. For that matter, I was not the only one to give her lessons. And at first I was glad to be helped in this respect [. . .]. Jacques had managed to break his arm while skating during the Christmas holidays, which he was spending with us; for during term time he goes to Lausanne, where he received his early education, and where he is studying at the Faculty of Theology. [. . .] He now suddenly began to take an interest in

Gertrude, to whom he had hitherto paid no attention, and occupied himself with helping me to teach her to read. (38–9; 27)

We recall that the initial subject of the tale was 'the whole history of her formation and development'. The Pastor specifies now that, in order to instruct her, he must himself 'learn the Braille alphabet', that is to say that he will not be capable of deciphering the blinded writing of his relations with Gertrude until he recognizes his own blindness, in the final lines of his text. In the meantime, Gertrude will be able to decipher it better than he; she it is who sees through him as a source of writing. She will become capable of doing so as a result of the rivalry between father and son.

From the outset the latter in effect duplicates the Pastor in all respects, establishes himself as a successor, that is to say, as a rival. And the tension created at this point in the text by the play of references back to the opening pages adumbrates the unfolding of the narrative. 'Studying at the Faculty of Theology' to become a Pastor himself, he 'helps' his father with Gertrude's education owing to his enforced leisure following on from his having 'managed to break his arm while skating during the Christmas holidays'. Now the beginning of the text was initially dated 25 December, and the scriptural work, at that time due to the snow, is now due to the ice. What is more, the action of skating refers back to the initial lake, and in this reading Jacques would thus represent the Pastor as adolescent. But this is where he first differs from his father: the latter did not break his arm, and the lake had thawed on the threshold of his narrative enabling him to write it. Thus the Pastor-narrator had been able to take in hand all the characters of his story, Jacques in particular, illuminating them in his own way. If, by contrast, Jacques broke his arm on what, according to the internal economy of the text, appears to be the same lake, he is thereby deprived of writing. Seeking to repeat his father's trajectory on his own account, he has encountered a writing which is already accomplished, that is to say frozen. He can only be presented to us through the scriptural flow directed by his father. It is therefore as if the Pastor, sensing that Jacques will supplant him in the religious domain (he is a future pastor, an expert in biblical exegesis), and in his love for Gertrude (she makes 'very marked progress' on contact with him, and is filled with an 'extraordinary zeal'), had contrived to mutilate him in this way. He tries to forestall the murder of the father, the condemnation he will be subjected to, by breaking the arm of his son who is thus unable to present his point of view. This perspective remains a minor one, subordinated so far as the reader is concerned to the angle of the father-scriptor who hopes thereby to restrict it to his own biased viewpoint as an unconscious rival. Thus it is that his two encounters with Gertrude will be truncated and presented indirectly.

This rivalry gives rise to a combat in which the words inscribed in the text accurately represent the unequal status of the two characters in relation to writing. The Pastor uses and abuses his scriptural monopoly over the word/writing, employing it as a weapon: 'Jacques has one excellent point – that the simple words I often used to him as a child: "I appeal to your conscience," have always been sufficient to check him' (68; 41). On this occasion too he achieves the result expected:

> 'Very well, Father, I will obey.'
> [. . .] I was touched by his obedience.
> 'That's the child I love.'

But contrary to the Pastor's Machiavellian calculations, his words like his writing unmask him in the reader's eyes instead of justifying him.

This play of truncated writing will be denounced by Gertrude in the dual domain of theology and love. In the entry for 3 May, the Pastor could still present himself as the winner in the theological duel and could mock his son's choices. But this is also the moment when the narrative lurches into a new phase, and by 10 May it is Jacques who, in his written note, has the last word. And when Gertrude recovers her sight, it will be to pass from Saint John to Paul the Apostle, from the laxity of the Pastor to the dogmatism of his son: the teaching of Jacques has triumphed over that of his father. Similarly, love will be transferred from the Pastor to Jacques, but not without the young woman having explicitly established their interchangeable character: 'He had your face – I mean the face I imagined you had . . . ' (128; 70).

The flux of the writing has thus escaped the designs of the narrator. The ice from which he freed himself at the start to enable the narrative to flow takes hold of him again, grips him at the end of his story, after serving him to break his son's arm. When about to see Gertrude again, he 'consult[s] the mirror' (118; 65), in other words his diary, the mirror of himself. For ice[30] is the image of writing which is accomplished, crystallized, frozen. But he encounters merely a surface and understands nothing in depth yet, until the ice finally gains possession of him: 'I shivered and my heart froze in a kind of terror' (128; 70). By now it is too late: caught in the net of his narrative, condemned by it, he must now bring it to a conclusion and hand it over, as he must hand himself over, to the public. Akin to the narrator of Agatha Christie's *The Murder of Roger Ackroyd*, he has been trapped by his own writing: he has given himself away while seeking to conceal himself, he has condemned himself by trying to prove himself beyond suspicion. This is one more illustration of a principle dear to Gide: 'I also like each book [that is to say, in this instance the will to press his case which governs the Pastor's narrative] to contain, though hidden within it, its own refutation. [. . . .] I like it to contain within it the wherewithal to negate and suppress itself altogether.'[31] At the same time, into his glacial imprisonment the Pastor also drags Gertrude, who dies from immersion in the 'icy' water of the river, and Jacques, shut away in his monastery, dead to the fiction. All that remains of the narrative is the 'cristal' of the work of art.

Thus in the works of fiction of this disciple of Mallarmé, this friend and contemporary of Valéry, is carried out a scriptural process which furnishes a metaphor, *en abyme* within the text, for the work of the text itself. Objects and characters are removed from the rut of realism and, by virtue of the internal play of words and themes, assume a symbolic signification, emblematic of itself, which offers within the work, insights into the meaning of the fiction. [. . .] In a *récit* such as *La Symphonie Pastorale*, literature is an end in itself. The circuit of water links the fiction to the process of its enunciation, and the discourse constructs its own signification on the basis of the internal systems formed by its constituent *signs*. [. . .] Starting from a theory of the symbol,[32] Gide progressed to the deployment of signs;[33] from a transcendant conception of the literary phenomenon, he progressed to a writing practice based on immanence. Literature is henceforth in search of its own signification; it creates its meaning instead of being the reproduction of a meaning which has supposedly existed for all eternity. This is why Gide can give the following advice to a young writer: 'Concern yourself only with form; emotion will naturally inhabit it. A perfect residence always finds a tenant. The business of the artist is to construct the residence; it is for the reader to provide the tenant.'[34] The work of literature, symbolic of itself, has become the object of the artist's 'adoration' instead of merely being the simple reflection of higher realities.[35]

The adventure of writing[36] has no preexisting object in view [. . .] from the moment one takes up the pen, one is taking a risk: one must agree to let oneself be guided, lured by the words which lead one where one had not initially anticipated going. The Pastor's adventure is exemplary; it is also that of Gide:

> As for me, I do not know where I am going; but I am making progress. I am perhaps merely an adventurer.
> It is only in adventure that some people succeed in knowing themselves – in finding themselves.[37]

It was also for Gide the only way of finding his salvation.

NOTES

1. Page references in the text are to the critical edition of *La Symphonie Pastorale* by CLAUDE MARTIN, Paris, Minard, 1970, followed by page numbers in the English translation.

2. Letter to André Rouveyre, 5 November 1924, *Correspondance 1909 1951*, édition établie, présentée et annotée par Claude Martin, Paris, Mercure de France, 1967, p. 87.

3. See, for example, the opposition between literature and life, between 'dream' and 'reality', in *Caractères* (*Divers*, p. 11–12).

4. Cf. this admission by Gide to André Rouveyre: '[. . .] you will understand better the need for justification that bothers you in my writings. For it is not the fact of being homosexual that matters, but rather, having established one's life in the first place as if one were not. That is what constrains one to dissimulation, trickery, and . . . art.' (*Correspondance*, op.cit., p. 89–90.) It is a simple matter to apply this to the love the Pastor does not yet admit to himself, which leads him into a self-justifying narrative.

5. One of the direct consequences is that the text is clearly distinct from life, even when it is grafted upon it. It is of another order, and one cannot pass directly from one to the other. Referential studies of the text are therefore to be distrusted.

6. This is what justifies, in the final analysis, the notorious 'contraction' of the conclusion in Gide's *récits*. The narration is consigned to 'falsehood' by opposition to the 'Truth' of life (the *envoi* to *Le Voyage d'Urien* [1893]), a leitmotif which we find, in diversely modulated forms, at the end of *La Tentative Amoureuse* [1893], *El Hadj* [1899], *L'Immoraliste* [1902], *Les Caves du Vatican* [1914], and even *Les Nourritures Terrestres* [1897]. To experimentation via writing is opposed 'desire', that is to say direct participation in life. On this point, one could refer to my study on *Les Caves du Vatican d'André Gide*, (Paris, Larousse, coll. Thèmes et Textes, 1972), pp. 34, 78.

7. I underline here, as in the following quotations, the terms on which my analysis places emphasis. [Quotations given in **bold italics** indicate a published translation which has been modified.]

8. See KEVIN O'NEILL, *André Gide and the 'Roman d'Aventure'* (Sydney, Sydney University Press, 1969). The Pastor's leap into the unknown is not unlike that of Julius de Baraglioul, and the question is the subject of chapter: 'La déconstruction du roman d'aventure', in my study of *Les Caves du Vatican*, op.cit.

9. Is it necessary to dispose of the traditional dual objection according to which one can invoke the 'realist' character of the description and the author's intention? Indeed Claude Martin notes quite rightly that 'the very topography is fairly accurately transcribed and even today one can follow the route taken by the Pastor at the start of *La Symphonie*: leave La Brévine heading south-west, and one can perceive "two kilometres away, on the left, a mysterious little lake", the Lac des Taillères, then proceed, "alongside a peat-moss", towards the forest of Cornées' (p. xxxvii); but that does not rule out the polysemy of the signs, and Gide declared many times that 'there is not a single one of the obligations to explain that one should not turn to advantage' (p. 206), and that he 'takes as a symbol *everything that appears*' (*Le Traité du Narcisse*). Cf. also in this regard the *avant-propos* of *Paludes*. What matters for the reading proposed here is the congruence of our explanation with the textual elements.

10. *Le Dialogue avec André Gide* (Paris, Corrêa, 1947), p. 7, reprinting a study published in *La Revue Romaine* in January 1921.

11. Letter from Anna de Noailles to André Gide, January 1919, quoted by Claude Martin, op.cit., pp. 157–8.

12. This is why a reading of the scenario imagined by Gide for the film adaptation

is so disappointing. The text has lost its false transparency, everything is pointed out, underlined, and ultimately flattened. One should note, however, that it is not written to be read, but to be interpreted, that is to say transposed into another language which possesses its own means of recreating allusions, ellipses, and ambiguities. The text can be found in Claude Martin's edition, op.cit., pp. 179–218.

13. André Fontainas wrote to Gide, on 23 July 1920: '[. . .] despite the pleasure I have in reading a language which is so precise (sic), so certain and so pure, in perceiving your mastery in it, I find it stifling and feel a need to breathe the open air.' (Ibid., p. 168.)

14. The use of this word does not mean that the characters have an autonomous existence, that they have a fully-constituted psychology independent of the indications of the discourse which creates them. But it is undeniable that Gide sought, through his characters, to portray certain problems of psychology, morality and theology.

15. This substitution only occurs in 1929, after three different editions reproducing the manuscript. However, the ms. B, containing a draft of the last third of the book, already had *'pleurer'* (weep). See Note 3, p. 133.

16. Which will enable her to represent Condilhac's 'animated statue' (p. 26; 20). [The philosopher Condilhac (1714–1780) used the example of an animated statue to illustrate how the human personality could be the product of accumulated sense impressions, rather than the manifestation of an innate essence deriving from God.]

17. Georges Raillard has formulated in the following terms the general problem of the title: 'A "short text" which interacts with the "long text" of the novel itself. Its function in relation to the latter is always ambiguous: it both "sums up" the book, exhibits the theme-word around which it crystallizes, and marks the distance separating the "short text" from the "long text". Every novel, by its very existence, expresses the inadequacy of the title, every title expresses the inadequacy of the novel: a variation on a word or phrase which, having served as a support, as a pointer enabling the reader to get his or her bearings, invariably remains in its unaltered form at the end of the book.' (*La Nausée de J.-P. Sartre*, Paris, Hachette, coll. Poche critique, 1972, p. 36.)

18. The 'as though' is important, since it underlines the process of metaphorization which is in play in the other references to water we have commented on above. These metaphors, whether explicit (i.e. comparisons) or not, unite the two indissoluble levels of writing: the narrative fiction, which observes the norms of verisimilitude, and the indications of its meaning, which departs from them. In this sense, poetic activity is essentially work on metaphor and it is as a function of the reciprocal relations which unify the different elements of the textual whole that we can understand this latter, that is to say interpret it.

19. In the film adaptation, this is how Charlotte justifies the choice of the name Gertrude: 'Where did you get that name?' (*Charlotte*) – In a fairy-tale I like. Ursula. . . or, no! no. . . Gertrude, I mean' (p. 215). One can probably see in this an admission by Gide as to the origin of his choice of the name. Gertrude remains, throughout the story, a fairy-tale character.

20. LAFFONT-BOMPIANI, *Dictionnaires des Oeuvres*, Paris, S.E.D.E., 1954, vol. IV, p. 491.

21. Translation of an extract from the first biography of Beethoven, by his friend

Anton Schindler, 1840: quoted in the booklet accompanying *Beethoven, 9 Symphonies,* Gewandhausorchester Leipzig, Wing Spezial, 96 600 SAE, and in *Konzertbuch,* Henschelverlag Berlin, 1961, vol. 1, p. 334.

22. We shall limit ourselves to recalling two examples of the productivity of words. Gide recounted several times how *Paludes* came into being: 'A certain sense of the grotesque, which had already manifested itself in *Le Voyage d'Urien,* dictated the first sentences to me, and as if in spite of myself, the book formed itself in its entirety around these, which I wrote down in the course of a walk in the public park in Milan, where I stopped off prior to my stay in Champel:

    "A path bordered with aristolochia" and
    " – Why bring only a parasol when the weather is always so unpredictable?
    – It's a stand-by, she told me . . . " ' (*Si le Grain ne Meurt, JII*, p. 576.)

    He also recounted the following example of Valéry's writing method: 'Paul tells me (as I already suspected) that *La Pythie* issued entirely from one line:

    Pâle, profondément mordue. (Pale, profoundly bitten)

    He sought the rhyme, then the rhymes. They dictated the form of the stanza, and the whole poem developed without his knowing at first how it would be nor what he was going to say in it' (*JI*, p. 751; J2 p. 319: 2 January 1923).

23. From time to time, however, the depths of the sub-text were indicated by expressions such as 'It was not till later that this became clear to me' (66; 40) or 'What did she mean by this insinuation? I did not know or care to know [. . .]' (72; 43).

24. Textually speaking, this can only be a resurgence of the initial 'stream'.

25. Cf.: 'In sum, it is a tragedy in five acts which derives its value from the long night of the four first ones' (A. Gide, interview quoted by Claude Martin, op.cit., p. 181).

26. Note that 'like seaweed', which spells out Gertrude's identity as a water-sprite, is a late addition to the manuscript (Note 1, p. 125). Francis Pruner, in his study on *La Symphonie pastorale de Gide: de la tragédie vécue à la tragédie écrite* (Paris, Lettres Modernes Minard, 1964, 'Archives André Gide', 1), has clearly glimpsed the thematic links between the different mentions of the stream ('[. . .] Gertrude's plunge into the water of a stream relates thematically to the waters of Siloe, the pool of Bethesda and the second movement of the Sixth Symphony by Beethoven in which the Pastor has sensed a profound analogy with the sacred texts of Saint John [. . .]', p. 25), but he has not drawn all the consequences from this: the angel has become an undine and the writing signifies its self by means of the water.

27. This is a theme of very long standing in the writer's fantasms. (It is the basis of his depiction of the Garden of Eden in *Le Traité du Narcisse.*)

28. 'After this, Jesus knowing that all things were now accomplished, that the scripture might be fulfilled, saith, I thirst' (John, XIX: 28). In pronouncing the same words, Gertrude also 'accomplishes' her scriptural function.

29. [The one word *ciel* signifies both sky and Heaven in French.]

30. [The French word *glace* signifies both 'mirror' and 'ice.']

31. Postface to a second edition of *Paludes*, p. 1479.

32. *Le Traité du Narcisse, théorie du symbole* was published in 1891.

33. 'The sign is a ternary structure for it necessarily implies three terms, and two radically different sets of relationships. The signifier enters into a relationship of *signification* [. . .] with the signified; the entity they form can enter into a relationship of *denotation* with the "referent"; the two relationships are not reducible to each other. [. . .] On the other hand, the symbol involves only one relationship, between its two constituent terms, which we might call *symbolizer* and *symbolized*.' T. TODOROV, 'Introduction à la symbolique', *Poétique*, no. 11, 1972, p. 277.

34. [*Divers*, Paris, Gallimard, 1931, p. 17.]

35. 'Perhaps, after all, my belief in the work of art and the cult that I make of it prevent that perfect sincerity which I henceforth demand of myself. What interest have I in any limpidity that is not a quality of style?' (*J1*, 388; *J1, 339: 26 June 1913.*)

36. [A reference to Ricardou's formulation of the writing practice in question here: the author of the modern novel is involved not in the writing of an adventure, but in the adventure of writing. Cf. *Problèmes du nouveau roman*, Paris, Seuil, 1967, pp. 23–43.]

37. *JI*, 791; *J2*, 356: 26 October 1924.

13   Jean Hytier on Gratuitous action and the aesthetic perspective in *Les Caves du Vatican**

The book from which this extract is taken comprises lectures given at the University of Algiers in 1938. It was the first to take as its guiding principle – and quote as its epigraph – Gide's assertion: 'The aesthetic point of view is the only one from which to speak of my work soundly' (*JI*, 653; *J2*, 229: 25 April 1918). Gide added as an important afterthought: 'It is, moreover, the only point of view that does not exclude any of the others' (*JI*, 658; *J2*, 235: 13 October 1918).

One of the most provocative ethical issues which Gide subordinated to aesthetics in this way was the *acte gratuit*, or gratuitous action. He toys with the idea as early as *Paludes* and *Le Prométhée mal enchaîné*, in which the protagonists wonder whether it is possible to achieve – or even contemplate – an action which escapes from the determinisms of motive and circumstance. The paradoxes provoked by the so-called 'free act' are argued over by the narrator and the philosopher Barnabé in the former text, and are pondered by the café waiter in *Prométhée*, who suggests that only Zeus, being a god, might be capable of committing one.

In *Les Caves du Vatican* Gide has his novelist-character Julius de Baraglioul theorize on the motiveless crime he intends to base a novel on; meanwhile another character, Lafcadio, commits what might pass for a gratuitous action: on a whim, he pushes out of a moving train an elderly fellow-passenger with whom, it later transpires, he is connected by circumstance and indirect family links. The two domains, of aesthetic speculation and defiantly immoral action, run in parallel throughout the novel, generating a series of comic and other ironies. Jean Hytier takes this material as his subject in a chapter of his book which he devotes to the *sotie*. Starting with an analysis of the implications of Gide's hypothetical notion, Hytier characterizes it as a matter for both

*[Text reproduced from chapter 4 of his *André Gide*, (London, Constable and Company, 1962) translated by Richard Howard from the French edition, first published by Edmond Charlot in Algiers in 1938. Quotations are in the versions given by the translator, intercalated page numbers refer to texts indicated in the Bibliography]

psychological and criminological examination. In the ensuing discussion, he concludes that it is a conceptual non-sequitur – invoking, in support of his argument, Gide's own subsequent admission to this effect.

However, the ultimate assessment of this element in the novel, as Hytier is committed to demonstrating, is a matter of artistic merit. First, is the action made plausible: has Gide achieved the aesthetic illusion? A lengthy passage quoted from the novel (not reproduced here) enables the critic to conclude that Gide has made the crime incredible precisely by removing from his narrative all hint of motivation, bringing it about only by technical contrivance and chance. There is a lack of fit between the character of Lafcadio, which seduced an entire generation of contemporary readers, and the nature of the action which remains logically inadmissible. On the other hand, the moral scandal is reinforced, and the action made more unacceptable, by the touching haplessness of the victim, Amédée Fleurissoire. Finally, Lafcadio's character is found wanting in his behaviour following the crime. His inconsistency, a feature of his characterization by which Gide sets great store, makes of him, in Hytier's view, an imperfectly realized character – or rather, means that he is realized with insufficient irony, so that in the end Gide's efforts may be judged an artistic failure.

Gide himself responded to Hytier's assessment with the comment 'Nothing else that has been written about my work has given me anywhere near as much satisfaction'.

In *Les Caves du Vatican* the theory of the free act [. . .] is applied to a particular kind of act: the wicked act, the crime. [. . .]

On the whole, the concept of the free act is not metaphysical in Gide, it is *psychological*, by its connection with the idea of disinterestedness, by its rejection of motivation by interest alone, and it is *juridical* by the connection between the crime's incomprehensibility and the criminal's being above suspicion. For Gide, a free act, whether a crime or not, is an act accomplished in such a way that other men do not see why a particular man should have committed it and consequently do not assert him to be its author.

Yet the act has been committed by a particular man. For it to be the *product* of this man, Gide finds himself obliged to obey two contradictory conditions: 1) to maintain the act's absurd aspect in the individual by stripping it of all those motivations, like vengeance, rage, jealousy, cupidity, which would permit its rationale to be grasped; 2) to make us feel how *this* individual could have committed *this* action which would not have been committed by any other man, which could have been committed only by this man: that is, *to link this surprising action to a particular human nature*, which comes down to an explanation by personality. The free act is the act of a *certain* personality. It is upon this personality that Gide will focus all his effort of explanation; he will determine it as much as he can, he will particularize it to the point of singularity – so that its incomprehensible action will not seem improbable to us.

This is a difficult challenge, for it means creating an exceptional being whose nature could explain how he might commit an exceptional action, yet without the latter's being explicable to himself. This attempt at *squaring the circle* is indicated by the formula: 'I don't want any motive for the crime, it is enough for me to motivate the criminal' [837–9; 204–5] employed by Julius de Baraglioul in a conversation with Lafcadio. 'Yes, I want to make him commit the crime gratuitously; I want him to try to commit a perfectly unmotivated crime.' There follows the strange dialogue in which Julius and Lafcadio give themselves up to an astounding intellectual leapfrog, but whose entire significance is in creating for the imagined criminal, the prototype of whom Julius does not suspect is his interlocutor (hence the zest of the scene), *a personality which might produce such an action*: acting in play – preferring pleasure to interest – taking pleasure in self-discipline to the point of dissimulation – loving risks – heeding the demon of curiosity; Julius sketches his criminal's beginnings as a *free man*: minor thefts, and rare ones, for they are committed only if they require skill and cunning, and only if they reveal him somewhat; – more of a juggler than a crook; – encouraged, but also exasperated by his impunity; – finally driving himself on to greater dangers, he will act all the more adroitly for having a cool head. 'Just think: a crime motivated by neither passion nor need. His reason for committing it is precisely to commit it without having a reason.' But here Lafcadio makes a crucial remark: 'It's you who are reasoning his crime for him; he merely commits it.'

The gratuitous crime by definition has no reason, but this absence of reason is not reasoned; the crime is spontaneous; it is the fruit of a personality in which *spontaneity* is the distinctive characteristic, although Gide, to my amazement, never uses this word apropos of Lafcadio. The difficulty of reconciling spontaneity with the lack of impulsiveness, with *sang-froid*, is precisely what makes the criminal of *Les Caves* so exceptional; one would have to speak of a spontaneity *à froid*. Is such a thing possible? Is it conceivable? We are still in a state of utter contradiction.

'To motivate the criminal and remove all motive from the crime' is possible only by a paradox that consists of making *non-motivation*, gratuitousness, the *psychological law* of such an individual. As Barnabé said, he must be constrained to freedom – an untenable position. Gide has made his Lafcadio into 'a creature of inconsistency,' [744; 83] but inconsistency can only be exceptional. Even in the most capricious person, actions can be established only in sequences. Logic always succeeds in asserting itself among them. And this is what Julius declares to Amédée '. . . no doubt this apparent inconsistency conceals a subtler and more secret consistency . . .' [813; 171]. We need not suspect Gide of irony here, for like his Julius, he himself ended by establishing determinism at the heart of the gratuitous act. In the *Préface* to the first volume of the *Ne Jugez pas* series, *L'Affaire Redureau*, he frankly asserts: 'Of course no human action is strictly unmotivated; no act is gratuitous save in appearance.'[1] As I was saying, ultimately the gratuitous act is merely the act witnesses find inexplicable, or even, still more simply, merely the act as yet unexplained. [. . .]

In his Lafcadio, Gide has subtilized, refined, quintessentialized gratuitousness; he has aspired to a crime that is committed absolutely without reason. He is alone in thinking so. Julius has never been convinced of the gratuitousness of actions; as soon as he learns that Fleurissoire has been murdered, he decides that the motive is theft; influenced by a conversation with Lafcadio, he thinks he has arrived at the notion of inconsistent characters on his own, but when he is told that theft was not the motive of the crime, he exclaims: 'There is no crime without a motive,' [842; 209] as any judge would, as Gide himself does later, and he supposes Amédée has been murdered by the gang that has kidnapped the pope and wanted to get rid of a witness who knew too much. Of course Gide ridicules Julius by making him fundamentally incapable, despite his – quite temporary – pretensions to create an inconsistent character, of understanding an action without a motive. But Gide's quarrel with Julius, as with the judges who believe only in the interestedness of an action, is not very fair, for he himself admits that there are always secret motivations. All he can reproach them for is their lack of a sense of complexity, their insufficient concern with rare or obscure motives. . . . Even so, we should no longer doubt these insufficiencies so much, for after all, many of these gentlemen have read Gide.

By an aesthetic attitude – a gratuitous one, we might say – Gide has dug an artificial moat between two kinds of actions, some familiar and classified, others exceptional and obscure; all relate to one and the same psychology, without which, moreover, any attempt at explanation would have to be abandoned. There is no gratuitous act, no free act, no inconsistent act, no detachable act – this is the very postulate of science. And Gide knows this is true, despite his reserve about a basic and inexpressible residue, the metaphysical extension of problems of action and personality which, on the psychological level, cannot be posited or even conceived, save according to a determinism of principle and of method. In positing the gratuitous act as a distinct entity, Gide has thereby based his work on a paradox. It remains for us to see if Gide has managed to give it the appearance of truth, or, if one prefers, to confer upon it that artistic truth which satisfies the reader and which is the emotional equivalent of truth; for in the domain of the imagination, the power of illusion precedes authenticity. Has Gide at least given us the *aesthetic illusion of the gratuitous act*, or has he merely implanted a disappointing hypothesis in a skilful fable?

It will be recalled that Lafcadio's crime is inserted in a huge comic apparatus intended to lead the victim into the adventurer's hand. This encounter is a pure effect of chance. [. . .]

From the analysis of the crime, we must conclude that Lafcadio did not know Fleurissoire and had no reason to kill him. This is what makes the act gratuitous. But by *demotivating the crime*, Gide has *made it incredible*. It is only by the artifice of the narrative that he establishes its genesis. [. . .]

On the other hand, everything which concerns Lafcadio's profoundest self is here expressed in order to bring the gratuitousness of the act into play. *By motivating the character, Gide thereby impels the reader to fill the gap between the act and its author*. If the act is disinterested, it seems no less interesting for Lafcadio. Fleurissoire's personality is relegated to the background; it plays no role; anyone else might have suffered the same fate – with this reservation, that he be as anonymous, in order not to have awakened any powerful effect in Lafcadio's mind which might have deprived him of the freedom to make the individual into a mere pretext. It was essential that sooner or later Lafcadio take this step, and it is in doing so that this so-called free man is a slave. The key lies in that passage where he discovers the distance between imagination and the act, and where he is tempted to prove to himself that nothing is stopping him. All the rest is accessory, the velleities of prudence; perhaps they merely augment, in fact, the *temptation* (it is surprising that Gide doesn't use this word) by the notion of risk they inspire in our gambler.

But why, we may ask, does he commit this crime precisely at this moment, upon this victim? *By chance*, or, more precisely, because circumstances lend themselves to it; further: they suggest the notion of the crime, doubtless not for the first time (although Gide has not informed us on this point). Lafcadio has nevertheless experienced the instability in the equilibrium of two contrary actions when, having taken on his shoulders an old woman's bag, he felt in kissing her that he might just as well have strangled her. In any case, the circumstances are presented with enough consistency so that the act can be introduced here with the *maximum* of facility. This is the meaning, in my opinion, of such details as the shadow projected on the slope and the play with the lock on the door – added, of course, to the wretched Fleurissoire's *optimum* position in front of the glass. Analogous circumstances would inevitably have presented themselves one day or another; one may suppose that Lafcadio would not have yielded – and then one diminishes his profound motivation – or think that he might have behaved in the same way, in which case one reinforces his tendency to commit the gratuitous act. In either case it is a second reason for regarding this free man as a slave: here a slave of 'circumstantial determinism', as before of the fatality of his nature.

The pretext of Fleurissoire and suggestive circumstances – such are the modes of an act whose essential and permanent element is Lafcadio's personality, or, if one prefers, the system of ideas which proliferates in his thought like a cancer and which lives there in an independent manner, without criticism whatever he may think of it, without links to the rest of his being, and which must conclude so dangerously in what Renouvier would have called 'a mental vertigo.'[2] He himself will say later that he 'did it very quickly' while he had a desire to do it; 'I was living unconsciously, I killed as in a dream' [871; 248]. He yields to the hypnotic fascination of an idea. Certainly he is not mad; on the contrary he is quite lucid, but only exceptional, abnormal, monstrous – which would not keep him from seeming true if Gide had convinced us.

One may cite analogous cases, but the problem is to know, in these cases, whether one does not always find a motivation, not only in the character (as Gide has done so superbly), but also in the *action* which he commits (which Gide has refused on principle to do), and particularly a motivation for the latter in the former. Now if Gide has admirably succeeded in the character (consider the full-length portrait of Lafcadio to be found in the book, which is sufficiently lifelike to have escaped its author and perilously influenced an entire generation of writers after World War I), he has not won our adherence to the action, and he has not really succeeded in relating them to one another. This is the weakness of *Les Caves*. Lafcadio exists; his gratuitous crime seems unreal to us, and we have particular difficulty in believing that he committed it.

I think that Gide might have come to realize the contradiction in which he was to imprison his hero if, instead of starting from the critique of ideas of psychology and justice, he had started from the critique of a logical idea such as causality. It is in fact astonishing that Gide never uses the word *cause* apropos of Lafcadio's actions. Criticism of the notion of cause has led certain philosophers to denounce its imprecision and to substitute for it the notion of function and of variable factors (in the mathematical sense of the phrase). Thenceforth the psychological progression is no longer the simple succession of motive and act; the act is the product of a great quantity of factors, almost impossible to measure, but whose existence prevails at any moment of our lives and whose complexity leaves no flaw through which a truly undetermined action might slip.

If Lafcadio's gratuitous crime distresses us, in short, as a logical scandal, it also shocks us as a moral scandal. Though we may tolerate the event with a maximum of complacency, may rival the author in broad-mindedness, Fleurissoire's murder is hard to swallow. In the first place Gide has made Amédée absurd, but he has not made him odious; and by accumulating his misadventures, in which his good faith is constantly ridiculed, he has finally made him touching; this effect is reinforced by the sympathy he wins from Carola, the good-hearted whore who can recognize a saint in this ninny; by launching Amédée on his nonsensical crusade, Gide has made him into a kind of burlesque hero who approaches Quixote in disinterestedness[3] (here is the true gratuitous act) and Parsifal in chastity.[4] Next, Lafcadio, by an inverse error, has been burdened with too many attractions. The reader is suspicious of his good deeds, and it must be admitted that the scene of the rescue of the two children from the fire is terribly contrived. As for the petty dishonesties committed out of bravura, they are amusing from only one point of view, and disagreeable from all others. The sympathy we are supposed to accord them is not steadfast, nor can it be; it is only a quite temporary complicity. Finally, Gide proposes an untenable bargain. He was no doubt artistically justified in taking his adventurer to the extreme limit of his tendency, but the act itself changes everything. One is no longer the same before and after a crime. Lafcadio's crime may be gratuitous, but to us it appears unjustifiable. Apropos of Merimée's *Partie de tric-trac*, Gide writes in his *Journal*: 'There is no *essential* difference between the honest man and the scoundrel. That the honest man may *become* a scoundrel is what is terrible and true. In the paths of "sin" it is only the first step that counts. As someone has already remarked, it is easier for a woman to have no lover than to have only one. That is the story of Lafcadio' [*JI*, 277; *J1*, 241: 3 December 1909]. But progression into evil cannot pass for an excuse. Moreover it is not between the honest man and the scoundrel that there is no difference, it is between the honest man and the *criminal*, for we can all commit a crime – by a sudden lapse of conscience, by a mental deficiency, by a lack of resistance to circumstances – but we will become scoundrels only by maintaining a profound solidarity with the crime. Now Lafcadio, if he is more or less sickened by his crime, if he has difficulty explaining it to himself, and if he is thereby shocked to hear himself called a *criminal*, feels absolutely no remorse for it and, faithful to his nature, regrets only that the contest should be simplified by the arrest of Protos in his place, which diminishes his risks and the pleasures of the game. If he were a Russian, he would confess publicly or turn himself in. If he momentarily thinks of doing so, it is only to show himself worthy of the respect which, in spite of everything, Julius' daughter Geneviève shows him. But once she has given herself to him out of love, he thinks only of freeing himself from this new connection, for 'he esteems her a little less now that she loves him a little more' [873; 250]. This is not only disagreeable but actually impious, although still within the logic of the character, for there is a terrible and inescapable logic of inconsistency which condemns Lafcadio to perpetual evasion; and at the end there is no longer any question for him of sacrificing his freedom and the promises of life by giving himself up to the police for the meagre pleasure of deserving his mistress' approval.

Gide's indulgence for his hero must not make us forget that he condemns him, however modestly. Such indulgence derives from the notion of *the virtue of evil*, which Gide has acknowledged elsewhere and in which he sees a resource that may serve the good, on condition that its energy be directed toward it, thereby becoming more capable of serving its cause than the lukewarm conformity of an untested honesty. This is the first lesson that can be learned from *Les Caves du Vatican*. It is indeed about Lafcadio that one can say, with Gide, that 'collaboration with the demon is necessary in the work of art,' and that 'it is with good intentions that one makes bad literature'.[5] But Lafcadio by his very inconsistency, is essentially a *virtual* being. To Julius, who sees him as ready for anything, he answers, 'Ready for nothing' [744; 83]. It is not impossible that Lafcadio may be saved. His crime has suddenly limited him, reduced him to the unilaterality of the determining action and separated him from the love of men, whom he despises but whom he needs. It is not impossible that he should one day put the virtue of evil to the service of good, if he consents to forget himself a little. In any case Gide does not mean to identify himself with his young hero, and it is altogether an error, as Gide has remarked, to regard *Les Caves* as 'an affirmation of nihilism'. Despite appearances, Gide does not intend to destroy; he aims at constructing; above all he aims at moral progress.

Ultimately, in this critical work, Gide has not shown enough irony with regard to Lafcadio – there are only traces of it – and this is what risks blurring the book's meaning. [. . .]

Notes

1. [André Gide, *Ne Jugez pas*, Paris, Gallimard, 1969, p. 143.]

2. [Charles Renouvier (1818–1903), one of the principal French representatives of philosophical idealism in the nineteenth century.]

3. [Don Quixote, the eponymous hero of the novel by the Spanish writer Cervantes, published between 1605 and 1616. The character embodies the extravagant unworldliness of an idealistic imagination at odds with real life.]

4. [Parsifal or Perceval, one of the knights in the legend of the Holy Grail, the embodiment of extreme purity, naïvety and religious devotion.]

5. [*Dostoïevski*, in *OCXI*, pp. 279–80.]

14 David H. Walker on Challenging the novel in *Les Faux-Monnayeurs**

In writing *Les Faux-Monnayeurs*, Gide explicitly set out to test the conventions of the novel as a genre. He was to refer to this book as his only novel, hinting thereby that it attained a summit of accomplishment surpassing that of his earlier narratives – but also implying that the majority of his writing was not that of a novelist as such. The uniqueness Gide claimed for *Les Faux-Monnayeurs* therefore suggests – was intended to suggest – both that he set high standards for the realization of what he considered a true novel, and that he found himself ill-suited to the form. This text thus sets a considerable critical challenge. Is Gide seeking to parody the novel, or extend its bounds? Is he hoping to take the form to unprecedented heights of sophistication, or simply undermine its pretensions as a record or example of human endeavour? Critics have adopted a variety of approaches to reading *Les Faux-Monnayeurs*, and the study reproduced here aims in part to take into account the substantial contribution others have made to our understanding of this paradoxical work. Surveying the extent to which Gide excludes from his narrative those dimensions which normally constitute the mainstay of the genre, it analyses the flamboyant narrative techniques through which Gide seeks nonetheless to maintain contact with the reader who risks being alienated by his novel's departures from the norm. However, the entertaining reading thus constructed is ultimately seen to be a diversion from another, rather different experience of the text; and the novel itself furnishes, within its repertoire of self-conscious musings on its own workings, pointers to the different ways in which a novel can be read. It is on this basis that the analysis presented here seeks to trace the effects of Gide's deliberate attempt to criticize the notion of plot in the novel. Through his depiction of the events leading up to the climactic suicide of the young Boris, the author has produced a narrative structure which points to an inexorable process implicating all the characters in guilt for his death. At the same time, however, the presentation of the plot's

---

*Adapted from texts previously published in *French Studies*, XL (1986), pp. 413–26; and David Walker, *André Gide* (Basingstoke, Macmillan, 1990), pp. 136–160.

intersecting strands is such as to question the very notion of deterministic causality. Moreover, Gide casts doubt on the novel's capacity to deal with such matters while adhering to the codes and conventions the reader has come to expect of it.

Gide was disappointed by what he had produced in *Les Caves du Vatican*. The *'grand roman d'aventures'* he had spoken about to Du Bos in 1912 turned out to be what Hytier has called a 'parody of the picaresque novel'.[1] It is true that Gide had realized he was producing something other than what may have been expected: 'These *Caves* [. . .] can't be and mustn't be a 'masterpiece' – but rather a bewildering book, full of holes and gaps, but also full of amusement, strangeness and partial successes'.[2] He was splitting the seamless fabric of traditional aesthetic theory, offering a text which did not present itself as complete and conventionally structured, but which questioned expectations and forced the reader to participate in making sense of it. Such qualities have become the criteria of value for **post-structuralist** critics, and for this reason Gide deserves a place as a pioneer in **deconstruction**. But in producing a critique of the novel, Gide was aware that he had in some sense failed actually to write a novel, and had therefore not succeeded in realizing his long-standing ambition.[3] Already around 1911, after writing the first-person narrative *Isabelle*, he had adjusted his aesthetic sights in order that such works should not be taken as indications of his true ideal: he published *Isabelle* as a *récit*, and in a sketch for a preface wrote, 'Why did I take care to entitle this little book a *récit*? Simply because it does not correspond to my idea of a novel; no more than did *Strait is the Gate* or *The Immoralist*; and because I did not want people to be misled'.[4] His dissatisfaction following *Les Caves du Vatican* prompted him once more to reconsider the nature of his achievement thus far, and led him to reclassify his works, referring again to the first-person narratives as *récits*, and baptizing *Les Caves* a *sotie*, a term borrowed from a burlesque satirical form of medieval drama which he also applied retrospectively to *Paludes* and *Le Prométhée Mal Enchaîné*. He explains himself in a preface to *Les Caves du Vatican*: 'Why do I call this book a *Sotie*? Why *récits* the three preceding ones? In order to demonstrate that they are not novels, properly speaking. [. . .] *Récits, soties* [. . .] it seems to me that up to now I have only written ironic (or if you prefer, critical) books, of which this is doubtless the last.'[5] It was to the novel – now defined largely negatively as a genre at which he had not yet exercised himself – that he turned once more, this time as a vehicle for an affirmative statement of his views.

Les Faux-Monnayeurs, which Gide was to call his 'first novel', was the product of such efforts. Even so, Gide could not resist his inclination to banish from it the stuff of which traditional novels are made. Description is dismissed by Édouard, the novelist-protagonist, as being irrelevant to the novel, as is dialogue; 'outward events, accidents, traumatisms' are the prerogative of cinema, and should be left to it (990; 70–1). In the *Journal des Faux-Monnayeurs*, Gide expresses his wish to 'purge the novel of all elements that do not belong specifically to the novel' (57; 31), just as he has Édouard do (989–90; 70–1). But, as Gide was to realize with hindsight, his difficulty arose from the fact that the very essentials of narrative were uncongenial to him. Most of the elements he resists incorporating in *Les Faux-Monnayeurs* are indispensable constituents of the genre. 'The novel requires a certain slowness of progress that allows the reader to live with the characters and become accustomed to them,' he later wrote (*JI*, 1050; *J3*, 165: 12 June 1931). Creating the impression of time passing much as it does in real life requires precisely a mixture of description, dialogue and incident, the writing of which calls for what Gide termed 'a large proportion of adipose tissue',[6] the retailing of banal padding merely for the sake of making reading time approximate to living time. 'What a success I could have had with my *Faux-Monnayeurs* if I had been willing to lay out my picture somewhat more', he commented. 'This stretching of the story allows the reader to keep contact with the characters over a greater surface' (*JI*, 991–2; *J3*, 113–14: 23 June 1930). What Gide notes here coincides with a comment by Barthes on the function of the secondary elements in a narrative structure which he calls 'catalysers'. Their role is a phatic one: they maintain the contact between the narrator and the addressee.[7] The seamless continuity of a text composed in this way draws the reader along with it; but Gide had a horror of the encumbrances that such a text is charged with, and refused to clutter up his narrative with inert, 'adipose' tissue. He was quite clear about his aim, discussing his novel in these terms as early as 1919: 'I would like the reader to have the feeling that it is coming into being before him; I would like to cut out the inert sections in a novel'.[8] Looking back later, he saw the risks he had taken, but did not retreat from his position: 'I recognize that those neutral passages are the very ones that rest, reassure and win over the reader [. . .] What is easier than to write a novel like others! I am loath to do so, that's all, and no more than Valéry can I resign myself to writing "The Marquise went out at five o'clock" ' (*JI*, 1068; *J3*, 181: 1 August 1931). The fact is that the notion of reality as a chronological continuum, which the traditional narrative techniques tend to articulate and reinforce, ran counter to Gide's views on the discontinuous manner in which significant events actually occur. The author who prizes '*inconséquence*' and '*imprévu*' above all, as Gide did, is bound to have problems when operating with a literary form whose readers are conditioned to expect continuity. Like Édouard, Gide is caught between 'two incompatible requirements' (1083; 169): the ways in which he copes with such contradictions are one source of the richness of *Les Faux-Monnayeurs*.

The salient features of Gide's text have been greatly illuminated by critics such as Michel Raimond[9] and more recently, by David Keypour and Michael Tilby. There is general agreement as to the 'extreme briskness in the development of the narrative';[10] and Tilby in particular analyses the means by which the action is presented as non-sequential, lived by the characters as a succession of present moments and perceived by the reader in such a way that the past and present of the story are continually confused.[11] There is, in fact, very little of the explicitly retrospective in this narrative; background is not construed as such, but is filled in via letters, diaries, dialogues, in which the information comes across with the same air of immediacy as in the novel's opening paragraphs. The multiplicity of narrative viewpoints, one of the constants in Gide's definition of the novel, is used by him in such a way as to fragment the diegesis: elements of the story are communicated piecemeal as they crop up seemingly by chance in the conversation or correspondence of characters who are themselves engaged upon unrelated narrative lines.[12] Hence the story of Bernard's illegitimate origins emerges from ten retellings in the course of the narrative; and the details of the affair between Laura and Vincent are sketched in cumulatively over a similar number of disparate allusions. At the same time, the text as a whole performs repeated rapid leaps from one set of characters to another. 'On all sides life offers us many beginnings of drama but only rarely do these continue and take shape as the novelist is accustomed to spin them out', Gide writes in the *Journal des Faux-Monnayeurs* (80; 47). A somewhat neglected commentator, André Julien, writing in 1951, brings out forcefully the key aspects of the presentation Gide devises as a means of remaining faithful to the true nature of reality, and reminds us at the same time of the model of the *roman d'aventure* which has played so important a part in enabling Gide to break away from conventional patterns of narrative: 'Fragment the action into adventures and write everything in the present', is his summary of Gide's method.[13] But given that the action is broken up in this manner, the question of transitions necessarily arises.

We know that Gide was preoccupied with the work of '*jointoiement*' between scenes, episodes and characters,[14] and part of the attraction of the novel stems from the devices he hits upon to accomplish this without having recourse to 'adipose tissue'. Indeed he attached great artistic importance to success in this domain, being inclined as he put it 'to devote the most care to just what most discourages me: the transitions, the welding of joints, everything in which Flaubert recognized the master writer' (*JI*, 92; *J3*, 49: 10 April 1929).

From the end of one chapter to the beginning of the next, and sometimes in the middle of chapters, we are pulled along by a variety of more or less ostentatious methods, such as in the statement: 'No, it was not to see his mistress that Vincent Molinier went out' (959; 39). This declaration, which

forces us to acknowledge that we had taken Olivier's story at face value –
whether we had or not –, is an example of the strategies whereby a text
presents or points to possible readings of itself.[15] Transitions like this serve
to foreground the narrator's voice; but, equally important, they serve to
construct a narratee[16] who is very much at the narrator's beck and call.
What might be termed the 'co-optive us' is strongly in evidence, from 'Let
us follow him' (959; 39) and 'Let us leave them' (950; 28. 1145; 235) to 'Let
us make use of this [. . .] season' (1109; 196) and '. . . Bernard's father (we
need not concern ourselves with him)' (950; 29). 'Let us follow him' and
'Let us leave them' blur the distinction between the represented world and
the world of the reading experience, just as the transitions involving 'It is at
this same hour [. . .] It is time to return to Bernard' (974–5; 54–5), for
example, cause representations of chronology to dissolve into reading time.
The narrator constructs an intermediate zone, somewhere between the
'real' world and that represented by the text, where a conversation-cum-
commentary on events takes place between himself and the narratee. This
latter is told he is moving from one element to another, but that does not
make the shift more intelligible: if anything it heightens the impression of a
random succession of items.

But if the narrator browbeats the narratee in order to maintain cohesion
in the narration, the remarkably fluid forms of free indirect speech and
dramatic monologue which have increasingly commanded critics'
attention[17] also reveal him to be in the habit of exploiting metalepsis and
taking liberties with different levels of the narrative. Gide's brand of free
indirect speech in the present tense[18] effectively runs together the narrator's
voice and that of the character: 'Heavens! How hot he is! Where shall he go
now? . . . What shall he do with it [the suitcase]? . . . No! No! Certainly not!
He will not break open the lock; what the devil, he isn't a thief! [. . .] And
now that he has the wherewithal – quick! a hotel' (996; 78–9).

This serves as another means of moving the text along between
episodes. It is used frequently with Bernard, but also with M. Profitendieu
(944–5; 23–4. 948; 27), Olivier (1141; 231), Vincent (1045–6; 129–30) and
Édouard (991; 72. 1191; 284). The device has two significant effects. First, it
confuses the locus of the narrative: are we in the world of Bernard or in the
world of the narrator recreating Bernard's words and actions? Secondly, it
confers on the narrator something of the prestige and status of a
protagonist. In a sense the novel is performed before our eyes by this
narrator-showman; he might be said to absorb rather than describe his
characters. When he does not actually imitate their way of speaking but
presents their words in more conventional forms, his presiding presence is
none the less evident in the ironic intrusions and the framing devices used.
These implicitly include epigraphs, chapter headings, editorial comments
('We have already seen the first pages; this is what followed' (997; 79)),
dates and phrases such as *'Ce même soir'* in Édouard's diary.[19] But above all,

in this text in which quotation is far from being an innocuous mimetic device, the narrator's appropriation of the words of his characters is marked by the ubiquitous *guillemets*, which have an overdetermined ironic impact.[20] They are especially noticeable around the extracts from Édouard's diary, which have – not entirely convincingly, perhaps – been taken by some critics to constitute a competing focus of narration.[21] One has only to look at a page of this diary in the French text to see how firmly it is subsumed under the category of secondary material and subordinated to the narrator's discourse by the insistent quotation marks at the start of each indented line. This is essentially a one-man show. Thus the disquisitions on characters and events, the disruptions of the narrative fabric, the nudges and winks aimed at the reader, the general ironic chattiness of the text have the effect, not primarily of distancing the reader from the story, but rather of involving him or her in the narration. They are bids to establish a form of collusion between the reader and the narrator. In other words, the obtrusive discourse of the narrator has a phatic function:[22] it bears the hallmarks of language used to keep in contact with the addressee. It is Gide's answer to the problem of maintaining the reader's attention without providing a uniform diegetic world in which the reader can immerse himself or herself. The technique of the playful narrator does not fracture the text; it permits a certain discontinuity at the level of the action but reestablishes contact, maintains continuity, at the level of reading.

Viewed from this angle, the text encourages a purely 'superficial' reading. The narrator's elegant patter and the fluency of his technique tend to elide questions of representation, of narrative chronology and causation. The position constructed for the reader is reminiscent of La Fontaine's lines about the 'Butterfly of Parnassus' of which Olivier offers an idiosyncratic gloss when he discusses them after Bernard's *baccalauréat* exam: 'The artist [. . .] the man who consents to take merely the outside of things, their surface, their bloom' (1142; 232). We slide off into the pleasures of parody and the ironic intricacies of a citational text[23] as illustrated, for example, in the opening paragraph of Chapter 3, Part II: 'Notwithstanding first appearances, and although each of them, as they say, "did his best", Uncle Édouard and Bernard were only getting on together fairly well' (1076; 163). Here the text makes a spectacular display of its polyphonic characteristics – 'as they say', unattributable quotation marks, 'Uncle Édouard' evoking yet another voice. The focus is clearly less on events than on the imbricated discourses which seek to speak about them: ' "Benefits", *says Tacitus, through the mouth of Montaigne*, "are only agreeable as long as one can repay them" ' the paragraph continues (1076–7; 162: my italics). The characters' as well as the narrator's language constantly overflows into, or is invaded by, other forms of discourse. Laura's 'J'ai un amant' (955; 34–5. 972; 51) echoes Emma Bovary; Bernard parodies Rastignac in *Le Père Goriot* with his 'Maintenant, valise, à nous deux' (997; 79) and repeatedly finds his impulse to self-expression embarrassed by the clutter of quotations to which he is reduced (1088; 175). All this calls into question the very power of language to do anything other than engage in a dialogue with other texts.[24] In this sense the wide range of quoted discourse and the high proportion of dialogue – 'There are nothing but conversations', Gide remarked to Dorothy Bussy about the novel[25] – are merely the most explicit manifestations of the text's essentially dialogic character: in the final analysis discourse itself is posited as the object of representation. *Les Faux-Monnayeurs* is also rich in puns, which render explicit the interplay between signifiers and signifieds, thereby short-circuiting the arbitrary link between sign and referent and disrupting the referential function of language which is crucial to realistic texts. Instead of pointing towards elements of a putative reality beyond the text, the words interact with each other in such a way as to highlight the relational structure of language in general and its 'signifying rather than indexical character'.[26] Apart from the word-play in the novel's title, pride of place is given to a number of key puns which generate the ethical basis of the entire work. Thus the family, the basic 'cell' of society, is seen as a prison cell (1021; 104) from whose injurious influence only the *'enfant naturel'* – 'How full of meaning is the expression "a natural child"!' (1022; 105) says Édouard – remains free to follow his 'inclination' – in either direction, but preferably upwards (1204; 298: 'a slippery slope' would better convey what is rendered as 'a downhill course'. 1215; 310). The moral decadence into which the adolescent is in danger of sliding is in turn highlighted through the punning on the Biblical image of salt which groups Passavant and his ilk among the *'dessalés'* (1031; 113. 1052–3; 136–7). The novel presents itself therefore as an assemblage of signifiers whose meaning is intrinsic to the structures in which they are incorporated, rather than dependent on and determined by the normal referential use of language characteristic of narrative. There are passages where the text appears quite deliberately to follow the momentum of the writing alone. An elaborate semantic and phonetic game concerning Édouard's case generates repetitions and variations of the words *clef, serrure, faix, porte, portefeuille, portefaix,* etc., and play around images of closure and containment: the hotel room containing the case containing the wallet which formerly contained the banknotes (996; 79). Similarly, in the proliferating parenthesis on the chair in Laura's hotel room (1035; 117–18) the transition ceases to be a mere accessory and acquires primary status.

The work on transitions produces, then, a text in which the signifier has a certain autonomy, a text which points towards the non-mimetic relations within language. These ludic elements furnish an entertaining continuity of surface texture, divorced in many respects from events in the story. The narrator's manipulation of language, like the conjuror's patter, actually distracts us from the implications of what is happening elsewhere nonetheless:

'it won't be of any consequence' (cf. 970; 50) is the general impression. 'The kaleidoscopic flux has something irremediably inconsequential,' Holdheim says.[27]

But things are happening elsewhere, and there are, in the course of the text, indications that it can be read in other ways – as indeed can the lines from La Fontaine, Olivier's interpretation of which so incenses Bernard (1142–3; 232–3). The incident of Olivier's essay is obviously intended to raise the possibility of the alternative readings to which a text like *Les Faux-Monnayeurs* can be subjected. Gerald Prince has shown that reading is a significant motif throughout the novel,[28] but two examples in particular merit further analysis. Bernard, when he leaves home, writes a letter to Profitendieu explaining his action. Profitendieu reads it once – with the reader of *Les Faux-Monnayeurs* looking over his shoulder – and is distressed; reads it again and sees in it the qualities that endeared Bernard to him; and when his wife arrives, he shows it to her. She reads it and says, 'Oh! why did you tell him?', whereupon Profitendieu replies, 'But you can see for yourself that I never told him anything. Read his letter more carefully' (948; 26). It would be a curious reader who did not turn back at least once in the course of these four readings to peruse Bernard's letter again in the light of subsequent comments on it. The text virtually urges us to interrupt our linear reading and interpolate an earlier section. Here it is calling for a reader other than the narratee invoked elsewhere: it elicits a different reader, for a different reading.[29]

A related phenomenon occurs, with more far-reaching effects, in connection with the letter to Édouard in which Laura appeals for his help. This we first hear of as Édouard rereads it 'on the deck of the ship which is bringing him back to France' (974–5; 54); we do not have the opportunity to read it ourselves until Édouard rereads it again on the train (984–5; 65–6). At this stage it comes as the culmination and confirmation of a series of fragmentary narratives whereby we have learned of Laura's affair with Vincent and her ensuing pregnancy. We are told that 'The place for this letter is not among coats and shirts [. . .] Laura's letter will find its proper place' between those pages of Édouard's diary written the previous year (986; 66). This we can take as a signal to the reader. However, we read the diary only after the letter, which means we see things in the wrong order. The letter is read again, by Bernard, but after he has read at one sitting – unlike us – 'the notebook into which Édouard had slipped Laura's melancholy letter' (997; 79). Some fifty pages after we first read it, we learn that 'the truth flashed upon' Bernard as he finds it in Édouard's diary (1032; 115). This is the moment when Bernard is alone in seeing the connection between the Molinier side of events, which he has heard about from Olivier, and that concerning the pension Vedel-Azaïs, as set out in Édouard's diary. But for the reader who follows up the thrice-repeated hint to reread Laura's letter in its appropriate position in Édouard's diary, its significance is transformed as we see in it, not so much an immediate consequence of Laura's seduction by Vincent, as a long-term repercussion of events during the previous autumn when Édouard contrived to wriggle out of his relationship with Laura by urging her to marry Douviers. Laura's distress which at first sight had appeared to be a contributory factor in Édouard's return to France actually emerges as a consequence of his leaving for England in the first place. The text is constructed in such a way as to encourage us to embark on a mimetic reading and reconstitute the reality of events behind the printed page. Discontinuities introduced into our reading of the novel prompt questions, therefore, about the causal links between otherwise disparate incidents: and in particular the example of Laura's letter points to the fact that causality is established retrospectively, after we have read all the relevant material. This of course is the pattern that governs the entire novel, for nothing illustrates the principle more clearly than the death of Boris. The random, disjointed succession of adventures, each of which seemed less consequential or even less significant than the narrator's discourse which knitted them into his act, suddenly emerges, in the light of Boris's enforced suicide, as an ineluctable progression whereby each unthinking or deluded gesture contributes to the catastrophe.[30]

At this point, moreover, we see that the phatic continuity established by the narrator's self-flaunting discourse is actually a deception, a sleight of hand whose effect is to conceal the proper dynamic of events in the story.[31] This aspect of the novel's duality, not to say duplicity, is hinted at in the final chapter of Part II, when the narrator 'wonders with some anxiety where his tale will take him' (1108; 195) and suggests that things are getting out of hand. But even taking this into account, it seems reasonable to argue that another function of the playful narrator- figure was precisely to keep these ominous developments out of sight as far as possible, so that Boris's death, occurring in dramatic contrast to the inconsequential tone, should trigger all the more effectively certain reflections on its causation.

When we seek to establish retrospectively the causality behind Boris's suicide, our chief concern is to discover what exactly it is that links the actions of each character with his death. Insofar as connections of whatever kind can be made, then it is possible to speak of collective responsibility for the tragedy, as Philip Thody has done.[32] But a sense of moral responsibility is not the same thing as an understanding of cause and effect connections, though the former can render more urgent a consideration of the latter. Such is the effect of Boris's death and the backward-reaching ramifications it precipitates. On the one hand, *Les Faux-Monnayeurs* reiterates the lesson of Gide's previous narratives: contingency characterizes human affairs, the consequences of actions and events cannot be predicted as they happen, and therefore it is misguided for human beings to feel responsible for chance. On the other hand, the novel's very structure demonstrates how, objectively speaking, a wide range of individuals contribute to the death of a young innocent. The dialogue between these theses is woven into the fabric of *Les Faux-Monnayeurs*. Claude-Edmonde Magny refers to the connections between the different lives and the poignant death as 'the merciless picture of novelistic causality'. She says: 'Because Bernard, in order to repair a clock, has lifted up the top of a chest of drawers [. . .] little Boris will commit suicide at the end of the novel'.[33] But clearly this is no mechanical cause and effect connection, and equally clearly something else is involved in the discrepancy of scale and significance between the two events; between, for that matter, the death of Boris and any other sin of omission or commission with which it might, with hindsight, be linked. Germaine Brée seems to come closer to the crux of the matter when she proposes the model 'If Bernard had been more conscious of his responsibility towards Boris, if La Pérouse [. . .] had not loaded the pistol . . .'.[34] The nature of this view of causation, and the leap from the trivial to the tragic plane which it entails, are illuminated by the conversation which Olivier has with Armand in the latter's room – a room which in this respect as in several others is the locus of a *mise en abyme*.[35]

Armand is obsessed by a theory of what he calls the *point-limite* in any progression: the point at which an entity comes into being or at which one state changes into another. He speaks of 'that dividing line between existence and non-existence . . . A tiny bit less – non-existence. God would not have created the world. Nothing would have been. "The face of the world would have been changed", says Pascal' (1162–3; 254–5).[36] It can be argued that this generates a conception of cause and consequence upon which the novel is based. What happens was not bound to happen: the effects of contingency and chance, which Gide has been at pains to illustrate in his earlier fiction, make it clear that events could have turned out differently. Mechanistic causality, in any case more properly considered as a trope constructed a posteriori,[37] gives way to a non-deterministic vision, like that informing Lafcadio's adventures in *Les Caves du Vatican*, which plots events as emerging from a range of possibilities. This is what makes Brée's rendering of the plot particularly pertinent. The conditional note is repeatedly sounded in the text: in declarations such as Bernard's 'If I hadn't read the letters, I should have had to go on living in ignorance' (977; 58), or the narrator's 'We should have nothing to deplore of all that happened later if only . . .' (991; 73), or again: 'Why did he not simply return home? He would have found his Uncle Édouard' (1153; 243); and elsewhere: 'If he had understood what was going on, he would certainly have been able to prevent it' (1244; 340). Boris's death is, in essence, only one possibility among many equally plausible alternatives.[38] Perhaps this is why Gide was so keen to make his own a quotation from the critic Thibaudet: 'The genius of the novel makes the possible come to life; it does not revive the real'.[39] By stressing the contingency of the events depicted, Gide is, in one sense, further championing the right of fictional causality to be read as hypothetical, as he had done in *Les Caves*.[40] One has only to recall the comical effects that ensue when a character like Pangloss in Voltaire's *Candide* mistakes the gratuitous determinants of fiction for the laws of physics or the dictates of Providence. But at the same time, by substituting indeterminate possibilities for the mechanistic one-dimensional laws of cause and effect in the world the novel constructs, Gide remains faithful to the Darwinian evolutionary narrative and moves in the direction in which physics itself developed with the elaboration of quantum theory at the beginning of the twentieth century. Replacing determinism or fate with uncertainty and chance relaxes the rigour of the otherwise bleakly pessimistic depiction of human affairs which the novel appears to present. As in the world of sub-atomic physics, the transitions between states are governed by the statistics of random processes.[41] Things could have been otherwise.

But Boris does die, and matters do develop to a tragic outcome. It is not enough, as Armand says, to declare like Pascal ' "If Cleopatra's nose had been shorter" '. He goes further: 'I ask: shorter, by how much?'. For it is clear that other possibilities are open only up to a point; beyond that point it is too late, a development becomes irreversible. In this sense *Les Faux-Monnayeurs* goes beyond *Les Caves du Vatican*, which, celebrating the gratuitous act, revelled in the possibilities available to the characters, proposed and retracted hypotheses for actions and consequences, and left the future open for Lafcadio at the end of the novel. In the later work, the strategic placing of Boris's death at the conclusion of the narrative sends the reader with renewed urgency to a consideration of questions the *sotie* deliberately left out of the account. Armand uses the example of a man who was electrocuted because of the film of perspiration that enveloped his body. 'If his body had been drier, the accident wouldn't have taken place. But now let's imagine the perspiration added drop by drop'. He sums up: 'Gradation; gradation; and then a sudden leap. . . . *natura non fecit saltus.* What absurd rubbish!' (1162–3; 254–5). This is the issue on which Gide parts company with Darwin.[42] Through Armand he asserts his belief in the discontinuity of phenomena in the natural world, and rallies to a principle which the theories of quantum physics were to confirm. For it is precisely the kind of jump envisaged by Armand, a quantum jump from the miniscule to the momentous, that allows Boris's death to arise from an accumulation of banal misadventures and misdemeanours. As Vincent reflects on the situation which is the outcome of his affair with Laura, he is led to conclude: 'It very often suffices to add together a quantity of little facts which, taken separately, are very simple and very natural, to arrive at a sum which is monstrous' (960; 40). This is an observation which may be applied to many of the developments in the story.

The novel illustrates several ways in which the humdrum course of human affairs gives rise to the perception of a discontinuity marking a dramatic change: its concern with *les âges de la vie*[43] is an obvious example. The general view of personality which emerges from the text suggests that the characters are not individuals existing continuously through time, so much as aggregates of successive states. Bernard's development proceeds less through an accumulation of experience than through a discontinuous series of emotional and intellectual postures from which he successively detaches himself: 'Strange to himself [. . .] he glides into another day' (1178; 270) is a typical evocation of such mutations. As for the 'gradation' that culminates in the quantum leap, the text alludes frequently to this issue. Profitendieu, aware that if his investigation goes ahead he risks revealing more than he wishes to know, fears the irreversible consequences of excessive zeal: 'After a certain point a case escapes our control, so to speak; that is to say we cannot go back on the police court proceedings' (1204; 298). Similarly, Pauline Molinier is afraid it may be 'too late' for two of her sons to be redeemed (1155; 246. cf. 1222; 318); and Vincent has already discovered, through Laura's reply to his offer of money, that it is 'too late' (1049; 132) in that direction. Armand, for his part, derives a perverse pleasure from the prospect of being able to say that it is 'too late' for him to be cured (1232; 328). These examples are, arguably, fairly banal – even redolent of mere melodrama – but the fact that such patterns are fundamental to the conception of the novel is illustrated by the epigraph to Part III: a quotation from a book by Lucien Febvre entitled, appropriately enough, *La Terre et l'Evolution Humaine*: 'When we are in possession of a few more [. . .] monographs – then, and only then [. . .] we shall be able to reconsider the subject as a whole, and take a new and decisive step forward' (1112; 199).

All this evades a crucial issue, of course: what *is* this *point-limite* beyond which a phenomenon is qualitatively different? And in particular, what is the point beyond which Boris's fate is irreversible? The answer is, presumably, that we see it only when it has occurred, when it is too late; and on this score Gide may perhaps be excused for not being more precise, since in physics too the quantum calculations only map a field of probabilities for the electron's behaviour – no particular path can be predicted.[44] For the novelist the real problem lies elsewhere. It may be perceived in Bernard's ruminations after his night with Sarah. This 'unprecedented night' will not, we are told, 'find [a] place in the body of the book – a book where the story of his life will continue, surely, will take up the thread again, as if nothing had happened' (1178; 271). Narrative is by its nature continuous: how then can it be prevented from merely bridging discontinuities, inducing the reader to cover over blanks and fill in gaps? Gide touches on this difficulty in the *Journal des Faux-Monnayeurs* when he considers the shortcomings of plot, which is the only available mode for articulating events in a novel: 'I have felt more urgently the need of establishing a relationship between the scattered elements. Yet I should like to avoid the artificiality of a "plot" [. . .] Perhaps with the form I adopt I can find a way to have all that criticized indirectly' (18,25; 6,11). Nevertheless, critics have been at a loss to justify the means he uses to connect Boris's death with events that contribute to it. Surely this is plot as conventionally conceived, the vehicle for representing a purely mechanistic version of cause and effect?[45] And if it is, doesn't this mark most emphatically the failure of Gide's ambition to go beyond such devices and find a construction to accommodate a more radical view of causality?

What does seem clear is that the impression of immediacy created through the device of the playful narrator stresses the random, aimless, discontinuous way the characters live, and the ingenuous narratee reads, events.[46] At the same time every detail is shaped to fit into an overall continuous sequence. What we have here is a marked, indeed arguably self-conscious, example of the two contradictory kinds of causality inherent in narrative: the teleology or retrospective logic of plot, and the 'backward causality' of character motivation and the momentum of events in the story.[47] They both share a tendency to set up patterns of continuity, but Gide puts them to work against each other in order to prevent this. In *Les Faux-Monnayeurs* the story is dragooned into the service of the plot rather more noticeably than verisimilitude should allow. The mark of this untoward manipulation is coincidence: and on this score *Les Faux-Monnayeurs* has drawn the fire of more than one critic.[48] Overall, novelistic credibility is strained by the interconnection of so many characters and events alleged to have a bearing on Boris's fate. But in the course of a page-by-page reading, the coincidences abound: Bernard happens to be on the scene as Édouard distractedly throws away his left-luggage ticket (995; 77); he happens to find a coin in his pocket when he needs one, although he had spent the last of his money earlier (996; 78). Of all the shores he could have been washed up on, Vincent happens to be shipwrecked in Alexandre Vedel's vicinity (1233–4; 329–30). There are negative coincidences too: Olivier happens to stay out looking for Édouard when Édouard decides to call at the Molinier home to see him – on two separate occasions . . . (1040; 123. 1153; 243). Bernard happens to be preoccupied in wrestling with his angel on the night when Boris has heard of Bronja's death and is in particular need of comfort (1212; 307). Perhaps each coincidence contains or marks one of the *points-limite* at which events take a decisive turn: certainly they are the points at which we are inclined to say – assuming we take them seriously – 'if only. . .'. Indeed the narrator sometimes says this for us, as has been indicated above. And ultimately Boris's death, the most dramatic *point-limite*, is brought about by an appropriately calamitous accumulation of coincidences. But such a proliferation of coincidences can hardly be a . . . coincidence.

The fact is that this structure provides Gide with precisely the kind of parodic critique of conventional plots he sought. The systematic foregrounding of coincidence splits the seams of the narrative. It shows up the tension between story and plot, the conventional way in which the teleology of form masquerades as psychological motivation, fate, and so on. As Jonathan Culler has shown, the perception of such features as coincidence in a narrative lays bare 'the rigorous deployment of two logics, each of which works by excluding the other'.[49] It unsettles the priority habitually accorded to story over plot. Clearly the story is not preformed, waiting for the narration to set it down as it happened, since it is compelled to satisfy the requirements of a plot by coming to a significant conclusion. At the same time we are made aware of the contradiction, inherent in some of the narrator's paradoxical assertions, that while characters may be pronounced autonomous and free, their behaviour is constrained by foreordained patterns beyond their control.[50] Furthermore, by highlighting the contrived nature of the encounters (or failed encounters) in which the story abounds, this device underlines the contingent nature of fictional causation.

In terms of narrative structure, then, as a technical device that is part of the novelist's stock-in-trade, coincidence serves to signal more or less self-conscious contrivance. However, in discourses of life, real or depicted, coincidence confirms the contrary view: it exemplifies the authentically random character of day-to-day events. In this perspective, coincidence is an instrument for breaking the chains of mechanical determinism; it injects Gide's cherished *imprévu* into the succession of events.

Each coincidence therefore marks the point at which the narrative advances via an articulation which is essentially self-contradictory, being so obviously unforeseeable as an event, so flagrantly purposive as a structuring device. This double-edged quality is illustrated when Édouard discovers that the boy he has spotted stealing a book is actually his nephew Georges whom he has not met before. He acknowledges that such an event, though true, would be difficult to justify in a novel (1001–2; 80–4). It is in a case like this that we are made aware of the two incompatible domains the realistic novel seeks to run together: the *vrai* and the *vraisemblable*, the authentic and the conventional.[51] Thus it is very much in keeping with the spirit of *Les Faux-Monnayeurs*, positing as it does 'the rivalry between the real world and the representation of it which we make to ourselves' (1096; 183), that the novel's very structure should hinge on a phenomenon whose implications are mutually contradictory when viewed from each of these angles. Borrowing our terminology from Barthes, we could say that the text mobilizes two kinds of necessity in a conflict which is undecidable: and 'good narrative writing is of this very undecidability'.[52] In essence what this novel does is deconstruct the opposition between life and art by offering itself as a third, undecidable term, what Barthes calls 'a third term which however is not a term of synthesis, but an eccentric, extraordinary term'.[53]

The important point about Gide's use of coincidence is that it is an appropriate response to the problems of reconciling chance and contingency in life with the deliberate contrivance inherent in any narrative that seeks to depict them. Coincidence signals that essential disjunction at the heart of narrative between the mutually exclusive type of logic of which it is constituted. For this narrative to produce its meaning, the story must lead to Boris's death; but none of the events in the story is bound to happen; it is only by chance that they occur. Thus the plot of the novel connects all the characters with the death of Boris via a network of coincidences, establishing a pattern of collective responsibility; but the story, proceeding through the same coincidences but construing them as random occurrences, denies that pattern. It may well happen in real life that accidental, random events lead up to a tragedy for which large numbers of people can therefore be held responsible: the problem is that a novel cannot depict such patterns without infringing the very codes upon which a mimetic or realistic narrative is predicated. The use of coincidences introduces a fissure into the novel by making it impossible to decide which way it should be read. We are offered two incompatible readings depending on whether we consider the text as self-reflexive, foregrounding its own structures, playing with language and with narrative conventions, or whether, on the other hand, we see it as an account of chance happenings leading up to a tragic death. This novel is theoretically impossible, since it cannot do and be all these things at once: but it does, and is.

Notes

1. DU BOS, *Le Dialogue avec André Gide* (Paris, Corrêa, 1947, p. 161; Hytier, op.cit., p. 104.

2. Letter to Copeau, 8 June 1912, *Correspondance*, p. 622.

3. The extent of his disappointment is chronicled in K. O'NEILL, *André Gide and the Roman d'Aventure*, (Sydney, Sydney University Press, Australian Humanities Research Council Monograph 15, 1969), pp. 47–9.

4. *OC, VI*, p. 361.

5. *RRS*, p. 679; also *JI*, 436–7; *J2*, 39: 12 July 1914.

6. *Le Journal de Robert Levesque*, in BAAG, *XI*, no. 59, July 1983, p. 337: the comments were made in a conversation of 31 August 1931.

7. 'Introduction to the Structural Analysis of Narratives', in *Image, Music, Text* (Glasgow, Fontana, 1977), p. 16; 95. Barthes borrows the term 'phatic' from Jakobson: see 'Linguistics and Poetics', in *Style and Language* ed. T.A. SEBEOK (Cambridge, Mass., M.I.T., 1960), pp. 353–9.

8. Maria van Rysselberghe, *Les Cahiers de la Petite Dame*, vol. 1, *Cahiers André Gide*, 4 (Paris, Gallimard, 1973), p. 28, 9 July 1919.

9. *La Crise du roman. Des lendemains du naturalisme aux années vingt* (Paris, Corti, 1966), pp. 356–63.

10. N. DAVID KEYPOUR, *André Gide: écriture et réversibilité dans 'Les Faux-Monnayeurs'* (Montréal, Presses de l'Université de Montréal, 1980), pp. 130–1. JEAN HYTIER, *André Gide* (Paris, Charlot, 1946) p. 271, underlines 'the discontinuity – sometimes rather wearisome – of the development'.

11. MICHAEL TILBY, *Gide: 'Les Faux-Monnayeurs'* (London, Grant and Cutler, Critical Guides to French Texts, 9, 1981), pp. 21–2; 75–6; 81.

12. In 1911 Gide wrote: 'The novel, as I recognize or imagine it, comprises a diversity of points of view, subject to the diversity of characters it presents; it is in essence a work of dispersion'. (*OC, VI*, p. 361). The *Journal des Faux-Monnayeurs* takes up the point: 'I should like events never to be related directly by the author, but instead exposed (and several times from different vantages) by those actors who will be influenced by those events' (28; 13: 21 November 1921). See FRANÇOIS MOURET, 'Gide à la découverte de Browning et de Hogg, ou la technique romanesque de la multiplicité des points de vue', *Cahiers André Gide*, 3 (Paris, Gallimard, 1972), pp. 223–39.

13. ANDRÉ JULIEN, *'Les Faux-Monnayeurs* et l'art du roman', in *Hommage à André Gide* (Paris, Nouvelle Revue Française, 1951), p. 128.

14. *JI*, pp. 790, 782; *J2*, pp. 355, 348 (1924). The issue is pinpointed by Julien, loc. cit., p. 127.

15. Cf. GERALD PRINCE, 'Notes on the Text as Reader', in *The Reader in the Text*, ed. SUSAN R. SULEIMAN and INGE CROSMAN (Princeton, Princeton University Press, 1980), pp. 225–40.

16. Cf. GERALD PRINCE, 'Introduction à l'étude du narrataire', *Poétique*, 154 (1973), pp. 178–96. Prince cites the sentence on Vincent as one of his illustrations (p. 184).

17. Cf. ALAIN GOULET, 'Lire *Les Faux-Monnayeurs'*, *André Gide 5*, Revue des Lettres Modernes, 1975, pp. 10–14; ARTHUR E. BABCOCK, *Portraits of Artists: Reflexivity in Gidean Fiction* (York, South Carolina, French Literature Publications Company, 1982), pp. 84–5. For a comprehensive overview and analysis, see Keypour, op.cit. The emergence of these techniques in the *récits* is examined by M. Maisani-Léonard, *André Gide ou l'ironie de l'écriture* (Montréal, Presses de l'Université de Montréal, 1976).

18. In this Gide's practice does not of course conform to standard conventions of free indirect speech which normally retains the 'back-shift' of tenses characteristic of indirect discourse. See S. RIMMON-KENAN. *Narrative Fiction: Contemporary Poetics* (London, Methuen, New Accents, 1983), p. 112. Raimond sees the feature as a 'prodigious technical success' on Gide's part: op.cit., pp. 353–4.

19. 1087; 173. The translation changes 'ce meme soir' to 'Tuesday evening', in order, presumably, to do away with the (deliberate?) metalepsis in the French.

20. It might be objected that direct speech is neutral presentation; but as Maisani-Léonard points out 'the direct and indirect styles are always a means of marking the appropriation of one discourse by another'; and a high proportion of dialogue. 'far from revealing a calm objectivity, betrays the illusion of objectivity, precisely the illusion denounced, moreover, in the *récits*' (op.cit., pp.

192–3). Bakhtin's analysis parallels this view: see 'Du discours romanesque', in M. BAKHTIN, *Esthétique et théorie du roman*, tr. Doria Olivier (Paris, Gallimard, Bibliothèque des Idées, 1978) pp. 82–233; 175.

21. Tilby, op.cit., pp. 90–93, holds that the tone and techniques of Édouard's narrative provide a contrast and a counterweight to the playful narrator's voice: see also his ' "Self-conscious" narration and "self-reflexivity" in Gide's *Les Faux-Monnayeurs*', *Essays in French Literature*, 15, November 1978, pp. 56–81. The argument is tenable up to a point; but the narrator's presence is constantly perceptible, even within Édouard's diary (see below). Keypour's contention is that the narrator's voice is attenuated by the discourses he quotes (but see previous note) and that in the final analysis Édouard can be viewed as the 'real' author of the novel. The subtle hypothesis of which this notion is part is built up ingeniously but on very insecure foundations, such as that the narrator cannot logically know more than Édouard about la Pérouse and the pension Vedel Azaïs (152–3) and that the epigraphs and other aspects of the editorial function must be seen as operating on a narrative level above that of the narrator (154–59).

22. See above Note 7.

23. The notion of the citational, dialogic or polyphonic novel derives from the work of Bakhtin. See 'Du discours romanesque', loc. cit.; *Problems of Dostoevsky's Poetics*, tr. R.W. ROTSEL (Ann Arbor, 1973); *The Dialogic Imagination*, four essays translated by CARYL EMERSON and MICHAEL HOLQUIST (Austin, University of Texas Press, 1981). A useful presentation of Bakhtin's work is contained in *Comparative Criticism*, ed. E.S. SHAFFER, vol 2 (Cambridge, Cambridge University Press, 1980): 'The Word in the Novel', tr. ANN SHUKMAN (213–20); Ann Shukman, 'Between Marxism and Formalism: the Stylistics of Mikhail Bakhtin' (221–34); ANN JEFFERSON, 'Intertextuality and the Poetics of Fiction' (235–50).

24. A particularly striking example of intertextual relations is provided by the story of how the actual suicide of a boy named Nény, which inspired that of Boris, found its way into *Les Faux-Monnayeurs* via a news report in the *Journal de Rouen* (reproduced in full in the *Journal des Faux-Monnayeurs*) and texts by MAURICE BARRÈS and JACQUES COPEAU: see BAAG, X, no. 55, July 1982, pp. 335–46; no. 56, October 1982, p. 523; *XI*, no. 57, January 1983, pp. 107–8.

25. *Correspondance André Gide – Dorothy Bussy*, 3 vols (Paris, Gallimard, Cahiers André Gide, 9, 10, 11, 1980–1982), vol. 2, p. 27.

26. BARTHES, 'Proust et les noms', in *Le Degré zéro de l'écriture, suivi de Nouveaux Essais Critiques* (Paris, Seuil, 1972), p. 133. For structuralist and post-structuralist critics, the 'caractère signifiant' of language is its capacity for generating meaning, rather than for simply transcribing preexisting meanings. The notion of language as a self-contained system of relational structures was most notably established by SAUSSURE in his *Course in General Linguistics* (Glasgow, Fontana, 1974).

27. W.W. HOLDHEIM, *Theory and Practice of the Novel. A Study on André Gide* (Geneva, Droz, 1968), p. 236.

28. 'Lecteurs et lectures dans *Les Faux-Monnayeurs*', *Neophilologus*, 57 (1973), pp. 16–23.

29. PRINCE, in his 'Introduction à l'étude du narrataire', loc. cit, p. 180, writes: 'The narratee can only follow a narrative in one clearly defined direction . . . he is

obliged to acquaint himself with events by proceeding from the first page to the last'. The exact status of the reader postulated here does not fall within the categories of much contemporary narrative poetics insofar as these are theoretical constructs encoded in the text, whereas the building up of this second reader for *Les Faux-Monnayeurs* requires some pragmatic components as well as hands to turn the actual pages. Eco's 'model of a possible reader' seems the most appropriate label: see *The Role of the Reader* (London, Hutchinson, 1981), pp. 7–11.

30. It is known that this pattern was part of Gide's intention. See his letters to Roger Martin du Gard in their *Correspondance*, vol. 1, p. 269; and to Jacques Lévy in his *Journal et Correspondance* (Grenoble, Editions des Cahiers de l'Alpe, 1954), p. 36. The *Journal des Faux-Monnayeurs* sets out the idea this structure is devised to illustrate. 'There is no act, however foolish or harmful, that is not the result of interacting causes, connections and concomitances. No doubt there are very few crimes of which the responsibility cannot be shared, to the success of which several did not contribute – albeit without their knowledge or will' 476–7; 44–5.

31. Prince indicates that textual reading signals 'may present a definition of the text that is at best superficial or off-base . . . In this case, rather than performing as readers, they perform as counterreaders' ('Notes on the Text as Reader', loc. cit., p. 239).

32. '*Les Faux-Monnayeurs*: The Theme of Responsibility', *Modern Language Review*, 55 (July 1960), pp. 351–8.

33. *Histoire du roman français depuis 1918* (Paris, Seuil, 1950), p. 253.

34. *André Gide, l'insaisissable Protée* (Paris, Les Belles Lettres, 1953), pp. 302–3. Elements of this argument are reproduced in Brée's 'Time sequences and consequences . . .' in the present volume.

35. On the walls are 'un tableau symbolique des âges de la vie' (1159) which Geneviève Idt comments on in her *André Gide: Les Faux-Monnayeurs* (Paris, Hatier, Profil d'une oeuvre, 1970), pp. 53–5; and a clinical picture of a horse in which 'the artist has concentrated on a single horse all the ills by means of which Providence chastens the equine soul' (1159; 251): this would appear to mirror Boris as the hapless victim of the repercussions of human weaknesses in the novel.

36. In *JI*, 1951, *J3*, 166: 16 June 1931, Gide accepts the Pascalian *pensée* as an expression of his own view of the world.

37. See Jonathan Culler, *The Pursuit of Signs* (London, Routledge and Kegan Paul, 1981), p. 183, where Nietzche's analysis of such tropes is considered. Barthes points out that narrative operates a related transformation of *post hoc* into *propter hoc*: 'Introduction to the Structural Analysis of Narratives' loc. cit., p. 16; 94.

38. Thematically this is underlined by the fact that the other illegitimate child, Bernard, with whom Boris is in this respect paralleled, does survive and flourish.

39. Quoted in *Journal des Faux-Monnayeurs*, p. 87; 51.

40. Cf. Gide's definition of the artist: 'he who does not believe, not completely, in the reality (in the *single* reality, at least) of the outer world . . . . How much more comforting is the idea of different possibilities' (*JI*, 801, 992, 1051; *J2*, 365, *J3*, 114, 116).

41. That Gide was aware of the advances in physics evoked here seems to be hinted at in *Les Caves du Vatican* by Julius de Baraglioul's remark – clearly not to be taken seriously – 'There is no such thing as inconsequence – in psychology any more than in physics' (744; 84). We may compare with the remark by Louis de Broglie, Nobel Prize for Physics in 1924, who wrote of 'the essential discontinuity in physics which today we call the quantum of action' (quoted in *Le Petit Robert*).

42. The expression 'Natura non fecit saltus' is quoted and endorsed by DARWIN in *The Origin of Species by means of Natural Selection* (London, Penguin Books, 1987), pp. 223–4.

43. See note 35 above.

44. See ROGER JONES, *Physics as Metaphor* (London, Sphere Books/Abacus, 1983), pp. 117–20.

45. See G. PAINTER, *André Gide. A Critical Biography*, (London, Weidenfeld and Nicholson, 1968), p. 93; Holdheim, op. cit., p. 241.

46. Édouard too claims that his novel has no plan, that nothing in it will be decided in advance (1082).

47. See Rimmon-Kenan, op. cit., pp. 17–18.

48. Holdheim, op. cit., p. 239; Tilby, op. cit., p. 27; Babcock, op. cit., pp. 87–89; Hytier, op. cit., pp. 296–7.

49. Op. cit., Chapter 9: 'Story and Discourse in the Analysis of Narrative', p. 175.

50. Barthes discusses this contradiction in *S/Z* (Paris, Seuil, 1970), pp. 183–4.

51. See Eric Marty, '*Les Faux-Monnayeurs*: Roman, mise en abyme, répétition', in *André Gide*, 8, Revue des Lettres Modernes, 1987, pp. 95–117 (102–4).

52. *S/Z*, op. cit., pp. 183–4.

53. *Le Plaisir du Texte* (Paris, Seuil, 1973), p. 87; *The Pleasure of the Text*, tr. Richard Miller (London, Jonathan Cape, 1976), p. 55. On the production of deconstructive undecidables in fiction and philosophy, see: *S/Z*, pp. 83–4, 169–70, 183–4, Vincent B. Leitch, *Deconstructive Criticism* (London, Hutchinson, 1983), pp. 110, 180, 280 n. 2, Rimmon-Kenan, op. cit., pp. 121–2, Graham Falconer, Flaubert, James and The Problem of Undecidability', *Comparative Literature*, vol. 39, no. 1, Winter 1987, pp. 1–18.

Glossary

BARTHES, ROLAND (1915–1980)   Literary theorist and essayist intrumental in founding structuralist literary criticism. In *S/Z* (1970), he analyses a novella by Balzac in terms of a set of narrative 'codes'. However, in the course of this study he brings to light a series of ironies, uncertainties and inconsistencies in the work, revealing that beyond the demonstrable structural patterns within it are flaws and irregularities which escape systematic categorization. Ultimately, such undecidable features prove more interesting to pursue: and in going on subsequently to make them the object of study, as in *Le Plaisir du Texte* (1973), Barthes begins to highlight the criteria which became the hallmark of deconstruction or post-structuralist criticism.

CATHARSIS   In the sense given to it by the writings of the Ancient Greek philosopher Aristotle, the term refers to the purging of emotion which the audience in the theatre derives from the performance of a tragedy. Referring to this definition, Gide explains that he purges himself of latent tendencies and temptations in his personality by isolating them in his books, where he can give them unrestrained expression, developing them to the extremes which demonstrate their dangers and shortcomings. See Gide's letter to Scheffer, quoted in Chapter 8, p. 126. The ultimate effect of this systematic literary purging is the serenity Gide referred to in a letter to his friend André Ruyters: 'I am no longer uneasy today. I should probably still be so if I had not managed to liberate my various possibilities in my books and project outside myself the contradictory characters that inhabited me. The result of that moral purgation is a great calm and, if I dare say so, a certain serenity' (letter of 5 November 1924, in *OCXII*, 561).

DECONSTRUCTION   A post-structuralist approach to reading which seeks to highlight points at which inconsistencies, contradictions and flaws within texts reveal underlying metaphysical assumptions often at odds with their surface sense. The practice and the term were propagated by Jacques Derrida (q.v.).

DERRIDA, JACQUES (1930 –) Post-structuralist philosopher who has written on a wide range of philosophical movements and literary works. His approach consists of applying to their texts the analytical method he calls deconstruction, based on linguistic strategies whereby unacknowledged contradictions and unspoken assumptions can be highlighted. This makes them available for rereading and reinterpretation as it becomes clear that the meaning of any text is endlessly deferred. First came to prominence with his books *Writing and Difference* (1967) and *Of Grammatology* (1967); he later wrote *Dissemination* (1972).

IRONY In its fundamental manifestation, can be perceived in a text which says one thing while implying a second meaning differing from, or contradicting, the apparent sense. Gidian irony of this kind is associated with his *récits* or first- person narratives, in which the protagonist tells his or her story but the reader can discern, through what is recounted, a different version or interpretation of the events depicted. In this sense Gide refers to his texts as ironic and suggests that they offer a critique of the narrator's position, in that the reader does not take it at face value. This sense of irony is developed into satirical comedy in the *soties*. It is also relevant to Gide's work as a whole, in which this 'creature of dialogue' manifests his equivocations and ambiguities on the topics that concern him through the contrasting perspectives that can be discerned between different works. Insofar as irony entails more than one point of view on a given issue, then Gide's cultivation of narrative techniques involving intersecting perspectives (as in *La Porte Étroite* or *Les Faux-Monnayeurs*) can be seen as a refinement on it. Similarly, the *mise en abyme* (q.v.), making elements of the text into mirrors of the text itself, provides a form of structural irony.

LACAN, JACQUES (1901–1981) Psychoanalyst, who built on the work of Freud, combining it with the work of structural linguistics to argue in his *Ecrits* (1966) and elsewhere that the unconscious is structured like language and that the individual subject is constituted in and through language. The subject is therefore in flux, pursuing an impossible quest to construct a fixed individual identity while forever caught up in the ceaseless circulation of signs.

LUTHER, MARTIN (1483–1546) German theologian, who triggered the Reformation and founded Protestantism through his opposition to the doctrine of the Catholic Church. Among his ninety-five theses he nailed to the church door at Wittenberg in 1517 were the principles of free interpretation of the Scriptures and free examination of the individual conscience. Gide saw these as the key to his own emancipation from dogma – even the way to atheism. (See p. 5.)

MISE EN ABYME A phrase applied by Gide to a device whereby one element of a text mirrors the text as a whole or features of it. See Chapter 6.

NARRATOLOGY The study of the formal properties of narrative. The basis of its method is a distinction made between narration (the mode of presentation) and narrative (the events or actions in themselves). The former is designated by the terms discourse or plot; the latter by the terms story or diegesis. Confusingly, among French narratologists the word *récit* is used sometimes to refer to the former (in opposition to *histoire*) and sometimes to the latter (in opposition to *discours*). Both these uses of this term have nothing to do with the label *récit* which Gide gave to his own first-person narratives such as *L'Immoraliste* and *La Symphonie Pastorale*.

PHATIC The linguistician Roman Jakobson distinguishes a number of codes in language, corresponding to various functions inseparable from the communication of a message. The phatic function is associated with those features of speech or writing that fulfil the need to maintain contact with the person to whom the message is addressed.

POST-STRUCTURALISM In a development from the perspective of structuralism (q.v.), Jacques Derrida (q.v.) argued that the binary oppositions providing the basis for these theories were demonstrably unstable and founded on arbitrary hierachies of value. The application of this critical technique, known as deconstruction (q.v.), ushered in post-structuralism which posits the uncertain, slippery nature of a meaning, arguing that sense is forever deferred by virtue of the infinitely regressive relations within language, and prizing the problematic, inconsistent and undecidable features of texts where flaws open up perspectives on this ungraspable horizon.

SCRIPTURAL A term deriving from the conceptualization by Barthes and Derrida of writing as *écriture,* a system of signifying relations producing meaning internally rather than representing or expressing meaning by transcribing a reality beyond itself. The idea of an author who stands outside his/her text and dictates its meaning is thus replaced by the notion of a *scriptor* whose identity is bound up with, and enmeshed in, the workings of language; the *scriptural* experience is that of being caught up in the generativity of language that produces meanings, and it tends to blur, indeed banish, the traditional distinction between a writer who produces the text and a reader who consumes it. See Chapter 12, pp. 174–5.

STRUCTURALISM   A school of thought which brought the theories of Saussure and structural linguistics into critical writing in the arts and the social sciences in the 1960s. It analysed cultural manifestations in terms of structures deriving from binary oppositions, showing that underpinning patterns of behaviour and thought were sets of conceptual relations, rule-governed systems working at unconscious levels, independently of human volition.

Bibliography

Works by Gide

The major extensive bibliographies of Gide's works are:

ARNOLD NAVILLE, *Bibliographie des écrits d'André Gide (depuis 1891 jusqu'en 1952)* (Paris: Guy Le Prat, 1949).
JACQUES COTNAM, *Bibliographie chronologique de l'oeuvre d'André Gide (1889–1973)* (Boston, Mass:, G. K. Hall and Co., 1974).

Most of Gide's prose fiction is available in French in the following edition:
ANDRÉ GIDE *Romans, récits et soties, oeuvres lyriques*. Introduction par Maurice Nadeau, Notices et Bibliographies par Yvonne Davet et Jean-Jacques Thierry (Paris: Bibliothèque de la Pléiade, 1958).

Other editions referred to
ANDRÉ GIDE, *Journal, 1889–1931* (Paris: Bibliothèque de la Pléiade, 1951).
ANDRÉ GIDE, *Journal 1939–1949, Souvenirs* (Paris: Bibliothèque de la Pléiade, 1954).
ANDRÉ GIDE, *Oeuvres Complètes*. Edition augmentée de textes inédits, établie par L. Martin-Chauffier (Paris: Nouvelle Revue Français, 15 volumes, 1932–39).
ANDRÉ GIDE, *Corydon* (Paris: Gallimard, 1947).
ANDRÉ GIDE, *Journal des Faux-Monnayeurs* (Paris: Gallimard, 1927).
ANDRÉ GIDE, *Ne Jugez Pas* (Paris: Gallimard, 1969).
ANDRÉ GIDE, *Dostoevski* (Paris: Gallimard, Collection Idées).
ANDRÉ GIDE, *Théâtre* (Paris: Gallimard, 1942).
ANDRÉ GIDE, *Prétextes, suivi de Nouveaux Prétextes* (Paris: Mercure de France, 1963).
ANDRÉ GIDE, *Les Cahiers et les Poésies d'André Walter*. Edition établie et présentée par Claude Martin (Paris: Gallimard, Collection Poésie, 1986).

André Gide

ANDRÉ GIDE, *La Symphonie Pastorale*. Edition critique de Claude Martin (Paris: Minard, Collection Paralogue, 1970).
ANDRÉ GIDE, *Retour de l'URSS* (Paris: Gallimard, 1936).
ANDRÉ GIDE, *Retour de l'URSS suivi de Retouches à mon Retour de l'URSS* (Paris: Gallimard, Collection Idées, 1978).
ANDRÉ GIDE, *Littérature Engagée*, textes réunis et présentés par Yvonne Davet (Paris: Gallimard, 1950).

The majority of Gide's fiction, as well as some works of non-fiction, is available in French paperback editions (Gallimard, Collection Folio), and almost as much is available in English (Penguin Books). Translations to which reference is made in the present volume are listed below.

Les Cahiers d'André Walter
The Notebooks of André Walter. Translated from the French and with an Introduction and Notes by Wade Baskin (London: Peter Owen, 1968).

Le Traité du Narcisse, La Tentative Amoureuse
The Return of the Prodigal, preceded by Five Other Treatises, with Saul, a Drama in Five Acts. Translated by Dorothy Bussy (London: Secker and Warburg, 1953). *Narcissus, The Lovers' Attempt, El Hadj, Philoctetes, Bathsheba.*

Paludes, Le Prométhée Mal Enchaîné
Marshlands and Prometheus Misbound, translated by George D. Painter (London: Secker and Warburg, 1953).

Les Nourritures Terrestres, Les Nouvelles Nourritures
Fruits of the Earth and *Later Fruits of the Earth*, translated by Dorothy Bussy (Harmondsworth: Penguin Books, 1970).

L'Immoraliste
The Immoralist, translated from the French by Dorothy Bussy (London: Cassell and Co, 1953).

La Porte Étroite
Strait is the Gate. Translated by Dorothy Bussy (London: Secker and Warburg, 1948).

La Symphonie Pastorale
La Symphonie Pastorale and *Isabelle*. Translated by Dorothy Bussy (Harmondsworth: Penguin Books, 1963).

Les Caves du Vatican
The Vatican Cellars. Translated from the French by Dorothy Bussy (London: Cassell and Co, 1952).

Les Faux-Monnayeurs
The Counterfeiters. Translated from the French by Dorothy Bussy (Harmondsworth: Penguin Books, 1966).

Journal des Faux-Monnayeurs
Logbook of the Coiners, translated and annotated by Justin O'Brien (London: Cassell and Co., 1952).

Journal 1889–1939, Journal 1939–1949
The Journals of André Gide. Translated from the French, with an Introduction and Notes, by Justin O'Brien.

    Vol. 1: 1889–1913 (London: Secker and Warburg, 1948).
    Vol. 2: 1914–1927 (London: Secker and Warburg, 1948).
    Vol. 3: 1928–1939 (London: Secker and Warburg, 1949).
    Vol. 4: 1939–1949 (New York: Alfred A. Knopf, 1951).

Et nunc manet in te
Et nunc manet in te and *Intimate Journal.* Translated from the French by Justin O'Brien. (London: Secker and Warburg, 1952).

Prétextes
Pretexts. Reflections on Literature and Morality. Selected, Edited and Introduced by Justin O'Brien (London: Secker and Warburg, 1959).

Ainsi soit-il ou Les Jeux sont faits
So Be It: or The Chips are Down. Translated, with an Introduction and Notes, by Justin O'Brien (London: Chatto and Windus, 1960).

Geneviève
The School for Wives, Robert, and Genevieve. Translated by Dorothy Bussy (London: Cassell and Co., 1953).

Retour de l'URSS
Back from the USSR. Translated by Dorothy Bussy (London: Martin Secker and Warburg, 1937).

Retouches à mon Retour de l'URSS
Afterthoughts. A Sequel to Back from the USSR. Translated by Dorothy Bussy (London: Martin Secker and Warburg, n.d.).

Correspondence

Gide was a prolific letter-writer, and more than 20,000 letters from him have so far been inventoried. For the complete list, see:

JACQUES COTNAM, *Inventaire bibliographique et Index analytique de la Correspondance d'André Gide (publiée de 1897 à 1971)* (Boston, Mass: G. K. Hall and Co., 1975).

CLAUDE MARTIN, *La Correspondance générale d'André Gide (1879–1951): répertoire, index, notices* (Lyon: Centre d'Etudes Gidiennes, 6 vols., 1984–85).

Numerous volumes of correspondence with particular individuals have been published, including:

Francis Jammes–André Gide, *Correspondance 1893–1938* (Paris: Gallimard, 1948).

Paul Claudel–André Gide, *Correspondance 1899–1926* (Paris: Gallimard, 1949).

Paul Valéry–André Gide, *Correspondance 1890–1942* (Paris: Gallimard, 1955).

Arnold Bennett–André Gide, *Correspondance 1911–1931* (Geneva: Droz, 1964).

Roger Martin du Gard–André Gide, *Correspondance 1913–1951* (Paris: Gallimard, 2 vols, 1968).

François Mauriac–André Gide, *Correspondance 1920–1950* (Paris: Gallimard, Cahiers André Gide, 2, 1970).

Henri Ghéon–André Gide, *Correspondance 1897–1944* (Paris: Gallimard, 2 vols, 1976).

Jacques–Emile Blanche–André Gide, *Correspondance 1891–1939* (Paris: Gallimard, Cahiers André Gide, 8, 1978).

Justin O'Brien–André Gide, *Correspondance 1937–1951* (Lyon: Centre d'Etudes Gidiennes, 1979).

Dorothy Bussy–André Gide, *Correspondance 1918–1951* (Paris: Gallimard, 3 vols., Cahiers André Gide, 9, 10, 11, 1979, 1981, 1982).

F.-P. Alibert–André Gide, *Correspondance 1907–1950* (Lyon: Presses Universitaires de Lyon, 1982).

Jacques Copeau–André Gide, *Correspondance Décembre 1902–Octobre 1949*, 2 vols (Paris: Gallimard, Cahiers André Gide, 12 & 13, 1987, 1988).

Critical material on Gide

The critical material on Gide is enormous. Useful lists can be found in:

CLAUDE MARTIN, *Bibliographie chronologique des livres consacrés à André Gide (1918–1986)* (Lyon: Centre d'Etudes Gidiennes, 1987).

CATHERINE SAVAGE BROSMAN, *An annotated bibliography of criticism on André Gide, 1973–1988* (New York and London: Garland Publishing, 1990)

Regular publications devoted to Gide include:

BULLETIN DES AMIS D'ANDRÉ GIDE. Founded in 1968 by Claude Martin. Published three times yearly by the Association des Amis d'André Gide. Currently edited by Pierre Masson and published at the Centre d'Etudes Gidiennes, Université de Lumière (Lyon II).

CAHIERS ANDRÉ GIDE (Paris: Gallimard).

ANDRÉ GIDE, *Revue des Lettres Modernes* (Paris: Minard).

Archives André Gide, Archives des Lettres Modernes (Paris: Minard).

Works On Gide

ANGLÈS, A., *André Gide et le Premier Groupe de 'La Nouvelle Revue Française'*, I. *La formation du groupe et les années d'apprentissage (1890–1910)* (Paris: Gallimard, 1978).

— II. *L'âge critique (1911–1912)*, (Paris: Gallimard, 1986).

— III. *Une inquiète maturité (1913–1914)* (Paris: Gallimard, 1986).

BABCOCK, ARTHUR E., *Portraits of Artists: Reflexivity in Gidean Fiction, 1902–1946* (York, South Carolina: French Literature Publications Company, 1982).

BASTIDE, R., *Anatomie d'André Gide* (Paris: Presses Universitaires de France, 1972).

BELL, W. M. L., 'Convention and Plausibility in *Les Caves du Vatican*', *Australian Journal of French Studies*, vol. VII, nos. 1–2, 1970, pp. 76–92.

BOOKER, J. T., 'The Generic Ambiguity of Gide's *La Symphonie Pastorale*: Reading the pastor's first cahier', *Symposium*, 40 (1986), pp. 159–71.

BOROS AZZI, MARIE-DENISE, *La Problématique de l'écriture dans 'Les Faux-Monnayeurs'* (Paris: Lettres modernes, Archives André Gide, 6, 1990).

BRÉE, G., *André Gide l'insaisissable Protée* (Paris: Les Belles Lettres, 1953).

CANCALON, E. D., *Techniques et personages dans les récits d'André Gide* (Paris: Lettres modernes Minard, Archives André Gide no. 2, 1970).

— 'Les Formes du Discours dans *Le Prométhée Mal Enchaîné*, *BAAG*, vol IX, no. 49, January 1981, pp. 35–44.

CIHOLAS, K. N.. *Gide's Art of the Fugue. A Thematic Study of 'Les Faux-Monnayeurs'* (Chapel Hill: University of North Carolina Department of Romance Languages, 1974).

CORDLE, T., *André Gide* (New York: Twayne, 1969)

CRUICKSHANK, J., 'Gide's Treatment of Time in *La Symphonie Pastorale*', *Essays in Criticism*, VII, April 1957, pp. 134–43.

DAVET, Y., *Autour des 'Nourritures Terrestres'*, (Paris: Gallimard, 1948).

DAVIES, J. C., *Gide, 'L'Immoraliste' and 'La Porte Etroite'* (London: Edward Arnold, 1968).

DELAY, J., *La Jeunesse d'André Gide* (Paris: Gallimard, 2 vols, 1956–7); *The Youth of André Gide*, abridged and translated by June Guicharnaud (Chicago and London: University of Chicago Press, one volume, 1963).

DU BOS, C., *Le Dialogue avec André Gide* (Paris: Corrêa. 1947).

FAWCETT, P., 'Gide et Stevenson', in *André Gide et l'Angleterre*, ed. Patrick Pollard (London: Birkbeck College, 1986).

FILLAUDEAU, B., *L'Univers ludique d'André Gide* (Paris: José Corti, 1985).

GOULET, A., 'Les premiers vers d'André Gide (1888–1891)', *Cahiers André Gide*, 1 (Paris: Gallimard, 1969), pp. 123–49.

— '*Les Caves du Vatican*' *d'André Gide* (Paris: Larousse, 1972).

— 'Lire *Les Faux-Monnayeurs*', *André Gide 5*, Revue des Lettres Modernes, 1975, pp. 10–14.

— 'Le Prométhée Mal Enchaîné: une étape vers le roman', *BAAG*, vol. IX no. 49, January 1981, pp. 45–52.

— *Fiction et Vie sociale dans l'œuvre d'André Gide*, (Paris: Minard, Publications de l'Association des Amis d'André Gide, 1986).

GOUX, JEAN-JOSEPH, 'Les Faux-Monnayeurs' in *Les Monnayeurs du Langage* (Paris: Editions Galilée, 1984).

HARVEY, L. E., 'The Utopia of Blindness in Gide's *La Symphonie Pastorale*', *Modern Philology*, 55, February 1958, pp. 188–97.

HOLDHEIM, W. W., 'The Dual Structure of the *Prométhée Mal Enchaîné*', *Modern Language Notes*, vol. LXXIV, December 1959, pp. 714–20.

— *Theory and Practice of the Novel. A Study on André Gide* (Geneva: Droz, 1968).

IDT, G., *André Gide: 'Les Faux-Monnayeurs'* (Paris: Hatier, Profil d'une œuvre, 1970).

IRELAND, G. W., *André Gide. A Study of his Creative Writings* (Oxford: Clarendon Press, 1970).

JULIEN, A., '*Les Faux-Monnayeurs* et l'art du roman', in *Hommage à André Gide* (Paris: Nouvelle Revue Française*, 1951), pp. 122–9.

KEYPOUR, N. D., *André Gide: Ecriture et réversibilité dans 'Les Faux-Monnayeurs'* (Montréal: Presses de l'Université de Montréal, 1980).

LACHASSE, P., 'L'ordonnance symbolique des *Cahiers d'André Walter*', *BAAG*, no 65, January 1985, pp. 23–38.

LEJEUNE, P., *Exercices d'ambiguïté. Lectures de 'Si le grain ne meurt'* (Paris: Minard, coll. 'Langues et styles', 1974).

LÉVY, J., *Journal et Correspondance* (Grenoble: Editions des Cahiers de l'Alpe, 1954).

LÉVY, Z. H., *Jérôme Agonistes; Les structures dramatiques et les procédures narratives de 'La Porte Étroite'* (Paris: Nizet, 1984).

MAILLET, H., *'L'Immoraliste' d'André Gide* (Paris: Hachette, 1972).

— '*La Symphonie Pastorale*' d'André Gide (Paris: Hachette, 1972).

MAGNY, C.-E., *Histoire du roman français depuis 1918* (Paris: Seuil, 1950).

MAISANI-LÉONARD, M., *André Gide ou l'ironie de l'écriture* (Montréal: Les Presses de l'Université de Montréal, 1976).

MARTIN, C., *André Gide par lui-meme* (Paris, Seuil, 1963).

— *La Maturité d'André Gide. De 'Paludes' à 'L'Immoraliste'* (1895–1902) (Paris: Klincksieck, 1977).

MARTY, E., 'Mythologie d'André Gide', in *André Gide, Qui étes-vous?, avec les entretiens Jean Amrouche-André Gide* (Lyon, la Manufacture, 1987), pp. 11–135.

— '*Les Faux-Monnayeurs*: Roman, mise en abyme, répétition', *André Gide 8*, Revue des Lettres Modernes, 1987, pp. 95–117.

MASSON, P., '*Le Prométhée Mal Enchaîné*, ou du détournement d'un mythe à des fins personnelles', *BAAG*, vol. IX, no. 49, January 1981, pp. 5–29.

MOURET, F. J.-L., 'Gide à la découverte de Browning et de Hogg, ou la technique romanesque de la multiplicité des points de vue', *Cahiers André Gide*, 3 (Paris: Gallimard, 1972), pp. 223–39.

MOUTOTE, D., *Le Journal de Gide et les Problèmes du Moi (1889–1925)* (Paris: Presses Universitaires de France, 1968).

— *André Gide: l'engagement 1926–1939* (Paris; SEDES, 1991)

OLIVER, A., *Michel, Job, Pierre, Paul: intertextualité de la lecture dans 'L'Immoraliste'* (Paris: Archives des Lettres modernes, Archives André Gide no. 4, 1979).

O'NEILL, K., *André Gide and the Roman d'Aventure* (Sydney: Sydney University Press, Australian Humanities Research Council Monograph 15, 1969).

PAINTER, G., *André Gide. A Critical Biography* (London: Weidenfeld and Nicolson, 1968).

— 'Lecteurs et lectures dans *Les Faux-Monnayeurs*', *Neophilologus*, 57 (1973), pp. 16–23.

POLLARD, P., *André Gide, Homosexual Moralist* (New Haven and London: Yale University Press, 1991).

PRUNER, F., *'La Symphonie Pastorale' de Gide, de la tragédie vécue à la tragédie écrite* (Paris: Lettres Modernes Minard, 1964).

SAVAGE BROSMAN, C., 'The Novelist as Natural Historian in *Les Faux-Monnayeurs*', *Essays in French Literature*, no. 14, November 1977, pp. 48–59.

— *André Gide: l'évolution de sa pensée religieuse* (Paris: Nizet, 1962).

SEGAL, N., 'Gide and women', *Paragraph*, vol. 8, October 1986, pp. 62–74.

STEEL, D.A., ' "Lafcadio ludens": Ideas of Play and Levity in *Les Caves du Vatican*', *Modern Language Review*, vol. 66, no. 3 July 1971, pp. 554–64.

— 'Gide and the conception of the bastard', *French Studies*, July 1973, pp. 238–48.

— 'Gide et Freud', *Revue d'Histoire Littéraire de France,* January-February 1977, pp. 48–74.

THODY, P., *'Les Faux-Monnayeurs:* The Theme of Responsibility', *Modern Language Review,* 55 (July 1960), pp. 351–8.

TILBY, M. J., ' "Self-conscious" narration and "self-reflexivity" in Gide's *Les Faux-Monnayeurs*', *Essays in French Literature*, 15, November 1978, pp. 56–81.

— *Gide: 'Les Faux-Monnayeurs'* (London: Grant and Cutler, Critical Guides to French Texts, 1981).

VAN RYSSELBERGHE, M., *Les Cahiers de la Petite Dame*, 4 vols., Cahiers André Gide, 4–7 (Paris: Gallimard, 1973–7).

WALKER, D. H., 'The Dual Composition of *Les Nourritures Terrestres*: Autour du 'Récit de Ménalque', *French Studies, XXIX* (1975), pp. 421–433.

— 'Subversion of narrative in the work of André Gide and John Fowles', in *Comparative Criticism*, ed. E. Schaffer, vol. 2 (Cambridge: Cambridge University Press, 1980), pp. 187–212.

— *Gide: 'Les Nourritures terrestres' and 'La Symphonie pastorale'* (London: Grant and Cutler, Critical Guides to French Texts, 1990).

WATSON-WILLIAMS. H., *André Gide and the Greek Myth* (Oxford, Clarendon Press, 1967).

WILSON, W. D., *André Gide: 'La Symphonie Pastorale'* (London and Basingstoke: Macmillan, 1971).

WYNCHANK, A., 'Métamorphoses dans *Les Cahiers d'André Walter*. Essai de rétablissement de la chronologie dans *Les Cahiers d'André Walter*', *BAAG*, no. 63, July 1984, pp. 361–73.

Works Of Critical Theory, Literary History, etc.

ADAM, J. M., *Le Texte narratif* (Paris: Nathan, 1985).

BAKHTIN, M., *Problems of Dostoevsky's Poetics*, tr. R. W. Rotsel (Ann Arbor, 1973).

— *Esthétique et théorie du roman*, tr. Doria Olivier (Paris: Gallimard, Bibliothèque des

Idées, 1978).

— 'The Word in the Novel', tr. Ann Shukman, *Comparative Criticism*, ed. E. S. Shaffer, vol. 2 (Cambridge: Cambridge University Press, 1980), pp. 213–20.

— *The Dialogic Imagination*, four essays translated by Caryl Emerson and Michael Holquist (Austin: University of Texas Press, 1981).

BAL, M., *Narratology*, tr. Christine van Boheemen (Toronto, London: University of Toronto Press, 1985).

BARTHES, R., *Mythologies* (Paris: Seuil, Collection Points, 1957).

— *Essais Critiques* (Paris, Seuil, 1964); *Critical Essays*, tr. Richard Howard (Evanston: North Western University Press, 1972).

— *S/Z* (Paris, Seuil, Collection Points, 1970); *S/Z*, tr. Richard Miller (London: Jonathan Cape, 1975).

— 'Introduction à l'analyse structurale des récits', in *Communications*, 8 (Paris: Seuil, Collection Points, 1981), pp. 7–33; 'The Structural Analysis of Narratives', in *Image-Music-Text*, ed. and tr. Stephen Heath (Glasgow: Fontana, 1977), pp. 79–124.

— *Le Degré Zéro de l'Ecriture, suivi de Nouveaux Essais Critiques* (Paris: Seuil, collection Points, 1972); *Writing Degree Zero and Elements of Semiology*, tr. Annette Lavers and Colin Smith (London: Jonathan Cape, 1984).

— *Le Plaisir du Texte* (Paris, Seuil, 1973); *The Pleasure of the Text*, tr. Richard Miller (London: Jonathan Cape, 1976).

— *et al.*, *Littérature et Réalité* (Paris: Seuil, Collection Points, 1982).

BELSEY, C., *Critical Practice* (London: Methuen, New Accents, 1980).

CULLER, J., *Structuralist Poetics* (London: Routledge and Kegan Paul, 1975).

— *The Pursuit of Signs* (London: Routledge and Kegan Paul, 1981).

DARWIN, CHARLES, *The Origin of Species by Means of Natural Selection* (Harmondsworth: Penguin Books, 1987).

DUCROT, O., and TODOROV, T., *Dictionnaire encyclopédique des Sciences du Langage* (Paris: Seuil, Collection Points, 1972).

EAGLETON, T., *Literary Theory: An Introduction* (Oxford: Blackwell, 1983).

ECO, U., *The Role of the Reader* (London: Hutchinson, 1981).

FALCONER, G., 'Flaubert, James and The Problem of Undecidability', *Comparative Literature*, vol. 39, no. 1, Winter 1987, pp. 1–18.

FORSTER, E. M., *Aspects of the Novel*, (Harmondsworth: Penguin, 1974).

FREEDMAN, R., *The Lyrical Novel* (Princeton: New Jersey, Princeton University Press, 1963).

FREUND, E., *The Return of the Reader* (London: Methuen, New Accents, 1987).

GENETTE, G., *Figures III* (Paris, Seuil, 1972); *Narrative Discourse*, tr. Jane E. Lewin (Oxford: Blackwell, 1980).

JAKOBSON, R., 'Linguistics and Poetics', in *Style and Language*, ed. T. A. Sebeok (Cambridge: Mass., M.I.T., 1960), pp. 353–59.

JAMESON, F., *The Prison-House of Language* (Princeton: Princeton University Press, 1972).

JEFFERSON, A., 'Intertextuality and the Poetics of Fiction', *Comparative Criticism*, ed. E. S. Shaffer, vol. 2 (Cambridge: Cambridge University Press, 1980), pp. 235–50.

LEJEUNE, P., *L'Autobiographie en France* (Paris: Armand Colin, 1971).

— *Le Pacte autobiographique* (Paris: Seuil, 1975).

LODGE, D., *The Modes of Modern Writing* (London: Arnold, 1977).

McHALE B., *Postmodern Fiction* (London: Methuen, New Accents, 1987).

MARTINS, L., *The Diary Novel* (Cambridge: Cambridge University Press, 1985).

PRENDERGAST, C., *The Order of Mimesis* (Cambridge: Cambridge University Press, 1986).

PRINCE, G., 'Introduction à l'étude du narrataire', *Poétique*, 154 (1973), pp. 178–96.

— *Narratology. The Form and Functioning of Narrative* (Berlin: New York, Amsterdam, Mouton, 1982).

RAIMOND, M., *La Crise du Roman, Des lendemains du Naturalisme aux années vingt* (Paris: Corti, 1966).

RICARDOU, J., *Problèmes du nouveau roman* (Paris: Seuil, 1967).

RIMMON-KENAN, S., *Narrative Fiction: Contemporary Poetics* (London: Methuen, New Accents. 1983).

SAUSSURE, F. de, *Course in General Linguistics*, tr. Wade Baskin (Glasgow: Fontana, 1974).

SULEIMAN, S. and CROSMAN, I., eds. *The Reader in the Text* (Princeton: Princeton University Press, 1980).

TADIÉ, J.-Y., *Le Roman d'Aventure* (Paris: Presses Universitaires de France, 1982).

VOLOSINOV, V. N., *Marxism and the Philosophy of Language*, tr. Ladislav Matejka and I. R. Titunik (New York: Seminar Press, 1973).

WELLEK, R., and WARREN, A., *Theory of Literature* (Harmondsworth: Penguin Books, 1973).

WRIGHT, E., *Psychoanalytic Criticism* (London: Methuen, New Accents, 1984).

INDEX

Indexer's Note: the various spellings of Dostoevsky in the Index reflect those in the text.